Breaking the Chains

Breaking the Chains

Slavery, Bondage, and Emancipation
in Modern Africa and Asia

Edited by

Martin A. Klein

THE UNIVERSITY OF WISCONSIN PRESS

The University of Wisconsin Press
114 North Murray Street
Madison, Wisconsin 53715

3 Henrietta Street
London WC2E 8LU, England

Library of Congress Cataloging-in-Publication Data
Breaking the chains: slavery, bondage, and emancipation in modern
Africa and Asia / edited by Martin A. Klein.
236 p.   cm.
Includes bibliographical references and index.
ISBN 0-299-13750-3   ISBN 0-299-13754-6 (pbk.)
1. Slavery—Africa—History. 2. Slaves—Africa—Emancipation—History.
3. Colonies—Africa—History. 4. Slavery—Asia—History.
5. Slaves—Asia—Emancipation—History. 6. Colonies—Asia—History.
                                                I. Klein, Martin A.
HT1025.B74   1993
306.3'62'096—dc20   93-15043

Contents

Maps

Tables

Preface

This collection developed from some conversations at the International Economic History Congress in Budapest in 1982 which brought home to me the range and importance of servile institutions throughout Asia. In the years that followed I was much stimulated by the works of Orlando Patterson, James Watson, Anthony Reid, and James Warren. I became increasingly aware of the extent to which the American experience shapes our understanding of slavery. I also realized that the experience of colonial Africa, which I was then researching, was closer to that of certain Asian societies than it was to the experiences of the Americas. I became convinced that this offered a fertile field for comparison, particularly in examining the poorly researched questions of how colonial regimes coped with servitude and how various slaves and masters coped with their colonial rulers. I then organized panels on the subject at the American Historical Association meetings in San Francisco in 1984 and at the International Economic History Congress in Berne in 1986. Six of the essays in this collection were first presented in Berne.

I am grateful to the Social Sciences and Humanities Research Council of Canada for years of support and to the Woodrow Wilson International Center for Scholars for the chance to develop some of my ideas. I first presented a version of chapter 8 at the Wilson Center, where it received very perceptive comments from Gillian Feeley-Harnik and Frederick Cooper. The refinement of the introduction was helped by comments from Richard Roberts, Suzanne

Miers, Paul Lovejoy, Frederick Cooper, Stanley Engerman, Dharma Kumar, Gervase Clarence-Smith, and David Feeny. They helped me hone my thoughts and saved me from some grievous errors, but the final synthesis is mine. I also appreciate the insights of those colleagues whose work does not appear in this collection but who contributed to the San Francisco and Berne panels: Robert Van Niel, Albertine Jwaideh, James Cox, Suzanne Miers, Jan Hogendorn, Babacar Fall, and K. K. N. Kurup. I also want to thank Hannah Searing for preparing the index.

Contributors

WILLIAM GERVASE CLARENCE-SMITH is Reader in the economic history of Asia and Africa at the School of Oriental and African Studies, University of London. He is the author of *Slaves, Peasants and Capitalists in Southern Angola, 1840–1926* (1979) and *The Third Portuguese Empire, 1825–1975* (1985).

DAVID FEENY teaches economics in the Department of Economics and the Department of Clinical Epidemiology and Biostatistics at McMaster University in Hamilton, Ontario. He is the author of *The Political Economy of Productivity: Thai Agricultural Development, 1880–1975* (1982).

MARTIN A. KLEIN teaches African history at the University of Toronto. He is the author of *Islam and Imperialism in Senegal: Siné-Saloum, 1847–1914* (1968). With Claire C. Robertson, Klein edited *Women and Slavery in Africa* (1983).

DHARMA KUMAR, Emeritus Professor of Economic History at the Delhi School of Economics, is the author of *Land and Caste in South India* (1965). She was one of the general editors of *The Cambridge Economic History of India*.

MOHAMED MBODJ teaches history at Columbia University. He has written extensively on Senegambian economic and demographic history and is now working on a study of the economic history of the Gambia.

GYAN PRAKASH teaches South Asian history at Princeton University. He is the author of *Bonded Histories: Genealogies of Labor Servitude in Colonial India* (1990) and the editor of *The World of Rural Labourers in Colonial India* (1992).

ANTHONY REID, Professor of Southeast Asian History at Australian National University, is the author of *Southeast Asia in the Age of Commerce* (2 vols., 1988 and 1993) and the editor of *Slavery, Bondage and Dependency in Southeast Asia* (1983).

EHUD R. TOLEDANO teaches Middle Eastern history at Tel Aviv University. He is the author of *The Ottoman Slave Trade and Its Suppression, 1840–1890* (1982) and *State and Society in Mid-Nineteenth Century Egypt* (1990).

Breaking the Chains

Martin A. Klein

Introduction: Modern European Expansion and Traditional Servitude in Africa and Asia

Different forms of servitude have existed in almost all parts of the world for thousands of years.[1] Though slavery, serfdom, and other forms of servitude have on occasion declined, only in the last two centuries has slavery been seriously called into question (Davis 1984: 107–8). The questioning came first from English-speaking religious dissenters and French philosophes. By the middle of the nineteenth century the major European powers had abolished slavery, and the abolition movement had begun to engage with both the slave trade and slavery in non-European societies. Most of the literature on emancipation deals with slavery in the Americas. This collection is concerned with emancipation in African and Asian societies which were either colonized or fell under the domination of European powers during the nineteenth century. In these societies emancipation involved the imposition on non-Europeans of a European discourse on slavery and, in most cases, a free labor ideology. The dominated societies all had their own servile institutions, in some cases a variety that bewildered European observers. With the exception of the study by Clarence-Smith (chap. 6), these essays deal with masters who were not European and accepted that discourse reluctantly, if at all. The process of change involved pressures from European abolition movements, the extension of capitalist relations of production, the concerns and perceptions of the colonial state, and the efforts of non-Western elites to modernize. Before considering the individual studies, we will look first

3

at forms of servitude found in Africa and Asia and then at the European
impact on these servile institutions.

Servitude in Africa and Asia

Servitude

The evolution of complex human institutions, most notably of the state and
of elite groups associated with the state, was in all parts of the world based
on the ability of those institutions to extract wealth from large numbers of
other people. In all complex preindustrial societies, some form of servitude,
sometimes several forms, has played an important role in the process of accumulation, of increasing economic rationalization, and of political centralization. Historically, the most important form of servitude and probably the
most widespread was slavery. Two factors stimulated the development of
slavery. War often made available a pool of prisoners, of which the most
desirable were women and children. Also, the existence of surplus land forced
ruling elites to seek control of labor rather than land.

Definitions of slavery usually stress any of three variables. First, the slave
was an outsider, someone who had no place in the kinship system. As Patterson
writes: "Not only was the slave denied all claims on, and obligations to,
his parents and living blood relations but, by extension, all such claims and
obligations on his more remote ancestors and on his descendants" (Patterson
1982:5; see also Finley 1964, 1968; Meillassoux 1986:23–42). For Miers
and Kopytoff (1977a), the slave's marginality decreased as he or she was
integrated into the kinship system. Meillassoux (1986:139–40), however, asserts that the slave was the antithesis of kin, an "antiparent." Watson (1980b)
sees these as two separate models and differentiates between open societies,
in which gradual integration took place, and closed ones, where slaves and
their descendants were kept forever outside the kinship system.

Second, the slave was seen as property. Feeny speaks of "property rights
in man." For Watson, the property relationship differentiates slavery from
other forms of involuntary labor (1980b:8–9). In chapter 2, Reid uses salability
to differentiate slavery from other forms of bondage. Most contemporary
writers see the idea of property as deriving from the slave's deracination,
but the two notions were linked. The marginality of the slave made him or
her dependent and thus exploitable and attractive (McCann 1988:342). The
property relationship maintained that marginality. Whatever the ideological
position, the crucial dimension was the reification of the person and the control
that gave the master.

Third, the dependence of the slave originated in an act of violence, and
its continuance required coercion (Meillassoux 1986:94–96; Watson 1980b:

8–9). The slave was torn from existing social relations and inserted in a new situation where he or she was powerless. This did not necessarily mean that slaves were poorly treated. Slaves often included both the wretched and the well-off, but the well-being of those who prospered depended on their lack of identity, which made them effective instruments of others.

In chapter 1, Toledano suggests that a continuum of forms of servility existed, rather than a dichotomy between slave and free. Reid (chap. 2), Feeny (chap. 3), and Kumar (chap. 4) stress that a range of forms of social domination encompassed slavery (see also Finley 1960; Ste. Croix 1988; and Miers and Kopytoff 1975a:7–11). Kumar speaks of "unfreedom of various degrees." Reid's analysis of Southeast Asia could be extended to other societies: "The key to Southeast Asian social systems was the control of men. Land was assumed to be abundant, and not therefore an index to power. . . . The wealth of the rich, and the power of the strong, lay in the dependent man- (and woman-) power they could gather around them. For the poor and the weak, on the other hand, security and opportunity depended upon being bonded to somebody strong enough to look after them. . . . the important question was to whom you were bonded rather than the abstract legal quality of your bondage" (1983b:8). After slavery, the most common forms of servitude were conceived in relation to debt. In India, a variety of relationships existed, some hereditary and some not, which are called bondage and which affected more people than slavery did. Writers on Southeast Asia refer to debt slavery or debt bondage, which resembled what Africanists would call pawnship. In some areas debt bondage could be hereditary, but in most the debtor or a member of his or her family worked for the creditor until the debt was repaid (see chapters by Reid, Feeny, Kumar, and Prakash). In theory, the primary difference between slavery and other kinds of bondage was that the slave was an outsider and was consciously kept marginal. The bonded person or pawn was part of a community and had kinship ties. The bonded person kept his or her name and identity. In practice, the lines between the two were more ambiguous. In parts of Africa, for example, a pawn could become a slave if the debt was not repaid or if the pawn was moved out of the area where he or she had kin. As Prakash makes clear, the debt often only symbolically represented a hereditary link that had deeper roots.

In addition, people in many areas had an obligation to labor for the state or its representatives that could last up to half of the year. In Thailand, this was the most common kind of coerced labor. The corvée was not slavery. Though Feeny (chap. 3) describes this as a kind of "property in man," it was only performed by free subjects in Thailand. The obligation was so heavy, however, that some persons bonded themselves to escape it. In Thailand, corvée was used more for public purposes, and bondage for private.

Finally, there were those called serfs. This term described persons attached to land who could not be sold independently of it. Forms of serfdom often evolved where conquered communities had a tributary relation imposed on them or where a servile community remained stable (Lasker 1950:69–73). Meillassoux (1986:73–78) suggests that slavery really existed only where it was reproduced by violence. His analysis implies that any stable slave community based on internal reproduction would evolve toward a form of serfdom. In much of Africa slaves born in a master's household were not supposed to be sold, though some were. The way in which the two kinds of slave were treated could depend on the character of the master, the local political economy, natural disasters, the age of the person at the time of enslavement, and the ability of the servile community to assert itself.

Of course, terms like *slave, pawn,* and *serf* come from English, and *corvée* is a French term that was used by the Dutch. They translate a variety of local terms, each with its nuances, its distinct social context, and its own definition of rights and obligations. Thus the term *serf* was used for eighteenth-century Russians who could be sold or given away. By contrast, in societies inhabiting areas as diverse as South China and the West African Sudan, terms translated as "slave" identified people who could not be sold or were not sold except in conditions of extreme distress (Klein and Lovejoy 1979; Miers and Kopytoff 1977a; Watson 1980c). Slaves often had rights and privileges, and the borders between slavery and other forms of exploitation were sometimes ambiguous and fluid. A trusted general, a beloved concubine, or a faithful retainer were usually well treated. A field slave in a plantation system could usually count on little more than subsistence. All, or almost all, were subject to arbitrary authority. In chapter 5, Prakash examines the linkages among the translation of terms, the perception of forms of bondage, and public policy.

The sources of slaves varied. In West Africa, most were produced by warfare. In the Middle East, the Islamic prohibition on the enslavement of Muslims limited capture, though such enslavement did take place. Most slaves were imported from elsewhere, primarily from the Black Sea area and from sub-Saharan Africa (see Toledano, chap. 1). This made the import slave trade a constant factor in Middle Eastern history. Like Africans, people living in the less centralized societies of South and Southeast Asia often fell victim to slave raiders. In Indonesia, pirate social formations lived off slave raiding much like their land-based African counterparts (Warren 1981). Nevertheless, the most important sources of slaves in India and Southeast Asia were debt and famine. Parents sold their children, husbands sold wives, and people put themselves independent relationships (see Reid, chap. 2 and Kumar, chap. 4). In modern China, the most important source of slaves was the sale of children by needy parents (Watson 1980c). Enslavement was also often a punishment for certain crimes.

Slave Systems

Other systems of bondage, which recruited within the community, did not require the violence or the brutal trade that slavery engendered in slave-producing areas. European public opinion was moved more by the horrors of warfare, trade, and brutality than by the fact of exploitation. The variety of slave systems thus demands a closer examination. Slavery was found even in small-scale societies that lacked structures of exploitation. War captives or men taken in raids were often killed. Women, children, and, in some cases, adult men were enslaved or absorbed into captors' communities. Differentiation was minimal. Though socially inferior, slaves in these societies lived with and worked alongside masters, and their offspring were absorbed, sometimes forming junior lineages (see African examples in Miers and Kopytoff 1977a).

The studies in this book do not focus on such societies. They deal mostly with two other kinds of slavery. First, they consider elite slavery. In both African and Asian societies, many of the slaves were found within the courts, in elite households, and within the political system (Toledano 1982; Fisher 1980; Watson 1980c). Slaves were concubines, officials, soldiers, servants, entertainers, and artisans. In some cases, this was the only kind of slavery that existed in the society. The wealth that supported the elite was produced in the form of taxation, tribute, or corvée or by other kinds of bondsmen. Slaves were important not as producers but as part of the structure that extracted wealth or spent it. Many exercised great power, particularly eunuchs and slave soldiers. Most played humble roles, but within the households of the rich and powerful. Thus, Wilbur writes that his thesis on slavery in Han China "was originally conceived of as one way to learn more about the condition of the lower classes in Han times, but it now appears to reveal much more about the ruling group, and to contribute only indirectly to a knowledge of the common people" (1943:243). This does not mean that slavery was unimportant. The existence of a mass of dependent persons was essential to the power of the state and the privileges of the elite. The Middle East and the Arab world rarely used slaves for productive activities (but see Fisher 1980; Inalcık 1979; and Clarence-Smith 1989), but the hunger of this area for slaves has been a factor in its history for over two thousand years and has influenced its relations with Slavic areas around the Black Sea and with Africa.

Many elite slaves achieved wealth and power, as Toledano discusses in chapter 1. It is easy to assume that these were not "real" slaves. In fact, those slaves who achieved prominence did so because they were slaves. Increasing political centralization invariably involved conflict between monarchy and aristocracy. Both kings and lords had to create groups on which they could depend, who had no ties to opposed kinship structures. Thus, slaves gained power because they were dependent, that is to say, because they were slaves. Many transcended their servile origins: concubines, for example, often managed to transcend both gender and servitude. Similarly, in commercial families, slaves could often become trusted traders, preferred over kin because their dependence made them trustworthy (Baier 1980: 176–79).

Second, this book examines societies that used slave labor primarily for productive purposes. In some, slave labor was the only important source of income for the state and the elite. In others, slavery functioned alongside other kinds of obligation, as in India and Southeast Asia, or alongside free labor, as in the southern United States. Reliance on slave labor in some societies, such as ancient Rome, resulted from military success (Hopkins 1978). In others, slave labor replaced other forms of labor: slaves were replenished by purchase, slave-producing societies developed to supply the market, and economic calculation imposed increasingly intensive labor on the slaves. As a result, increasing numbers of slaves were gathered in large units of production.

In chapter 2 Reid suggests that the rise in power of centralized monarchies led to "a decline of private slavery in favor of direct obligations to the Crown." This was certainly true in Thailand and was probably true for parts of India. It was not true for Africa, because the rise of powerful monarchies there was so often linked to their role as suppliers of slaves to the Americas and increased slave use was a by-product of those slaving activities. It was also not true for the Middle East, where a form of slavery provided officials who staffed the court and the administration.

Varieties of Servitude

China provides perhaps the most striking example of slavery as an extension of the elite (Wilbur 1943; Pulleyblank 1958; Watson 1976, 1980c; Eberhard 1962). According to Watson, the country had up to the establishment of the People's Republic in 1949 "one of the largest and most comprehensive markets for the exchange of human beings in the world" (1980c:223). Furthermore, it was an old market. Throughout Chinese history, slaves occupied many positions at court and in the imperial bureaucracy. In ancient China conquest usually provided slaves, but in recent centuries slaves came mostly from sale by indigent parents, especially during years of famine, or by kidnappers. Though some slaves were used in mines (Lasker 1950:337) and a trade in adult concubines existed, most transactions involved children under the age of ten. Adolescents and young adults were sometimes bound to a creditor, but only for limited periods of time. Male children could be assimilated as the heirs of childless men with the agreement of the men's families, but in that case the boys ceased to be slaves and became sons. Other males became servants. A female could be at different periods of her life a servant, a concubine, a wife, or a prostitute. Slaves were rarely used for productive activity. In Watson's words, they "did not generate any surplus; they consumed it" (1980c:238).

As Kumar (chap. 4) and Prakash (chap. 5) reveal, bondage in India was more varied (see Kumar 1965; Patnaik and Dingwaney 1985; Jha 1988; Sareen 1988–89). There was, after all, never a single India. Some people lived in temporary bondage, usually for debt, some were attached to land like European serfs, and some were hereditary chattel slaves. As in China, slavery in India seems to have originated in conquest. *Dasa,* which means "slave," also refers to indigenous peoples who fell under the sway of invading Aryans (Chakravarti 1985:35; Basham 1954:153). Slaves were both exported and imported, but most were Indian in origin. In recent centuries debt seems to have been the most important basis of servitude. As Kumar explains in chapter 5, Indian slavery was most distinctive because of its links to caste. While there were a few high-caste slaves, most were members of the scheduled castes, called untouchables by the British. Their status made them vulnerable: they could not own land and were restricted in the work they could do (see Kumar 1965). Caste also made difficult any internal opposition to systems of exploitation, because it divided the exploited from each other.

Reid (chap. 2) and Feeny (chap. 3) explore the variety of forms of obligation in southeast Asia, both public and personal (see Reid 1983b:8–12). Public obligation could involve payment of tribute by a conquered community, whose members were sometimes seen as slaves, or some form of corvée (Reid 1983b:18–19). The importance of corvée reflected the power of monarchic and often despotic states. The nature of personal obligations varied, depending on whether a person was born in slavery or whether enslavement originated in capture, condemnation for crimes, or the sale of dependents. Slaves were important at all courts and in the households of the wealthy, but they were also widely used for productive purposes. Slavery was particularly important in the Southeast Asian cities of the sixteenth and seventeenth centuries, as it was to be in the cities of eighteenth- and nineteenth-century Africa. Though slaving was less widespread than in Africa, the existence of a market for slaves stimulated predation. Slaves were taken by the armies of the powerful, by kidnappers and by pirates who ravaged the coasts for human booty (Warren 1981).

Slavery in the Middle East dates back to the origin of complex societies (Mendelsohn 1949; Dandamaev 1984). Islam confirmed the existence of the institution and provided a legal framework for it (Brunschwig 1960; Hunwick 1988). The wealthy urban society of the Islamic heartland attracted a constant flow of slaves from the fringes: from the Balkans, the Black Sea, the Caucasus, and Africa. By the nineteenth century Africa had become the major source of slaves, though Circassian women from the Caucasus still brought the highest prices (Toledano 1982:65–67). Most slaves were used within the courts and elite households. Only in Persia and in the date plantations of southern Arabia did many slaves work as agricultural laborers (Ricks 1988; Ewald 1988). Slave soldiers were widely used (Pipes 1981; Crone 1980), and slaves could become senior officials. Most women in harems and most servants were slaves. In the Persian Gulf, slaves were important as pearl-divers and sailors (Jwaideh and Cox 1989; Ricks 1988). Others became artisans or worked in commerce. Very few farmed. Within the Middle East during the modern period, agricultural slavery existed, though on a small scale.

The African continent has provided slaves since the end of the first millennium for the Mediterranean world, for India, and for the Americas (Lovejoy 1983; Harris 1971). The demand for slaves encouraged the development of systems of slave production. This was true in other areas, but probably nowhere on a greater scale than in those parts of Africa open to the Arab and European slave trades. Caravan routes penetrated deep into the hinterland of desert and sea and developed military systems specializing in enslavement. The growth of these networks made slaves available for other uses. African armies, much like the Sulu raiders of the South Seas, were recruited largely among slaves. Slave production became in many parts of Africa the major source of the comforts on which military and commercial elites depended (Meillassoux 1986). The more productive economies invariably relied on slave labor. Even during the peak years of the Atlantic trade, most of those enslaved were kept within Africa (Klein 1987).

A Slave Mode of Production?

The simplistic use of the concept of a slave mode of production by Communist scholarship has influenced many writers to reject the idea. It is clear, however, that a relatively small number of very powerful societies were based on slave labor, often to the point where the dominant social groups completely depended on slaves for their wealth and, as a result, for their power. In these societies slaves fed the courts and provided all of the trade goods and the revenue needed to pay for imports. Finley (1968) speaks of these as slave societies, avoiding the term *mode of production*. For these societies the significance of slavery is clear. The crucial question is whether slaves within them related to the society differently than other people did. Thus, Suret-Canale writes that "the state of being a captive, although widely prevalent in Africa, was essentially a legal category, and implied no well defined role in production such as could characterise a social class. The basic exploited class was the working peasantry, embracing at the same time 'free' tributaries and captives; while the dominant class was the aggregate of aristocracies—tribal, military and official—which included certain categories of royal captives who held public office" (1988:17). Slavery was widespread in post-Vedic India, but most Indian historians argue that a slave mode of production never existed (Jha 1988). Reid asserts similarly that "a slave mode of production did not exist in the sense of a significantly different production system from that of serfdom" (1983b: 23). Reid, however, makes an exception for the Banda Islands, and Warren (1981:221) uses the term to apply to the islands of the Sulu Archipelago.

In contrast, a large literature describes African societies that had a servile majority and in which almost all productive labor was done by slaves (Lovejoy 1978, 1983:9–11; Klein 1987; Cooper 1977; Roberts 1987; Pollet and Winter 1971; Meillassoux 1975b; Balde 1975; Fernyhough 1988; Cordell 1988). Makassar, Batavia, and many other early modern cities in Southeast Asia had populations the majority of whom were slaves (Sutherland 1983:268–69; Abeyasekere 1983:286; Reid 1983b:29). Some merchants and aristocrats owned six or seven hundred slaves (Manguin 1983:210; Sutherland 1983:269). The population of Thailand has been described as 25 to 50 percent slave in the eighteenth and nineteenth centuries (Reid 1983b:12), and a Chinese account of medieval Angkor stresses the importance of slavery (Mabbett 1983:44). In areas of India and Southeast Asia where slavery was more rare, other forms of bondage were prevalent and provided most of the productive labor.

One scholar has compared the slave plantation to a concentration camp (Elkins 1959). This is a deceptive comparison. The slave plantation, or any other kind of slave-based enterprise, was concerned either with profits or with the ability of the plantation to feed some group of nonproductive persons. A person became a slave through capture or purchase. The purchaser was concerned about productivity, essential for expansion and for reproduction. By contrast, the productive activity of the concentration camp was secondary to its intention to confine or break the will of its inmates. Profitability shaped the master's approach to the slave. Slaves had both will and intelligence. They could and did resist, rarely by taking arms, but often by flight or by shirking work. There was paradox to any slave system. As Reid puts it in chapter 2, the slave "is a commodity and yet human, exploited and yet loyal, inferior and yet intimate." In theory, masters considered slaves as things, but to get performance from slaves, it was necessary to recognize their humanity. Many recent works on slavery have stressed not only the world that the slave owners made, but also the world the slaves made (Genovese 1969, 1972; Sobel 1987; Cooper 1979). If slaves, by definition outsiders, constructed their own worlds, then so also did others in bondage. Prakash (chap. 5) argues that the essence of bondage in India was not debt but the quest for security.

There was also another variable. Those who controlled labor generally had a vision of a just social order, shaped in part by religion and community values. Slaves often had few sanctions to bring to bear on a cruel master, but they could resist, and they could sometimes count on collective action and the values of the community. Invariably, those worst treated were those recently captured, in the process of being traded, or newly acquired (Warren 1981: chap. 11; Miers and Kopytoff 1977b).

This obviously leaves the question of why slavery was important. I would argue that the preindustrial state was not as despotic as its own ideology claimed or, rather, that its despotism operated within limited areas, that large states were involved in a constant struggle with local communities, which often sought to maximize their autonomy without bringing down royal wrath. Most preindustrial societies had a surplus of land, and thus control of persons was crucial (Nieboer 1910; see Feeny, chap. 3, for an analysis based on Nieboer). Many writers on slavery quote approvingly Adam Smith's remarks about the inefficiency of slave labor.[2] Smith may well have been right, but the central question was usually not the productivity of slave labor but how much labor or how much surplus could be extracted from slaves. Neither slavery nor bondage gave the master total control, but the slaves or bonded persons could be forced to work longer hours or to give up a larger percentage of their production than they would have done if they had had a choice. Slavery was profitable not because slaves were more productive than free laborers, but because more was extracted from them or less was spent on their maintenance. The rootlessness and vulnerability of slaves subjected them to more intensive forms of labor and greater exploitation. This, in turn, made it desirable for masters to maintain that rootlessness.

Indigenous Slavery and European Expansion

Slave labor could, of course, be used by different people. Where slavery existed, different social groups struggled for the control of slaves' productivity and social services. Often struggles occurred between kings and aristocrats or between military, commercial, and agrarian elites. Soon after the first Portuguese ships made contact with African and Asian peoples, Europeans became part of this struggle (Sarkar 1985; Reid 1983c). From the beginning, European traders got involved with slavery in two ways. First, they became involved in moving slaves. In the fifteenth century the Portuguese on the coast of West Africa bought slaves not only for use in Portugal and the Atlantic islands but also for sale to labor-short Akan gold miners in what is now Ghana (Lovejoy 1983:35–43). In the East a slave trading economy evolved that linked the Indian Ocean and the South China Sea. Africans were sold in India, the Persian Gulf, and Indonesia (Harris 1971). Malays were sold in southern China and the Cape of Good Hope. Slaves were moved from various islands to Java and the trading cities. Second, Europeans living in both Africa and Asia used slave labor themselves. As outsiders, they had little control over local sources of labor, since labor was provided largely within social relationships. They used slaves as sailors and as laborers, but most important, they used slaves within their own households. The more successful and powerful maintained large and often lavish houses, staffed by slave gardeners, cooks, and servants. Even the more modest had slave concubines and servants (Reid 1983b:14–18, 25–27). The same was true of African coastal trading towns (see Mbodj, chap. 8; Brooks 1976). In Southeast Asia a Chinese diaspora was linked to the European one and, like it, involved mostly males, who often purchased sexual and domestic services.

Economic growth and a European taste for tropical products created increasing opportunities for Europeans to move from commerce to production. They tended to do so in areas where population was low or had been decimated by European conquest. Using the labor of slaves, first native peoples, then imported Africans, seemed the cheapest way to develop the Atlantic islands, Brazil, and then the West Indies (Dunn 1972; Schwartz 1985; Curtin 1990). Similarly, in the Banda Islands of Indonesia, Jan Pieterszoon Coen's brutal conquest left population so low that spice production could only be maintained by importing labor to produce the spices the Dutch wanted (Lasker 1950: 33–35).

From commercial empire in the sixteenth century and settlement in the seventeenth century, Europeans moved to control massive populations in India and Indonesia by the late eighteenth century. They were there to make money for shareholders and for themselves. Their intervention in local economies took two forms. First, they tended to rely heavily on traditional systems of general obligation. Forced labor, or corvée, was widely used in India and Southeast Asia for public purposes and, in time, to increase production. The new colonial rulers could use these systems to their own advantage. At the same time, colonial taxation and a new legal framework encouraged production of cash crops and the extension of market relationships. Many prospered, but debt, landlessness, population growth, and the restrictions of caste left most of the poor with few options. Though no statistics are available, it seems certain for India and probable for much of the rest of eastern and southern Asia that the extension of market relationships stimulated the growth of debt bondage, and perhaps also the sale of children (Sarkar 1985; Kumar et al. 1983; Watson 1980c).

The use of slave labor was expanding in eighteenth- and nineteenth-century Africa. Even after abolition, the slave trade was used to produce supposedly free labor in Senegal (Mbodj, chap. 8) and on the Atlantic islands (Clarence-Smith, chap. 6). The fiction of an indenture contract was used for migrants who had no choice (Renault 1976). By contrast, in India and Southeast Asia, use of servile labor declined. Feeny (chap. 3) argues that in Thailand other kinds of labor became cheaper, largely because of population growth and large-scale international migration. Clarence-Smith (chap. 6) asserts that the high cost of slave labor at a later period doomed the cocoa plantations of the Gulf of Guinea when those plantations had to compete with peasant production. In India the decline involved both a shift into debt bondage and more efficient systems of wage labor (Kumar, chap. 4).

Patterns of Emancipation

In all parts of the world, there were times when slavery expanded, and in many, there were times when it declined, as it was replaced or absorbed by other forms of exploitation. Southeast Asia offers only one example. During the late medieval period slavery disappeared in northern Europe (Bloch 1975; Pelteret 1981), and in seventeenth-century Russia it was absorbed within a rather harsh form of serfdom (Hellie 1982: chap. 18). There is no evidence, however, that slavery came under serious attack in any part of the world before the eighteenth century.

Slavery and Modern Religion

Both the existence of slavery and the question of how to treat slaves constituted problems for the universal religions. Hinduism did not question slavery but regulated the treatment of slaves. Vedic law confirmed the right of the master to sell, loan, or give away slaves, but it denied the master the right to kill a slave or to abandon an elderly slave. Sexual relations with slave women were forbidden, and manumission was recommended as a pious act (Basham 1954; Chanana 1960; Chakravarti 1985; Nair 1986).

Christianity, Buddhism, and Islam all questioned slavery, and tried to ameliorate the condition of slaves but ended up reinforcing the institution. Christ insisted on the equality of all before God, and Christianity experienced much of its early success among the disenfranchised of the Roman Empire. The church fathers, however, "tended to accept the institutions of state and society as a necessary framework for controlling sin and allowing the Church to perform its sacramental functions" (Davis 1966:88–89). By preaching kindness and insisting on religious equality, the Church legitimated the institution and provided a later justification for the enslavement of non-Christians.

Like Christ, Buddha created a world where all were equal regardless of origin, but this world was parallel to the existing world of exploitation and suffering. The Buddha forbade his followers to live on income derived from the slave trade. He recommended that slaves be treated with kindness but criticized slaves who envied their master's wealth. More important, Chakravarti writes, Buddha rationalized slavery itself by suggesting that a person was born a slave because of deeds in a previous existence (1985:66–69). Turton argues that in Thailand, Buddhism "had a mitigating effect on possible abuses of persons, slave and free, and . . . these are reflected to some extent in laws and reforms, in a way comparable to the effect of Christianity on medieval slavery" (1980:287). But Buddhist states participated in the slave trade, and Buddhist monasteries often owned large numbers of slaves. In nineteenth-century Burma, the slaves of the monasteries were harshly treated outcasts (Aung Thwin 1983:80–85; Lasker 1950:52).

The Prophet Muhammad forbade the enslavement of Muslims (Brunschwig 1960; Hunwick 1988). He did not recommend the enslavement of pagans, but in later centuries Muslims used his ban to justify slaving activities. He commended manumission as a pious act which could expiate various lesser sins. The following saying was attributed to him: "Fear God in the matter of your slaves. Feed them with what you eat and clothe them with what you wear and do not give them work beyond their capacity. Those whom you like retain, and those whom you dislike sell. Do not cause pain to God's creation. He caused you to own them and had He so wished He would have caused them to own you" (Hunwick 1988: n. 10). Islamic law recognized the slave's humanity both in recommending kindness and in suppressing such institutions as human sacrifice. Nevertheless, on the frontiers of Islam, enslavement was often widespread, not because Islam recommended it, but because it recognized the institution and did not forbid it (Cooper 1981). Muslims in Africa, India, and Indonesia had the power to impose themselves on others and controlled the institutions necessary to exploit slave labor.

The Abolition Movement

Abolition had its origins in a change in European consciousness. By the middle of the eighteenth century Enlightenment thinkers in England and on the Continent had called slavery into question. Montesquieu dissected classical justifications of slavery and attacked it as contrary to natural law (Davis 1966: 402–8). Adam Smith and his followers argued that free labor was more productive because it was better motivated (Smith [1776] 1937:365). More important for its later consequences, in 1758 the Philadelphia yearly meeting of the Quakers voted to exclude any members who bought or sold slaves (Davis 1984:107). Within a generation, abolition had a solid base in evangelical Protestant churches on both sides of the Atlantic.

Slavery was held to be illegal in England in 1772, and by the end of the century upper Canada and most of the northern United States had taken action against slavery. In 1794 revolutionary France abolished colonial slavery.

Though disapproval of slavery itself lay at the root of most abolitionist thought, the early abolition movement focused on ending the trade. The United States Constitution provided for the end of slave imports in 1808. The Danes abolished the colonial slave trade in 1803, the British in 1807, and the Dutch in 1814 (Rice 1975: chap. 6). The British and French abolition movements differed. In Britain a powerful movement based in the dissenting churches developed methods of shaping public opinion and proved a major force in British politics for fifty years. On the Continent abolitionism remained more a movement of ideas, which never mobilized masses. Napoleon reestablished slavery in the French colonies in 1802, and the Catholic church remained for much of the nineteenth century hostile to a movement it associated with the hated Revolution (Drescher 1980, 1986). Nevertheless, the heirs of the Enlightenment continued to see slavery as contrary to natural law and to reason.

Having abolished the British slave trade, the abolitionists turned to colonial slavery. Their success in 1833 did not end their struggle. The law passed was less than they wished. It provided for a period of apprenticeship and clearly called for continued pressure. More important, rival nations reaped the benefits. The slave trade continued in foreign ships, and this was only slightly riskier because of the efforts of the Royal Navy. Slave-based production also remained prosperous in the colonies of rival powers (Eltis 1987). The British and Foreign Anti-Slavery Society was formed in 1839 (Miers 1975; Temperley 1972). During its early years it was still concerned primarily with the Americas, particularly with Cuba, Brazil, and the United States. Increasingly, however, it had to confront other issues. European explorers described the horrors of the slave trade in Africa. James Richardson's account of Moroccan slavery and the Saharan slave trade turned British attention to the Muslim world (Richardson 1848). The 1833 abolition did not affect India and Ceylon, which were controlled by the East India Company. And wherever British authority was extended onto the African mainland, concern about relations with slaveholding neighbors compromised British policy (Dumett and Johnson 1988; Miers 1975:163–66).

By 1839 the United Kingdom had treaties with all major maritime powers except the United States providing for the right to search each other's merchant vessels (Miers 1975: chap. 11). The efforts of the Royal Navy eliminated the trade in some areas but were limited both by the skill of the slavers and by international law, which required that all slaving ships be taken to a Prize Court. The only one in West Africa was at Freetown, Sierra Leone. Under Palmerston, however, as the Royal Navy began to cut more deeply into the trade, British pressure extended its field of operations. In 1845 Sayyid Said of Zanzibar agreed to prohibit the export of slaves from his African territories (Cooper 1977:45). Similar treaties were signed with various West African rulers (Dike 1956; Miers 1975: chap. 2). The Ottomans refused any action against slavery, but in 1847 they closed the Constantinople slave market and banned the slave trade in the Persian Gulf. Ten years later they prohibited trade in African slaves. These actions had the effect of driving the slave trade into back alleys and private homes (Toledano 1982: chap. 3).

British attackes on the slave trade produced a particularly vehement response in the Muslim world, because slavery was seen as an institution legitimated by the Prophet. During the late nineteenth century the most persistent export trade from Africa was from the Horn across the Red Sea into the Hejaz (Austen 1988; Ewald 1988). The major effect of European intervention was to make the trade less public (Ochsenwald 1980). Finally, in 1880 a stronger treaty was signed. The trade declined, but its eventual demise came primarily from European intervention in Africa. The pilgrimage to Mecca remained the occasion for a clandestine slave trade. Egypt closed its slave markets in 1854 and in 1877 agreed to an antislavery convention with the United Kingdom. (Baer 1967). The slave trade was abolished in Tunisia in 1846, and French occupation in 1881 made this ban more effective. In Morocco, Islam bolstered a resistance to foreign intervention. For a long time British attentions only made the trade more secretive. A formal ban came only in 1922, but French occupation of the Niger Valley during the 1890s effectively reduced the scale of the trade (Schroeter 1988).

The British were often resented, but abolition made steady, if sometimes slow, progress. All of the newborn American republics abolished the slave trade and passed gradual emancipation laws at the time of their independence. By 1854 all of the Hispanic republics had abolished slavery (H. Klein 1986: chap. 11). Denmark and France abolished slavery in 1848, the Netherlands in 1863, and the United States between 1863 and 1865. The abolition of slavery in Cuba in 1886 and Brazil in 1888 resulted partly from internal forces, in Brazil's case, a mass abolition movement subsidized by the British (Eltis 1987: 207–17; see also Bethell 1970; Toplin 1972; and Conrad 1972). In Cuba, Eltis argues, it was because the price of sugar no longer adequately offset the cost of importing slaves (1987: 218–19; see also Scott 1985).

Also in 1888, a series of Catholic abolition societies were founded in Europe under the leadership of Cardinal Lavigerie and with the blessing of Pope Leo XIII (Renault 1971). The French Catholic antislavery movement, in particular, remained active well into the twentieth century. It used quiet pressure more than open propaganda, but it was backed by a strong missionary presence. It could mobilize Catholic opinion and put pressure on French colonial administrations. More important than any single movement was the equation in late nineteenth-century Europe of bondage and backwardness and the belief that slavery was profoundly immoral.

Motives for Abolition

The major debate on abolition has concerned whether it was a triumph of moral principle (Coupland 1933; Anstey 1975) or of economic interest. The debate was provoked by Eric Williams' *Capitalism and Slavery* (1944), which argued that accumulation of capital in the slave trade and in slave-based production was crucial to the Industrial Revolution but that by the end of the eighteenth century the West Indian slave plantations had declined in profitability and in their importance to Great Britain. Seymour Drescher (1977) has proven that there was no such decline at the time of the antislavery debate, and David Eltis (1987) argues that the period from 1820 to 1860 was the most profitable for the Atlantic slave trade.

Most contemporary writers accept the link between antislavery and industrial capitalism, while rejecting the economic determinism of Eric Williams. "The key to the timing of slavery's ultimate demise in the Western economy," Drescher argues, "lies not in its economic functioning but in its social peculiarity" (1986:5). David Davis writes: "Antislavery cannot be divorced from the vast economic changes that were intensifying social conflicts and heightening class consciousness. . . . in Britain it was part of a larger ideology that helped to ensure stability while accommodating society to political and economic change" (in Solow and Engerman 1987:218, citing argument in Davis 1966).

For Temperley, the key question was not what the abolitionists thought but why they were so successful at convincing others. The market, after all, did not end slavery. The state did (Temperley 1977:96). The two leaders of abolition, Britain and the northern United States, had free labor economies. They had experienced extraordinary growth and were convinced that individual freedom was crucial to that growth. Continental Europe was still freeing itself from traditional restraints on labor and lacked the organizational base provided by evangelical Protestantism, but a similar capitalist, free labor ideology predominated in Europe by the end of the nineteenth century and provided a clear ideological map. Slavery was seen as immoral and irrational. Public opinion shaped the strategies of imperial statesmen and proconsuls. Leopold, the king of the Belgians, made alliances with slave dealers when he first penetrated the Congo, but when confronted by the problem of how to finance his colony, he found it necessary to wrap himself in an antislavery cloak (Ascherson 1963: chap. 10). The French officers, who gave slaves to their soldiers and allies after military victories, often justified their actions by referring to an eventual abolition (see Klein, chap. 7). Lugard, who reinforced the control of slave owners over their "freed" slaves in northern Nigeria, sold himself at home as an antislavery crusader (Lennihan 1982; Lovejoy and Hogendorn 1988, 1989). Antislavery had become the heart of the civilizing mission.

This was most vividly illustrated by the Brussels Act of 1889–90, in which the major European powers agreed to measures against the internal African slave trade, the export of slaves from Africa, and the trade in arms and liquor (Miers 1967, 1975). The Brussels Act came a decade before most colonial powers were willing to act against the slave trade within Africa. It provided a cloak of moral legitimacy for the partition of Africa, but there was a gap between the rhetoric and the reality of Europe's moral crusade. The problem was that Europe's proconsuls lacked resources (Cordell 1985, 1988). The quest for African empire was often backed by well-organized public relations efforts, but the real interests involved were often very limited, and most European statesmen were well aware of this. Leaders like Bismarck and Salisbury viewed the claims of the colonial lobby with great scepticism. European parliaments were willing to approve colonies as long as they did not cost anything. Colonies were forced to pay their own way, but the revenue that could be extracted from most of these areas was limited. Thus, European armies were small and were made up primarily of soldiers recruited in the colonies (Echenberg 1986). Booty, particularly human booty, attracted allies. In addition, European generals were often anxious to prevent their enemies from uniting. It was therefore important not to undermine the existing social order, which depended on slaves (Twaddle 1988; Ohadike 1988; Heywood 1988). The rule was often to free the slaves of enemies, but to reinforce the control of allies or of those who submitted willingly over slaves.

European Abolition and Non-Western Slavery

Up to the middle of the nineteenth century the abolition movement was primarily concerned with the exploitation of slaves by Europeans or people of European descent. The act of 1833 did not apply to India. There were probably more slaves in India than in all of the Americas, but they were mostly owned by Indian masters (Temperley 1972:94; Banaji 1933:195–203). More important, British India was ruled by a small number of British officials allied to Indian princes, commanding Indian soldiers, and dependent on Indian subalterns and intermediaries. They lacked both the desire and the administrative capacity to force abolition on reluctant Indian ruling classes. When the issue of Indian slavery was raised in Britain, the response was vigorous. One official insisted that "the lower classes are glad to bind themselves and their posterity to such perpetual service, in order to be secure of subsistence in sickness and in old age . . . and in periods of scarcity" (Temperley 1972:95). Self-sale or the sale of children was seen as an effective way of dealing with such disasters as the Bengal famine of 1833.

The attack, however, was equally vigorous. The trade in women and children offended Christian sensibilities. So too did the castration of young boys and the operation of roving bands of Thugs, who made kidnapping a business. From the renewal of the East India Company charter in 1833, efforts were made to force the Company to act. Finally, in 1843 it did so, albeit reluctantly. As Kumar explains in chapter 4, the crucial provision of the abolition act was that the courts could no longer recognize claims rising out of slave status (Temperley 1972:107). No compensation was paid to slave owners, and no effort was made to provide alternative employment to the slaves. The hope was that slaves would not notice, that they would quietly continue to work under their masters, and that in the absence of recruits, slavery would eventually die out. Only in 1860 did it become illegal to own slaves. In fact, as Kumar argues, one effect of abolition was the increased reliance on other forms of bondage to control former slaves.

The Indian model became an important one. In 1874, under pressure, the governor of the Gold Coast forbade any court, British or African, to recognize slavery (Miers and Roberts 1988:13; McSheffrey 1983; Dumett and Johnson 1988). In 1859 the control of the former masters was strengthened by the Workman's Breach of Contract Act (Sarkar 1985). Such legislation affecting masters and servants was passed in most British colonies within a generation after the end of slavery (McSheffrey 1983; Pouncy 1981; Greenberg 1980: 73–78).

Contract Labor

This all took place while slavery was still profitable. Abolition was successful well before the demand for unskilled labor in the tropics could be met by an international free labor market. The most important problem was sugar. The intensity of labor on the sugar plantation and the distasteful nature of the work were such that it was difficult to recruit labor without coercion (Engerman 1986). When the slave trade was abolished, the continuing decline of local populations created a labor shortage. In the West Indies, this was intensified when many former slaves, particularly women, withdrew from the plantation labor force (Temperley 1972:124–36). Indentured labor systems were devised both to maintain old centers of sugar production and to provide labor for new ones. Those based in Africa resembled too closely the slave trade (Renault 1976; Asiegbu 1969; Miers 1975:28–30). Within Africa, other forms of recruitment were difficult, as Mbodj demonstrates in chapter 9.

Increasingly, labor was recruited in India, China, and, to a lesser degree, Java and Japan, where poverty and landlessness created a pool of willing migrants. The Chinese "coolie" trade involved people purchased and sold (Stewart 1951: chap. 2). The Indian indentured system was essentially a free migration. Emmer (1986b) argues that the Indian trade tapped into existing migration patterns within India and toward areas like Ceylon and the Straits

Settlements (see also Tinker 1974; Marks and Richardson 1985). The system provided labor for sugar plantations in the West Indies and the Indian Ocean, for tea plantations in Ceylon, for rubber plantations in Malaya, for railroad building in North America, for gold mining in South Africa. Watched by abolitionist interests, the British imposed controls on recruitment, which were often ineffective. The other powers were less conscientious. The French indenture system remained a disguised slave trade until 1862, and some slave trading continued in East Africa for another generation (Renault 1976). The Portuguese, as Clarence-Smith explains in chapter 6, abolished slavery in 1878 but continued what amounted to a slave trade until 1910 (see also Clarence-Smith 1985:74–76, 107–109; Vail and White 1980; Heywood 1988).

According to Kumar, twenty-eight million Indians emigrated within an eighty-six-year period, mostly as indentured laborers. This is more than twice the number of slaves estimated to have been exported in the Atlantic trade (Lovejoy 1989). In addition, there were large-scale movements in Indonesia, from Java to the outer islands (see Reid, chap. 2), and in India, to the jute industry of Bengal and the tea plantations of Assam. The hunger of capitalist enterprise for unskilled labor merely underlines Eltis' argument that slavery was abolished while it was still profitable.

The Persistence of Slavery

While European enterprise used new forms of labor and disguised forms of slavery, slave use and slave raiding expanded in many areas outside European control. In West Africa, the end of the Atlantic trade and the decline in the Saharan trade hardly affected the price of slaves, because demand within Africa was so high. Slaves were increasingly being used in West Africa to produce palm oil and peanuts for European markets, grain and cloth for Saharan markets, and soldiers for the slaving armies (see Klein, chap. 7; Roberts 1988; Ohadike 1988; Hopkins 1973:143–44). In East Africa, they produced cloves on Zanzibar and grain, coconuts, and sesame on the coast (Cooper 1977; Sheriff 1987). In the Arab world, markets were being closed, but slave use seems to have increased. Clarence-Smith suggests that the "rise in real incomes and the expansion in the numbers of the wealthy elite contributed to greater demand" (1988:5). Ricks (1988) describes an increase in slave use in Persia. With the slave trade restricted elsewhere, the Red Sea route expanded, and the Hejaz served as a base for trade to other parts of the Middle East (Ewald 1988).

James Warren's study of the Sulu sultanate gives us a similar picture. Located bewteen Borneo and the Philippines, the Sulu Islands were the base for slave-raiding pirates who ranged wide over the waters of Southeast Asia. In the eighteenth century the slaves they took were sold along with spices and other Indonesian goods to Dutch and Chinese merchants throughout Southeast Asia (Warren 1981:13–14). During the nineteenth century slave raiding expanded, but the export of slaves declined. The slaves were sold instead within the Sulu Zone, the coasts of Borneo, Celebes, and the islands inbetween. Many slaves took part in trading expeditions or manned the ships that enslaved others. Others gathered sea slugs, wax, birds' nests, and pearl shell. Many fished, made salt, or grew rice. Some were artisans or scribes, and women often became concubines or servants (Warren 1981: chap. 10).

European colonial enterprise was not threatened by slavery. It successfully exploited indigenous slavery. It did, however, consider slave raiding a menace, since it threatened depopulation and blocked the development of trade and production. The Sulu pirates took most of their slaves in the southern Philippines, where the Spanish were at first helpless to block them. Only the efforts of the Catholic friars to organize defense limited Sulu dominion. By 1860 steamships gave the European powers an increasing superiority over slavers in both Atlantic and Pacific waters. Spanish, English, and Dutch ships established control over large areas, and in 1875 the Spanish occupied Jolo, the Sulu capital (Warren 1981:122–25). Small-scale slave raiding persisted until after American occupation of the area in 1898.

Ending the Slave Trade

Slave raiding and the accompanying insecurity constituted more of a threat to the new colonial regimes than did slavery itself. Armies in the field were often reluctant to threaten the interests of slave-owning allies. Once in control, Europeans often, but not always, moved against slaving and slave trading. Sometimes local reasons inspired action. Thus, in Africa, freeing slaves was often a way to weaken enemies or leaders who remained too powerful. Forest (1980) argues that in Cambodia there was a desire to get slaves on the tax rolls. In most areas, however, Europeans felt reluctant to attack slavery itself (see Reid, chap. 2; Klein, chap. 7; Miers and Crowder 1988). Laws and edicts dealing with slavery were often not enforced (Klosterboer 1960:202–6). European administrators were few in number and feared the effects of social disruption. They also often felt sympathetic to the ruling elites and saw slavery as a benign institution. Pressures from home, however, often proved persuasive. Senior administrators feared that scandals might erode their political support at home or influence their careers. They often had to push reluctant subordinates to act.

In Indonesia, during British occupation, Sir Stamford Raffles had abolished the importation of slaves into Java in 1813, and the Dutch prohibited the slave trade in 1818. Dutch policy shifted increasingly during the early nineteenth century toward more intensive use of forced labor. Corvée labor was used for public works, and an elaborate system of compulsory cultivation forced all cultivators, bonded or free, to produce cash crops (see Reid, chap. 2). With high population densities, obtaining labor no longer required enforcing servitude. In spite of this, the Dutch did not prohibit owning slaves until 1860, and they immediately began making exceptions for indigenous slave ownership in the outer islands. Sutherland defines Dutch policy in the 1860s: the Dutch acted to "abolish slavery when it was possible, diminish it whenever the opportunity offered, pay compensation if it was necessary, and avoid regulation and publicity" (1983:277). A decade later there was a shift: "In directly ruled lands with real Dutch power, abolition was to be carried out quickly; in directly ruled lands . . . with little power, there was to be a gradual movement against slavery, with registration and compensation. In territories with self-rule but under contract to the Dutch, the tactic was to be one of limitation and amelioration when possible, but no abolition" (Sutherland 1983:278). Only after 1878 was antislavery policy pursued vigorously. In some areas, however, no serious action was taken until the twentieth century.

Elsewhere in Southeast Asia, abolition came later. In Cambodia, the French signed treaties in 1877 and 1884 which had antislavery clauses, but decisive legislation came in only with definitive occupation in 1897. The law prohibited the sale of persons but merely regulated debt slavery. With the imposition of taxes and the elaboration of a money economy, debt slavery increased much as it had earlier in India (Forest 1980:342–57). In British-ruled Malaya, abolition of slavery and debt bondage came piecemeal, state by state, and was not complete until 1915 (Endicott 1983:236). In Burma, the British moved with similar caution, acting in parts of eastern Burma only in 1926.

In Africa, serious abolition also came late. Slaves were freed at the Cape in 1833, a factor pushing Afrikaner farmers to trek into the interior, where they were less restrained in their efforts to coerce the labor of others. Britain's 1833 abolition act received limited application in Sierra Leone and the Gambia. In 1848 the French showed similar reluctance to apply the emancipation law which threatened the colony's relations with its neighbors. The legal status of slavery was abolished on the Gold Coast in 1874. The major concern of colonial administrations was often to limit the damage which these islands of liberty did to their relations with African states (see Klein, chap. 7 and Mbodj, chap. 8; Miers 1975:157–66). Africa was largely conquered with armies recruited from slaves. Many of these armies, like the French, rewarded their troops and allies with slave booty.

Conquest was usually followed by a ban on slave trading and slave raiding. Some acts, however, were clearly written for outside consumption, and local administrators were often reluctant to enforce others. As in Asia, colonial administrators in Africa distinguished slaving from slavery and argued that slavery was benign. Furthermore, they believed that compulsion was necessary to maintain production, and they tended to identify their own interests with those of slave-owning intermediaries. Invariably, slaves were seen as lazy. Even when forced to abolish slavery, colonial administrators tried to reinforce the control of former masters or to secure other forms of labor. This was particularly true in areas that were economically or strategically important. Thus, in East Africa, the British allowed slavery to die on the coast and killed it on Zanzibar, but they tried other ways to guarantee labor supplies to Zanzibar's clove plantations (Cooper 1980). In West Africa, the French recognized the property rights of the former masters in the fertile inner delta of the Niger, and former masters were able to use control over land to maintain control over labor. In the Sudan, a British administration tolerated both slavery and slave trade until about 1930 (Daly 1986:231–37).

Antislavery legislation often used the India formula of 1843. In West Africa, the French simply withdrew recognition of slave status, but with the state no longer standing behind the masters, hundreds of thousands of slaves were free to go home (Roberts and Klein 1980). In northern Nigeria, Lugard freed only slaves who had been mistreated but insisted on other slaves' right to purchase redemption. Many, however, fled (Lovejoy and Hogendorn 1988, 1989). Once slavery lost its legal status, the official line was that it no longer existed. Henceforth, colonial administrators were generally reluctant to involve themselves in conflicts that arose. In many areas, a small clandestine slave trade in children persisted well into the twentieth century, and slave status remains important even today.

The abolition of slavery did not usually constitute a rejection of coercion. Colonial regimes generally lacked the funds to develop infrastructure and to expand administration. They thus turned, often massively, to forced labor. In Indonesia, efforts to control slavery were paralleled by the rise in the coercive cultivation system (see Reid, chap. 2). In India, forced labor was particularly important in the early nineteenth century. All colonial regimes in Africa used forced labor. The Belgians relied heavily on forced labor (Northrup 1988a). The French also did so until 1946, and forced labor was used in Portuguese Africa into the 1970s (Clarence-Smith 1985:215). Systems of forced cultivation similar to the Indonesian cultivation system were also used (Clarence-Smith 1985:182–84; Jewsiewicki 1980).

Slavery and Reform

Neither the issue of slavery nor the slave trade was confined to colonial domains. During the nineteenth century much of the non-Western world struggled with the problem of how to limit, resist, and understand the West. At their most superficial, African and Asian rulers simply wanted to fend off international pressure and to create alliances. This was certainly true of Menelik of Ethiopia. From 1876 until his stroke in 1908, Menelik issued edicts restricting and banning the slave trade. During the same period the taking of slaves helped finance the conquest of southern Ethiopia and reward the military men responsible (Fernyhough 1988:115–25; McCann 1988). Khedive Ismail of Egypt actually asked for a British demonstration against Egyptian slavery in 1872, and one was arranged (Miers 1975:78). When Sultan Barghash of Zanzibar agreed to ban the slave trade in 1873, it only constituted recognition of British power.

Antislavery was also part of a more profound reaction. Just as the Russian reformers of 1861 saw emancipation of the serfs as a way of liberating productive energies from the restraints of an archaic social order, many reformers elsewhere saw abolition as part of a program of reform. Both the Turks and the Thais were anxious to fend off imperialist threats to their sovereignty, but in both cases, they sought to do so by transforming the nature of their own societies. Both Toledano in chapter 1 and Feeny in chapter 3 describe a groping with change. In China, the last years of the empire saw a series of sweeping reform proposals, one of which was finally approved in 1910 (Meijer 1980). Furthermore, some of these reformers looked to their own traditions to sanction antislavery action. Ottoman reformers sought justification in the humane principles of Islam. Chou Fu, a Chinese reformer, argued that Chinese practice had strayed from early principle (Meijer 1980:327). Ahmed al-Nasiri, a Moroccan historian, wrote: "The basic condition of the human being is freedom. . . . The reason in the Holy Law which existed in the Time of the Prophet and the pious forefathers for enslaving people— namely being capture in a jihad which has the object of making the Word of God supreme and bringing men to His religion—does not exist in these days" (cited in Hunwick 1988:5).

Class Struggle

The decrees of an alien European authority were not always the last word. In some areas, slaves left, usually to go home but sometimes to seek other opportunities. Many, however, were born in slavery or had spent long years in slavery. Throughout Asia and Africa, the vast majority of freed slaves remained where they were. Warren (1981: chap. 11) describes the tales of people enslaved as children who had lost all memory of their original homes. Endicott (1983) tells us that most freed slaves in Malaya had no desire to return to aboriginal homes in the hill region. The desire of freed slaves to remain where they were was particularly strong when they had been effectively assimilated into a new culture or where land was valuable or work remunerative. There were often new forms of class struggle as former slaves sought control over strategic resources and over their productive and reproductive lives. Mbodj in chapter 8 describes ways in which masters were able to maintain their control over labor. In India, it was through the extension of debt bondage; in Senegal, through control of the housing and job markets. In both cases, former masters were successful, but their success reflected their ability to protect and reward (see also Prakash 1990). In other areas, a complex process of negotiating new relationships began. In densely populated areas of Asia, the shortage of land restricted the freedom of the bonded. State and master struggled to develop new ways of expropriating the labor of their former dependents, while slave and bondsman sought to circumscribe their ability to do so or to extract in exchange a greater security. Even where masters were not successful in maintaining control of labor, they generally maintained a social ascendancy. The stigma of slave origins has persisted to the present (Watson 1980c:245–48; Miers and Roberts 1988).

Conclusion

Traditional forms of servitude survive in many parts of the world. Children are sold on the streets of Bangkok (Bond 1989). Bondage persists in India in spite of efforts to abolish it (Marla 1981; Kamble 1981). Mauritania "abolished" slavery in 1980, and forms of servitude continue in many parts of the Sahara (McDougall 1988). In chapter 2 Reid tells us that it persists in many isolated parts of Southeast Asia. In most conservative areas with a tradition of slaveholding, servants and family retainers remain in the service of the rich and powerful or maintain a client relationship. Slavery in these areas was rarely tied to race, but there is a stigma that persists and that forces the descendents of yesterday's slaves into new kinds of dependency. Mostly it persists in poor countries and the descendents of slaves and bondsmen cling to what little security their inferior status gives them.

Yet, though forms of bonded labor, mostly that of children, persist in the dark corners of some poor countries, probably no society depends on slavery for much of its labor. The transformation in the ways in which labor is organized and controlled has been profound.[3] From the slave plantation to modern apartheid, capitalist enterprise has not been reluctant to exploit coerced labor, but it has invariably extended, sometimes hesitantly, capitalist relations of production, which have eroded servile ties. Equally important, it created in Europe and North America a free labor ideology and convinced itself that free labor was essential to the dramatic growth and transformation of the capitalist world. This ideology was given its loftiest expression by the abolition movement, spawned by and consistently supported by Christian churches. It was also powerful enough that those non-Western elites who sought to understand Europe's ascendancy invariably saw free labor as a crucial part of that ascendancy. Ironically, that ideology was resisted most vigorously by colonial states quite willing to protect and to exploit different kinds of servitude. To be sure, the freeing of labor from traditional restraints was often part of the colonial agenda, but it was sometimes put off into the distant future. Dependent on democratically elected European parliaments for their budgets, colonial administrations were vulnerable to the pressures of abolitionist groups and increasingly had difficulty controlling the flow of information about their policies. Only these ideological agendas can explain why Europe turned against slavery when it was still very profitable.

The many tales told in this book are part of the same larger story, but each one responds to the rhythms of a different history. Change was dramatic in some areas, slow in others, though each responded within its particular historical tradition to the same world historical process. Bondage often proved more resilient than slavery, perhaps because slavery depended so much on the use of force and the maintenance of a constant supply of new slaves. Invariably, some form of struggle occurred. Landowners struggled to maintain control over labor. Servile groups struggled for security as well as for control of their productive and, in the case of slaves, their reproductive lives. And the state, the final arbiter, struggled to impose its will on both, often freeing the servile from traditional bonds in order to impose new ones.

If the tales are different, so too are the approaches our authors take. Reid, Kumar, Klein, and Clarence-Smith present broad regional overviews. Mbodj describes the struggle for control of the former slave's labor in a small trading community. Toledano and Prakash are concerned with the mind of the actor — Toledano with Ottoman reformers, Prakash with British colonial administrators. In both cases, policy was shaped by the way in which servile institutions were conceived. Feeny is an economic historian interested in examining the economics of decline of a well-established slave system. We hope that the combined effect will offer a fuller understanding of the decline of slavery and other servile institutions. Just as recent research on servitude has underlined the variety and ambiguity of different labor forms, so we have tried to confront the varieties and ambiguities of emancipation, to assess both persistence and transformation, and to look at emancipation in a world historical perspective. We hope that we will leave the reader asking more questions than we have answered.

Notes

1. The literature on comparative slavery is limited. The classic text is Nieboer 1910. The only comparable recent work to examine slavery in broad cross-cultural perspective is Patterson 1982. The literature is, however, growing rapidly. See especially Archer 1988; Meillassoux 1986, 1975a; Miers and Kopytoff 1977b; Lovejoy 1983; Robertson and Klein 1983; Watson 1980a; Reid 1983c; Finley 1968. For further bibliographical references, see Miller 1985.

2. "The work done by slaves, though it appears to cost only their maintenance, is in the end the dearest of any. A person who can acquire no property, can have no other interest but to eat as much, and to labour as little as possible. Whatever work he does beyond what is sufficient to purchase his own maintenance, can be squeezed out of him by violence only, and not by any interest of his own" (Smith [1776] 1937:365). See Williams 1944:6.

3. See Klosterboer 1960 for a survey of newer forms of compulsory labor in the twentieth century. On the link between capitalism and different forms of unfree labor, see Miles 1987.

References

Abeyasekere, Susan. 1983. Slaves in Batavia: Insights from a slave register. In *Slavery, bondage and dependency in Southeast Asia. See* Reid 1983c.

Anstey, Roger. 1975. *The Atlantic slave trade and British abolition, 1769–1810.* Atlantic Highlands, N.J.: Humanities Press.

Archer, Léonie, ed. 1988. *Slavery and other forms of unfree labor.* London: Routledge.

Ascherson, Neil. 1963. *The king incorporated.* London: George Allen and Unwin.

Asiegbu, Johnson. 1969. *Slavery and the politics of liberation, 1787–1861: A study of liberated African emigration and British anti-slavery policy.* New York: Africana.

Aung Thwin, Michael. 1983. *Athi, Kyun-Taw, Hpayà-Kyun:* Varieties of commendation and dependence in pre-colonial Burma. In *Slavery, bondage and dependency in Southeast Asia. See* Reid 1983c.

Austen, Ralph. 1981. From the Atlantic to the Indian Ocean: European abolition, the African slave trade, and Asian economic structures. In *The abolition of the Atlantic slave trade. See* Eltis and Walvin 1981.

Austen, Ralph. 1988. The 19th century Islamic slave trade from East Africa (Swahili and Red Sea coasts): A tentative census. In *The economics of the Indian Ocean slave trade.* See Clarence-Smith 1989.

Baer, Gabriel. 1967. Slavery in nineteenth-century Egypt. *Journal of African History* 8:417–41.

Baier, Stephen. 1980. *An economic history of central Niger.* Oxford: Clarendon.

Baldé, Mamadou Saliou. 1975. L'esclavage et la guerre sainte au Fuuta-Jalon. In *L'esclavage en Afrique précoloniale. See* Meillassoux 1975a.

Banaji, D. R. 1933. *Slavery in British India.* Bombay: Taraporevala.

Basham, A. L. 1954. *The wonder that was India.* London: Sedgwick and Jackson.

Bethell, Leslie. 1970. *The abolition of the Brazilian slave trade.* Cambridge: Cambridge University Press.

Bloch, Marc. 1975. How and why ancient slavery came to an end. In *Slavery and serfdom in the Middle Ages,* trans. W. R. Beer. Berkeley: University of California Press.

Bond, Peter. 1989. *Anti-slavery reporter,* ser. 7, 13, no. 5:26–36.

Brooks, George. 1976. The signares of St. Louis and Gorée: Women entrepreneurs in eighteenth-century Senegal. In *Women in Africa,* ed. Nancy Hafkin and Edna Bay. Stanford, Calif.: Stanford University Press.

Brunschwig, R. 1960. Abd. In *Encyclopedia of Islam: New edition.* 1:24–40.

Chakravarti, Uma. 1985. Of dasas and karmakaras: Servile labour in ancient India. In *Chains of servitude. See* Patnaik and Dingwaney 1985.

Chanana, Dev Raj. 1960. *Slavery in ancient India.* New Delhi: Peoples.

Clarence-Smith, William Gervase. 1985. *The third Portuguese empire, 1825–1975.* Manchester: Manchester University Press.

Clarence-Smith, William Gervase. 1988. The economics of the Indian Ocean and Red Sea slave trade in the 19th century: An overview. *Slavery and Abolition* 9:1–20.

Clarence-Smith, William Gervase. 1989. *The economics of the Indian Ocean slave trade.* London: Cass.

Conrad, Robert. 1972. *The destruction of Brazilian slavery, 1850–1888.* Berkeley: University of California Press.

Cooper, Frederick. 1977. *Plantation slavery on the east coast of Africa.* New Haven: Yale University Press.

Cooper, Frederick. 1979. The problem of slavery in African studies. *Journal of African History* 20:103–26.

Cooper, Frederick. 1980. *From slaves to squatters: Plantation labor and agriculture in Zanzibar and coastal Kenya, 1890–1925.* New Haven: Yale University Press.

Cooper, Frederick. 1981. Islam and cultural hegemony: The ideology of slaveowners on the East African coast. In *The ideology of slavery in Africa. See* Lovejoy 1981.

Cordell, Dennis. 1985. *Dar al-Kuti and the last years of the Atlantic slave trade.* Madison: University of Wisconsin Press.

Cordell, Dennis. 1988. The delicate balance of force and flight: The end of slavery in eastern Ubangi-Shari. *The end of slavery in Africa. See* Miers and Roberts 1988.

Coupland, Reginald. 1933. *The British anti-slavery movement.* London: Oxford University Press.

Crone, Patricia. 1980. *Slaves on horses.* Cambridge: Cambridge University Press.

Curtin, Philip. 1969. *The Atlantic slave trade: A census.* Madison: University of Wisconsin Press.

Curtin, Philip. 1990. *Rise and fall of the plantation complex.* Cambridge: Cambridge University Press.

Daget, Serge. 1980. A model of the French abolitionist movement and its variations. In *Anti-slavery, religion and reform: Essays in memory of Roger Anstey,* ed. Christine Bolt and Seymour Drescher. Folkestone: Dawson.

Daly, Martin. 1986. *Empire on the Nile: The Anglo-Egyptian Sudan, 1898–1934.* Cambridge: Cambridge University Press.

Dandamaev, Muhammad. 1984. *Slavery in Babylonia.* Trans. Victoria Powell. DeKalb: Northern Illinois University Press.

Davis, David Brion. 1966. *The problem of slavery in western culture.* Ithaca, N.Y.: Cornell University Press.

Davis, David Brion. 1984. *Slavery and human progress.* New York: Oxford University Press.

Dike, K. O. 1956. *Trade and politics in the Niger delta.* London: Oxford University Press.

Dingwaney, Manjari. 1985. Unredeemed promises: The law and servitude. In *Chains of servitude*. *See* Patnaik and Dingwaney 1985.

Drescher, Seymour. 1977. *Econocide: British slavery in the era of abolition*. Pittsburgh: University of Pittsburgh Press.

Drescher, Seymour. 1980. Two variants of anti-slavery: Religious organization and social mobilization in Britain and France, 1780–1870. In *Anti-slavery, religion and reform: Essays in memory of Roger Anstey*, ed. Christine Bolt and Seymour Drescher. Folkestone: Dawson.

Drescher, Seymour. 1986. *Capitalism and antislavery: British mobilization in comparative perspective*. London: Macmillan.

Drescher, Seymour. 1987. Paradigms tossed: Capitalism and the political sources of abolition. In *British capitalism and Caribbean slavery*. *See* Solow and Engerman 1987.

Dumett, Raymond, and Marion Johnson. 1988. Britain and the suppression of slavery in the Gold Coast colony, Ashanti, and the northern territories. In *The end of slavery in Africa*. *See* Miers and Roberts 1988.

Dunn, Richard. 1972. *Sugar and slaves: The rise of the planter class in the English West Indies, 1624–1713*. Chapel Hill: University of North Carolina Press.

Eberhard, Wolfram. 1962. *Social mobility in traditional China*. Leiden: Brill.

Echenberg, Myron. 1986. Slaves into soldiers: Social origins of the Tirailleurs Senegalais. In *Africans in bondage*, ed. Paul Lovejoy. Madison, Wis.: African Studies Program.

Elkins, Stanley. 1959. *Slavery*. Chicago: University of Chicago Press.

Eltis, David. 1987. *Economic growth and the ending of the transatlantic slave trade*. New York: Oxford University Press.

Eltis, David, and James Walvin, eds. 1981. *The abolition of the Atlantic slave trade*. Madison: University of Wisconsin Press.

Emmer, Pieter C., ed. 1986a. *Colonialism and migration: Indentured labour before and after slavery*. Dordrecht: Nijhoff.

Emmer, Pieter C. 1986b. The meek Hindu: The recruitment of Indian indentured labourers for service overseas, 1870–1916. In *Colonialism and migration*. *See* Emmer 1986a.

Endicott, Kirk. 1983. The effects of slave raiding on the aborigines of the Malay Peninsula. In *Slavery, bondage and dependency in Southeast Asia*. *See* Reid 1983c.

Engerman, Stanley. 1986. Servants to slaves to servants: Contract labour and European expansion. In *Colonialism and migration*. *See* Emmer 1986a.

Ewald, Janet. 1988. The Nile Valley system and Red Sea slave trade, 1820–1880. *Slavery and Abolition* 9:71–92. (Also in *The economics of the Indian Ocean slave trade*. *See* Clarence-Smith 1989.)

Fernyhough, Timothy. 1988. Slavery and the slave trade in southern Ethiopia in the 19th century. *Slavery and Abolition* 9:103–30. (Also in *The economics of the Indian Ocean slave trade*. *See* Clarence-Smith 1989.)

Finley, Moses. 1960. The servile statuses of ancient Greece. *Revue internationale des droits de l'antiquité*, 3d ser., 7:165–89. Reprinted in *Economy and society in ancient Greece*, by Moses Finley. Harmondsworth, Eng.: Penguin, 1981.

Finley, Moses. 1964. Between slavery and freedom. *Comparative Studies in Society and History* 6:233–49.

Finley, Moses. 1968. Slavery. In *International encyclopedia of the social sciences* 14:307–13. New York: Macmillan.

Fisher, Alan. 1980. Chattel slavery in the Ottoman Empire. *Slavery and Abolition* 1:25–45.

Fogel, Robert William, and Stanley L. Engerman. 1974. *Time on the Cross: The economics of American Negro slavery*. Vol. 1. Boston: Little, Brown.

Foner, Eric. 1983. *Nothing but freedom: Emancipation and its legacy*. Baton Rouge: Louisiana State University Press.

Forest, Alain. 1980. *Le Cambodge et la colonisation française*. Paris: Harmattan.

Genovese, Eugene. 1969. *The world the slaveholders made*. New York: Vintage.

Genovese, Eugene. 1972. *Roll, Jordan, roll*. New York: Random House.

Greenberg, Stanley. 1980. *Race and state in capitalist development*. New Haven: Yale University Press.

Harris, Joseph. 1971. *The African presence in Asia: Consequences of the East African slave trade*. Evanston, Ill.: Northwestern University Press.

Hellie, Richard. 1982. *Slavery in Russia, 1450–1725*. Chicago: University of Chicago Press.

Heywood, Linda. 1988. Slavery and forced labor in the changing political economy of central Angola, 1850–1949. In *The end of slavery in Africa*. *See* Miers and Roberts 1988.

Hopkins, A. G. 1973. *Economic history of West Africa*. London: Longmans.

Hopkins, Keith. 1978. *Conquerors and slaves*. Cambridge: Cambridge University Press.

Hunwick, John. 1988. Black slaves in the Mediterranean world: Introduction to a neglected aspect of the African diaspora. Paper presented to the Workshop on the Long-Distance Trade in Slaves across the Sahara and the Black Sea in the Nineteenth Century. December. Bellagio, Italy.

Inalcık, Halil. 1979. Servile labor in the Ottoman Empire. In *The mutual effects of the Islamic and Judeo-Christian worlds: The east European pattern*. ed. A. Ascher, T. Halasi-Kun, and Bela Kiraly. New York: Brooklyn College Press.

Jewsiewicki, Bogumil. 1980. African peasants in the totalitarian colonial society of the Belgian Congo. In *Peasants in Africa*, ed. Martin A. Klein. Beverly Hills: Sage.

Jha, Vivekanand. 1988. Slavery in precolonial India. Paper presented to the International Conference on Slavery, June. São Paulo, Brazil.

Jwaideh, Albertine, and Robert Cox. 1989. The black slaves of Turkish Arabia during the 19th century. In *The economics of the Indian Ocean slave trade*. See Clarence-Smith 1989.

Kamble, N. D. 1981. *Bonded labour in India*. New Delhi: Uppal.

Klein, Herbert. 1986. *African slavery in Latin America and the Caribbean*. New York: Oxford University Press.

Klein, Martin A. 1987. The demography of slavery in the western Soudan during the late 19th century. In *African population and capitalism: Historical perspectives*, ed. Dennis Cordell and Joel Gregory. Boulder: Westview.

Klein, Martin A., and Paul Lovejoy. 1979. Slavery in West Africa. In *The uncommon market: Essays in the economic history of the Atlantic slave trade*, ed. H. A. Gemery and J. S. Hogendorn. New York: Academic Press.

Klein, Martin A., and Richard Roberts. 1987. Pawning in the depression in French West Africa. *African Economic History* 16:23-37.

Klosterboer, Wilhelmina. 1960. *Involuntary labour since the abolition of slavery*. Leiden: Brill.

Kumar, Dharma. 1965. *Land and caste in south India*. Cambridge: Cambridge University Press.

Kumar, Dharma, H. Fukuzawa, B. Chaudhuri, and E. Stokes. 1983. Agrarian Relations. In *The Cambridge economic history of India*, vol. 2, ed. Dharma Kumar. Cambridge: Cambridge University Press.

Lasker, Bruno. 1950. *Human bondage in Southeast Asia*. Chapel Hill: University of North Carolina Press.

Lennihan, Louise. 1982. Rights in men and rights in land: Slavery, labor and smallholder agriculture in northern Nigeria. *Slavery and Abolition* 3:111-39.

Lovejoy, Paul. 1978. Plantations in the economy of the Sokoto caliphate. *Journal of African History* 19:341-68.

Lovejoy, Paul, ed. 1981. *The ideology of slavery in Africa*. Beverly Hills: Sage.

Lovejoy, Paul. 1983. *Transformations in slavery: A history of slavery in Africa*. Cambridge: Cambridge University Press.

Lovejoy, Paul. 1989. The impact of the Atlantic slave trade on Africa: A review of the literature. *Journal of African History* 30:365-94.

Lovejoy, Paul, and J. S. Hogendorn. 1988. The reform of slavery in early colonial northern Nigeria. In *The end of slavery in Africa*. See Miers and Roberts 1988.

Lovejoy, Paul, and J. S. Hogendorn. 1989. The development and execution of Frederick Lugard's policies toward slavery in northern Nigeria. *Slavery and Abolition* 10:1-43.

Mabbett, I. W. 1983. Some remarks on the present state of knowledge about slavery in Angkor. In *Slavery, bondage and dependency in Southeast Asia*. See Reid 1983c.

McCann, James. 1988. Children of the house: Slavery and its suppression in Lasta, northern Ethiopia, 1916-1935. In *The end of slavery in Africa*. See Miers and Roberts 1988.

McDougall, Ann. 1988. A topsy-turvy world: Slaves and freed slaves in the Mauritanian Adrar, 1910-1950. In *The end of slavery in Africa*. See Miers and Roberts 1988.

McSheffrey, Gerald. 1983. Slavery, indentured servitude, legitimate trade and the impact of abolition in the Gold Coast: 1874-1901. *Journal of African History* 24:349-68.

Manguin, Pierre Yves. 1983. Manpower and labour categories in early sixteenth-century Malacca. In *Slavery, bondage and dependency in Southeast Asia*. See Reid 1983c.

Marks, Shula, and Peter Richardson, eds. 1985. *International labour migration: Historical perspectives*. London: Maurice Temple Smith.

Marla, Sarma. 1981. *Bonded labour in India*. New Delhi: Biblia Impex.

Meijer, Marinus. 1980. Slavery at the end of the Ch'ing dynasty. In *Essays on China's legal tradition,* ed. Jerome A. Cohen et al. Princeton, N.J.: Princeton University Press.

Meillassoux, Claude, ed. 1975a. *L'esclavage en Afrique précoloniale.* Paris: Maspero.

Meillassoux, Claude. 1975b. "Etat et conditions des esclaves à Gumbu (Mali) au XIXe siècle." In *L'esclavage en Afrique précoloniale. See* Meillassoux 1975a.

Meillassoux, Claude. 1986. *Anthropologie de l'esclavage: Le ventre de fer et d'argent.* Paris: PUF.

Mendelsohn, Isaac. 1949. *Slavery in the ancient Near East.* New York: Oxford University Press.

Miers, Suzanne. 1967. The Brussels conference of 1889–1890: The place of the policies of Great Britain and Germany. In *Britain and Germany in Africa,* ed. Prosser Gifford and William Roger Louis. New Haven: Yale University Press.

Miers, Suzanne. 1975. *Britain and the ending of the slave trade.* New York: Africana.

Miers, Suzanne, and Michael Crowder. 1988. The politics of slavery in Bechuanaland: Power struggles and the plight of the Basarwa in the Bamangwato reserve, 1926–1940. In *The end of slavery in Africa. See* Miers and Roberts 1988.

Miers, Suzanne, and Igor Kopytoff. 1977a. African "slavery" as an institution of marginality. In *Slavery in Africa. See* Miers and Kopytoff 1977b.

Miers, Suzanne, and Igor Kopytoff, eds. 1977b. *Slavery in Africa.* Madison: University of Wisconsin Press.

Miers, Suzanne, and Richard Roberts, eds. 1988. *The end of slavery in Africa.* Madison: University of Wisconsin Press.

Miles, Robert. 1987. *Capitalism and unfree labour.* London: Tavistock.

Miller, Joseph. 1985. *Slavery: A world-wide bibliography, 1900–1982.* New York: Kraus International.

Miller, Joseph. 1988. *Way of death: Merchant capitalism and the Angolan slave trade, 1730–1830.* Madison: University of Wisconsin Press.

Nair, A. K. K. R. 1986. *Slavery in Kerala.* Delhi: Mittal.

Nieboer, Herman J. 1910. *Slavery as an industrial system: Ethnological researches.* 2d ed. The Hague: Nijhoff.

Northrup, David. 1988a. *Beyond the bend in the river: African labor in eastern Zaire, 1865–1940.* Athens, Ohio: Center for International Studies.

Northrup, David. 1988b. The ending of slavery in the eastern Belgian Congo. In *The end of slavery in Africa. See* Miers and Roberts 1988.

Ochsenwald, William. 1980. Muslim-European conflict in the Hijaz: The slave trade controversy, 1840–1895. *Middle Eastern Studies* 16:115–26.

Ohadike, Don. 1988. The decline of slavery among the Igbo people. In *The end of slavery in Africa. See* Miers and Roberts 1988.

Patnaik, Utsa, and Manjari Dingwaney, eds. 1985. *Chains of servitude: Bondage and slavery in India.* Madras: Sangam.

Patterson, Orlando. 1982. *Slavery and social death.* Cambridge, Mass.: Harvard University Press.

Pelteret, David. 1981. Slave raiding and slave trading in early England. *Anglo-Saxon England* 9:99–114.

Pipes, Daniel. 1981. *Slave soldiers and Islam.* New Haven: Yale University Press.

Pollet, Eric, and Grace Winter. 1971. *La société Soninke.* Brussels: Editions de l'Institut de Sociologie, Université Libre de Bruxelles.

Pouncy, Hilliard. 1981. Colonial racial attitudes and colonial labour laws in British West Africa, 1815–1946. Ph.D. diss., Massachusetts Institute of Technology.

Prakash, Gyan. 1990. *Bonded histories: Genealogies of labor servitude in colonial India.* Cambridge: Cambridge University Press.

Pulleyblank, E. G. 1958. The origins and nature of chattel slavery in China. *Journal of the Economic and Social History of the Orient* 1:185–220.

Reid, Anthony. 1983a. "Closed" and "open" slave systems in pre-colonial Southeast Asia. In *Slavery, bondage and dependency in Southeast Asia. See* Reid 1983c.

Reid, Anthony. 1983b. Introduction: Slavery and bondage in Southeast Asian history. In *Slavery, bondage and dependency in Southeast Asia. See* Reid 1983c.

Reid, Anthony, ed. 1983c. *Slavery, bondage and dependency in Southeast Asia.* St. Lucia: University of Queensland Press.

Renault, François. 1971. *Lavigerie, l'esclavage africain et l'Europe, 1868–1892.* 2 vols. Paris: Boccard.

Renault, François. 1976. *Liberation d'esclaves et nouvelle servitude.* Dakar: Nouvelles Editions Africaines.

Rice, C. Duncan. 1975. *The rise and fall of black slavery.* London: Macmillan.

Richardson, David, ed. 1985. *Abolition and its aftermath: The historical context, 1790–1916.* London: Cass.

Richardson, James. 1848. *Travels in the great desert of the Sahara in 1845 and 1846.* London: R. Bentley.

Ricks, Thomas. 1988. Slaves and slave traders in the Persian Gulf, 18th and 19th centuries: An assessment. *Slavery and Abolition* 9:60–70.

Roberts, Richard. 1987. *Warriors, merchants, and slaves: The state and the economy in the Middle Niger Valley, 1700–1914.* Stanford, Calif.: Stanford University Press.

Roberts, Richard. 1988. The end of slavery in the French Soudan, 1905–1914. In *The end of slavery in Africa. See* Miers and Roberts 1988.

Roberts, Richard, and Martin A. Klein. 1980. The Banamba slave exodus of 1905 and the decline of slavery in the western Sudan. *Journal of African History* 21:375–94.

Robertson, Claire C., and Martin A. Klein, eds. 1983. *Women and slavery in Africa.* Madison: University of Wisconsin Press.

Ste. Croix, G. E. M. de. 1981. *The class struggle in the ancient Greek world from the archaic age to the Arab conquests.* London: Duckworth.

Ste. Croix, G. E. M. de. 1988. Slavery and other forms of unfree labour. In *Slavery and other forms of unfree labour. See* Archer 1988.

Sareen, T. R. 1988–89. Slavery in India under British rule, 1772–1843. *Indian Historical Review* 15:257–68.

Sarkar, Tanika. 1985. Bondage in the colonical context. In *Chains of servitude. See* Patnaik and Dingwaney 1985.

Schroeter, Daniel. 1992. Slave markets and slavery in Moroccan urban society. In

The Human Commodity. Perspectives on the Trans-Saharan Slave Trade, ed. Elizabeth Savage. London: Frank Cass.

Schwartz, Stuart. 1985. *Sugar plantations in the formation of Brazilian society: Bahia, 1550–1835*. Cambridge: Cambridge University Press.

Scott, Rebecca. 1985. *Slave emancipation in Cuba: The transition to free labor*. Princeton, N.J.: Princeton University Press.

Sheriff, Abdul. 1987. *Slaves, spices and ivory in Zanzibar*. London: Currey.

Smith, Adam. [1776] 1937. *The wealth of nations*. Modern Library edition. New York: Random House.

Sobel, Mechal. 1987. *The world they made together: Black and white values in eighteenth-century Virginia*. Princeton, N.J.: Princeton University Press.

Solow, Barbara, and Stanley Engerman, eds. 1987. *British capitalism and Caribbean slavery*. Cambridge: Cambridge University Press.

Stewart, Watt. 1951. *Chinese bondage in Peru*. Durham, N.C.: Duke University Press.

Suret-Canale, Jean. 1964. Les sociétés traditionnelles en Afrique tropicale et le concept de mode de production asiatique. *La Pensée* 117:3–24.

Suret-Canale, Jean. 1988. Traditional societies in tropical Africa and the concept of the "Asiatic mode of production": Marxism and the study of African societies. In *Essays on African history: From the slave trade to neocolonialism*, ed. Jean Suret-Canale. London: C. Hurst.

Sutherland, Heather. 1983. Slavery and the slave trade in south Sulawesi, 1660s–1800s. In *Slavery, bondage and dependency in Southeast Asia*. *See* Reid 1983c.

Temperley, Howard. 1972. *British antislavery, 1833–1870*. London: Longmans.

Temperley, Howard. 1977. Capitalism, slavery and ideology. *Past and Present* 75:94–118.

Tinker, Hugh. 1974. *A new system of slavery: The export of Indian labour overseas, 1830–1920*. London: Oxford University Press.

Toledano, Ehud R. 1982. *The Ottoman slave trade and its suppression, 1840–1890*. Princeton, N.J.: Princeton University Press.

Turton, Andrew. 1980. Thai institutions of slavery. In *Asian and African systems of slavery*. *See* Watson 1980.

Twaddle, Michael. 1988. The ending of slavery in Buganda. In *The end of slavery in Africa*. *See* Miers and Roberts 1988.

Vail, Leroy, and Landeg White. 1980. *Capitalism and colonialism in Mozambique*. London: Heinemann.

Warren, James Francis. 1981. *The Sulu Zone, 1768–1898: The dynamics of external trade, slavery and ethnicity in the transformation of a Southeast Asian maritime state*. Singapore: Singapore University Press.

Watson, James L. 1976. Chattel slavery in Chinese peasant society: A comparative analysis. *Ethnology* 15:361–75.

Watson, James L., ed. 1980a. *Asian and African systems of slavery*. Oxford: Basil Blackwell.

Watson, James L. 1980b. Introduction: Slavery as an institution: Open and closed systems. In *Asian and African systems of slavery*. *See* Watson 1980a.

Watson, James L. 1980c. Transactions in people: The Chinese market in slaves, servants and heirs. In *Asian and African systems of slavery*. *See* Watson 1980a.

Wilbur, C. Martin. 1943. *Slavery in China during the former Han dynasty: 206 B.C.– A.D. 25*. Anthropological series no. 34. Chicago: Field Museum of Natural History.

Williams, Eric. 1944. *Capitalism and slavery*. Chapel Hill: University of North Carolina Press.

1 *Ehud R. Toledano*

Ottoman Concepts of Slavery in the Period of Reform, 1830s–1880s

One of the main themes of nineteenth-century Ottoman history is the process of change through reform from above. The period during which many reforms were carried out is known as the period of the Tanzimat, meaning in Turkish "reforms," "reordering," "reorganizations" (Lewis 1969; Davison 1963; Findley 1980). The Tanzimat is commonly considered to have been inaugurated by the Gülhane Rescript of 1839 and to have lasted through the first Ottoman Constitution of 1876 until the dissolution of Parliament and the renewal of sultanic autocracy in 1878, two years after the accession of Abdülhamit II (r. 1876–1909). Since reforms began in the 1830s and continued well into the reign of Abdülhamit II, we shall refer here to the long Tanzimat period, spanning approximately the half century from the 1830s to the 1880s.

The Tanzimat period is generally regarded as a time of change in many areas of Ottoman life, although it is not certain how deeply the reforms affected nonelite groups—the overwhelming majority of Ottoman subjects—or even peripheral groups within the Ottoman elite. Visible changes in the army, the bureaucracy, the economy, law and justice, education, communication, transportation, and public health accompanied the reinvigoration of central authority. While the government came to possess more efficient tools of repression, its reforms also sowed the seeds of political change, giving rise to a strong constitutional movement.

Too often, the Tanzimat was seen as a drive initiated and backed by Euro-

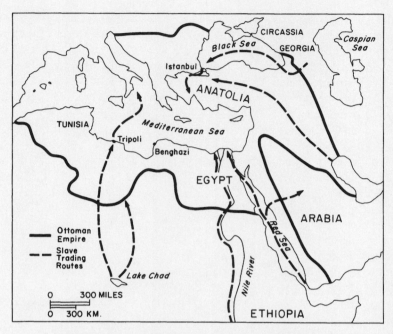

1.1 Major slave import routes, nineteenth-century Ottoman Empire

peans to import Western models and to "modernize" the Ottoman Empire.
Modern scholarship has shown, however, that the reforms were carried on
the shoulders of a strongly motivated, Ottoman-centered group of able
reformers, who were not merely the tools of Western influence but acted
to implement their own program and further their own political cause. On
the other hand, the extent to which Western ideas—not just technology and
fashion—were assimilated into Ottoman culture (integrated or "converted"
in semiotic terms) is still under debate. Ideas about the security of life, honor,
and property of the sultan's subjects figured already in the Gülhane Rescript
of 1839. The concept of equality among all subjects, including non-Muslims,
and constitutionalism took hold from the 1850s onward. Work is currently
under way to investigate how these products of Western culture were understood, converted to Ottoman categories, and then consumed and disseminated.

   A discussion of Ottoman slavery and the slave trade during the Tanzimat
offers a convenient opportunity to examine how the reformers contended with
political and cultural "interference."[1] Excepting the issue of equality for non-
Muslims, the call for the abolition of Ottoman slavery was perhaps the most
culturally loaded and sensitive topic processed in the Tanzimat period. Al-

though it was rarely debated in public, this was a matter of daily and personal concern, for both the public and private spheres of elite life were permeated by slaves at all levels.[2] Encapsulating British diplomatic pressure for the suppression of the slave trade into the Ottoman Empire and the zeal of Western abolitionism, it elicited a complex response from Ottoman reformers and thinkers on the political as well as the ideological planes.[3] In that sense, slavery is an interesting—though not in all aspects typical—example of the critical choices with which the Ottoman elite was being confronted during the Tanzimat.

From the rise of the Ottoman state in the thirteenth century, slavery was familiar to and widely accepted by people in all walks of Ottoman life. Several types of slaves were known to the sultan's subjects and lived among them. In fact, slavery had gradually become a differentiated and broadly defined concept in many Islamic societies since the introduction of military slavery into the Abbasid caliphate in the ninth century. In the Ottoman Empire, military-administrative servitude, better known as the *kul* system, coexisted with other types of slavery: harem, domestic, and agricultural (on a rather limited scale).[4] While the latter types of slavery remained much the same until the Tanzimat period, the kul system underwent profound changes.

From its inception, the kul system nourished itself on periodic levies of the unmarried, able-bodied, male children of the sultan's Orthodox Christian subjects, mostly from the Balkans. This child levy was known as the *devşirme*. The children were reduced to slavery, converted to Islam, and rigorously socialized in the palace school into various government roles, carrying elite status. Freeborn Muslims gradually entered government service, however, and the kul system evolved to accommodate this change, a process usually described as its decline. The child levy was abandoned during the seventeenth century, the palace school lost its monopoly on the reproduction of military-administrative slaves, and a new type of recruitment-cum-socialization pattern, what I describe below as the kul-type, prevailed.

What characterizes the evolution of the kul system, among other things, is that the classification of kuls as slaves was gradually becoming irrelevant. Gibb and Bowen's somewhat dated work provides what is still a useful reference to the point at issue. They write: "It is unfortunate that we should be obliged to use the word 'slave' for persons of this status. For it is appropriate only in some ways. . . . everyone that belonged to it [the ruling institution] was held still to be a slave of the Sultan, though only a small minority were really eligible to be any such thing. The conventional slavery of the rest has a painful and real quality, however. It was actual enough to cost them what may be termed their civil rights" (Gibb and Bowen 1950: vol. 1, pt. 1, pp. 43–45). This meant that the sultan could confiscate their property or take their lives, without legal process, whenever he wished. With time, confiscations and executions became infrequent, being reserved for exemplary cases of reminding Ottoman officials who was boss.

The persistence of this ambiguity regarding the servile status of Ottoman officialdom has spawned a scholarly debate over the categorization of slaves. The result is still a rather blurred picture. Hence, we need to digress briefly in order to clarify matters, before moving on to the situation which obtained in the nineteenth century. The controversy here concerns whether all men in government service, regardless of their origins, should be considered slaves, like domestic and agricultural slaves in the empire.

The noted Ottomanist Halil Inalcık stops short of arguing that military-administrative slaves were slaves in name only but states that there was much difference between them and "real" slaves. On the other end of the spectrum of opinion stand two relatively recent works by Daniel Pipes (1981) and Orlando Patterson (1982). In his study of military slavery in Islam, Pipes argues that the designation of a person as slave in Islam refers only to that person's origins, not to his or her experience in later life. He then poses the question whether military slaves were "true slaves," i.e., "persons in a state of legal and actual servility," or merely "persons of slave origins" (Pipes 1981:15–23).

The notion of control is central to Pipes's concept: to qualify as a true slave, a person must be both salable and lacking freedom of action. He writes that "though everyone is subject to innumerable restrictions and limitations, the [true] slave . . . consistently lacks the power to make his own most important decisions" (1981:17). These consist of decisions regarding location, occupation, marital status, and discipline. Military slaves thus differ from other types of slaves in their ability to gain control over their lives not only through manumission but also through the use of their own power base to liberate themselves. Accordingly, "a military slave remains a true slave as long as his master controls him" (Pipes 1981:23). Pipes concludes by cautioning against dismissing military—what I call military-administrative—slavery as mere formality or legal fiction.

This concept enables Pipes to maintain that it was quite possible for a person to possess wealth, social status, and power while at the same time being considered a true slave. Conveniently for our purposes, his most striking example is that of Ottoman grand viziers, whom, he asserts, the sultans could execute or reduce "to a kitchen aide" at the "merest whim" (Pipes 1981:18). Pipes's point is picked up and expanded by Patterson in his book *Slavery and Social Death*. Although quite problematic in its application to Ottoman slavery, this is perhaps the most stimulating contribution to the comparative study of the institution in many years. Patterson's definition of slavery is rather radical: it is "the permanent, violent domination of natally alienated and generally dishonored persons" (1982:13). Patterson insists that the concept of slavery should be applied to all kinds of slaves regardless of how elevated and powerful they might be.

Furthermore, in an example relevant to our discussion, Patterson argues that "Paul Rycaut's classic description of the Janissaries as men whom their master, the sultan, 'can raise without Envy and destroy without Danger' holds true for all slaves in all times" (1982:8). When he subsequently delves into the specific case of military-administrative slavery in Islam, Patterson inevitably finds himself profoundly disagreeing with Halil Inalcık and other Ottomanists. In his analysis, the concept of honor is central, and the assumption that grand viziers in the Ottoman Empire may have had considerable power but no honor is crucial to his argument. The only piece of evidence adduced for this far-reaching claim is the refusal of a Muslim high court to admit the testimony of the powerful Ibrahim Paşa, who served as grand vizier between 1523 and 1536, because he was a slave (Patterson 1982:308–14).

As is often the case, the great appeal of a universal model tends to wear off for specialists almost as soon as the theory is applied in their own scholarly territories. No matter how hard favorably disposed Ottomanists may try to shirk their preconceptions—and I have done my best—it would be quite difficult for them to accept Patterson's, and even Pipes's, position. The historian's concern here is to convey and interpret the peculiar situation in which, for much of Ottoman history, powerful, highly honored personages throughout the army and bureaucracy, in Istanbul as well as in the provinces, labored under certain legal impediments resembling servile status. That some of Patterson's assertions might be correct with regard to early Ottoman history and the emergence of the kul system does not make them valid for the overwhelming majority of historical cases.

In those, high-ranking Ottoman officials of kul origins and training held their elevated, powerful positions with all rights, privileges, and honors pertaining thereto. It was not common practice for grand viziers and other dignitaries—of free or of slave origin—to be humiliated after their dismissal from office. Kuls and nonkuls were subject to the sultan's "whims" to the same extent. Contrary to Pipes's view, kuls were not necessarily more at risk. Rather, the intimacy and mutual reliance of the master-slave relationship sometimes provided the kul who had slave origins with greater protection than that enjoyed by free officials. That intimacy seems to have been ignored in recent theoretical ventures, though there is considerable potential for accommodating it within Patterson's concept of "human parasitism." This concept deals in a more satisfying way with the complexities of master-slave relations by addressing the "cooperation and mutualism between holder/parasite and slave/host" (Patterson 1982:334–42). The problem with Pipes's position regarding the Ottoman kul system is his insistence that "grand viziers," as

members of a catchall category embracing all officeholders, were "true slaves"
and not merely "of slave origins," to use his own typology. He himself, however, seems to be aware that much of post–sixteenth-century Ottoman history
belies such a notion. To make amends, Pipes opines that during that period,
Ottoman military slaves reached the point of "self-assertion" and passed into
"domination," whatever that means (1981:20–21). He also provides some lee-
way by allowing that such slaves ceased to be true slaves when they were
no longer (directly?) controlled by their master. Thus, presumably, we could
mitigate the "true slavery" of the kuls who moved to the provincial administration and maybe even of those who served in the central government but not
immediately under the sultan. Moreover, the condition of salability did not
obtain with regard to officeholders unless they were of slave origins (the
kul-type), and even then it was rarely enforced.

In any event, the historical trend is clear. Even if the kul system might
have yielded an all-slave military-administrative establishment in early Ottoman history—and even that is under debate—it soon came to include an ever-
increasing number of freeborn men. As time went by, the "sultan's slaves"
(kuls) turned less kullike. As we approach the nineteenth century, their servility becomes more a symbol of their high status and less a practical fact of
life. Their job insecurity then derives from their position as servants of an
autocratic monarch, not from their formal servility. Even Carter Findley,
who takes the servile status of officeholders almost literally, can cite only
five cases during more than fifty years (1785–1837) in which highly prominent
personages were thus punished (1980:103).

To sum up this digression, we are dealing with a continuum of various
degrees of servility rather than a dichotomy between slave and free. At one
end of the continuum stand domestic and agricultural slaves, those most "slav-
ish" of Ottoman slaves. Officeholders stand at the other end, with very little
to tie them to the phenomenon of slavery. Not very far from these office
holders, we find our kul-type slaves, or state functionaries of slave origins.
Further down the steep road leading to the depths of slavery, we come upon
harem women of slave origins. The last three groups, however, are located
quite apart from the rest of those who populate our continuum. By walking
this path rather than following the dichotomous way, we avoid forcing rigid
categories upon a complex social phenomenon that rebels against them. In
so doing, we can also accommodate culture-bound historical nuances that
would otherwise elude us.

Thus, at the beginning of the Tanzimat, the "real slave" population in the
Ottoman Empire consisted of female and male, black and white, domestic
and what I call kul-harem slaves. The last category included officeholders
and harem women of slave origins. The overwhelming majority of Ottoman
slaves were female, black, and domestic; males, white females, and kul-harem

slaves constituted only a small minority. A steady stream of about eleven thousand to thirteen thousand slaves per annum entered the empire from Africa and the Caucasus. They were run via Sahara Desert routes, the Ethiopian plateau, the Red Sea, the Nile Valley, the Mediterranean, the Persian Gulf, the Black Sea, and the pilgrimage routes to and from Arabia (Toledano 1982). Slaveholding and the traffic in slaves were legal and socially acceptable. Except for cases of cruelty and ill usage, they were matters over which no serious moral question ever arose. The powers of Europe had then just passed the stage of abolition and were turning their political, economic, and moral zeal to slavery in the Americas.

By the end of the long Tanzimat period the history of Ottoman slavery had taken a major turn. The suppression of the importation of slaves into the empire had become a common item in dealings between Britain and the Ottoman government. Slaveholding was still legal, but the slave trade had been prohibited by law. The traffic in Africans and Caucasians died down, although it would pick up from time to time on a small scale. Slavery was gradually being transformed into free forms of service cum patronage, such as raising free girls in the household, socializing them into lower- or upper-class roles as talent and need determined, and later marrying them off and setting them up in life (*çırak/çıraǧ* and *besleme*). Ottoman elite culture was adopting a negative stance toward slavery and was gradually disengaging from it on moral grounds.

What happened during that half century? In the 1840s British public opinion and the British government began to take an interest in the abolition of Ottoman slavery. Attempts to induce the Sublime Porte to adopt measures to that effect soon proved futile.[6] Instead, and as an alternative method that would ultimately choke the institution for want of supply, a major effort was launched to suppress the slave trade into the empire. The essence of that long-term British drive was to extract from the Ottoman government edicts forbidding the trade in Africans and Caucasians on humanitarian grounds. The implementation of such edicts was then carefully monitored by British diplomatic and commercial representatives throughout the empire and was reported back to London. In turn, London would press Istanbul to enforce the edicts, and so on.

This pattern yielded the prohibition of the slave trade in the Persian Gulf in 1847, the temporary prohibition of the traffic in Circassians and Georgians in 1854–55, the general prohibition of the African slave trade in 1857, and the Anglo-Egyptian conventions for the suppression of the slave trade in 1877 and 1880. The campaign reached its climax with the participation of the Ottoman government in the negotiations leading to the conclusion of the Brussels Act against the slave trade, signed in 1890. It is immediately noticeable that from the mid-1850s onward, Caucasian slavery and the Caucasian slave trade were excluded from the realm of Anglo-Ottoman relations. In that area, the Porte initiated some major changes, acting alone and according to its own considerations.

One of the most important factors which forged the Porte's policy toward Caucasian slavery in the empire was the large number of Circassian immigrants—estimates range from five hundred thousand to one million—who entered Ottoman territory from the mid-1850s to the mid-1860s. That Russian-forced immigration contained about 10 percent unfree agricultural workers, which put the question of non-African slavery into a different perspective. Increased tensions between immigrant owners and slaves, at times causing violence and disturbance of public order, induced the Ottoman government in 1867 to design a special program for slaves who wished to obtain their freedom. Using an Islamic legal device, the Porte granted the slaves the land they were cultivating in order to purchase manumission from their masters.

In 1882 the authorities moved further in the same way to facilitate the conscription of Circassian and Georgian slaves. Such a step was necessary because only free men could be drafted into the army. Measures were also taken from the mid-1860s to restrict the traffic in Circassian and Georgian children, mostly girls. Thus, by the last decade of the nineteenth century the trade in Caucasian slaves was reduced considerably. The remaining demand was then maintained only by the harems of the imperial family and the households of well-to-do elite members. The imperial harem at the time contained about four hundred women in a wide array of household positions quite different from those consigned to them by Western fantasy. Those harems also continued to employ eunuchs, and as late as 1903 the Ottoman family alone owned 194 of them. In the nineteenth century a perceived decline occurred in the eunuchs' political influence, both as individuals and as a distinct corps in court politics (Toledano 1984:379–90). Whether officially abolished by the 1908 revolution or only later by the new Turkish republic, Ottoman slavery died piecemeal, not abruptly with the end of empire.

The history of Ottoman slavery and slave trade clearly belongs to the history of the Tanzimat. As such, it also reflects some of the larger issues of reform and change. Two of the most familiar themes immediately come to mind: European intervention and the reception or rejection of Western ideas. As regards the suppression of the traffic in Africans, the changes that took place mostly resulted from British pressure and deliberate effort to induce social reform in the Ottoman Empire. When we turn to Caucasian slavery and slave trade, however, it is obvious that reform was introduced on Ottoman initiative and according to Ottoman notions of the desirable and the possible. The second theme offers an opportunity to examine the extent to which Western values affected Ottoman culture during the Tanizmat. This case of "cultural interference" is discussed in the next section.

The study of slavery and the slave trade in the Ottoman Empire is only beginning. Its beginnings are related to recent developments in the study of slavery in general and the study of Islamic slavery in particular. The mid-1970s witnessed a renewed interest in the history of slavery, which was mainly stimulated by Fogel and Engerman's *Time on the Cross* (1974) and the rekindled debate over the volume of the Atlantic traffic (Curtin 1969; Inikori 1976; Curtin, Anstey, and Inikori 1976). In the area of Islamic slavery, a similar development took place. Here, however, Africanists and medievalists took the lead. In 1977 John Ralph Willis organized at Princeton University a conference on slavery and related institutions in Islamic Africa. The revised papers were published in two volumes eight years later (Willis 1985). Works by Patricia Crone and Daniel Pipes, both dealing with military slavery under Islam, appeared in 1980 and 1981, respectively, and were incorporated into the larger, comparative discussion which evolved in the 1980s. The importance of military-administrative slavery in Islam has drawn much scholarly attention, eclipsing in the process the less glamorous, though more widely prevailing forms of servitude.

Following the new wave of works on slavery both in its universal and its Islamic dimensions, the study of Ottoman slavery appeared even more neglected than before. My own work on the suppression of the Ottoman slave trade in the nineteenth century, along with more limited ventures into some aspects of Ottoman slavery, has attempted to rescue the topic from the oblivion it does not merit and to launch it into the orbit of slavery studies (Toledano 1982, 1980, 1984). Before a comprehensive work can be offered, however, many aspects of Ottoman slavery as a social phenomenon need to be studied on the basis of specific cases. The attitude of intellectuals to slavery had not been treated until the publication in 1987 of İsmail Parlatır's study of slavery in the literature of the Tanzimat period. Hakan Erdem is currently preparing at Oxford University a dissertation on the last phase of Ottoman slavery. These works and the references to Ottoman slavery in general works, such as Patterson's, may open the field to a promising, though belated, debate on substance and methodology.

The period of the Tanzimat is certainly one of the more eventful eras within the history of Ottoman slavery. It is, therefore, not surprising that students interested in the history of the institution have been attracted to the Tanzimat and the period that followed in its wake. With Parlatır's work at hand, we can now add the literary and intellectual to the political and social aspects and proceed to explore some of the more intriguing questions about the phenomena of Ottoman slavery and the slave trade: How did Ottoman elite culture deal with the Western campaign against Ottoman slavery? How were Western notions of slavery received and processed? How did those notions affect attitudes to slavery in Ottoman society?

In the following pages I examine the main reactions of Ottoman writers to slavery and to the European pressure to abolish it and offer a sociocultural interpretation of the complex and differentiated concept that was being formulated at the time. In the process, I explore the complex elite perception of military-administrative and harem slavery versus male and female domestic slavery. Finally, I argue that it was the defense of the kul and harem types of slavery that delayed full adoption of a clear abolitionist stance by the Ottoman governing elite. The slave turned general or minister and the harem woman were a small minority among Ottoman slaves and, in some fundamental aspects, were not "real" slaves nor conceived as such. The fact that the elite refused to surrender kul-harem slavery and the Western insistence on lumping this with the other, far more painful, types of slavery ensured that the one could not be abolished without the other. This inseparability only prolonged the suffering of domestic and agricultural slaves in the empire.

Ottoman Attitudes to Slavery

One can argue with foundation that strong moral sentiments nurtured the politics of abolition and suppression and that moral considerations moved the wheels of British pressure upon the Ottoman government on this issue, perhaps more overtly than on any other, excepting that of equality of non-Muslim Ottoman subjects. The antislavery lobby in Britain was often seen by British politicians and diplomats as overzealous and lacking a sense of realpolitik. They had to yield to its powerful evangelical appeal to the public, however, and press the matter abroad even when they believed it to be useless or inexpedient. Nonetheless, they too seem to have welcomed the opportunity to trade, even if temporarily, the image of Perfidious Albion for that of the champion of a humanitarian cause. But when they met their Ottoman counterparts to discuss the issue, they soon found that no common ground would be reached if the moral basis of slavery was broached. Perhaps no other issue during the Tanzimat so clearly pitted Ottoman against Western culture as did slavery. That moral flagship of Britain's civilizing mission sailed with all its zeal toward the Ottoman horizon, proudly flying its glorious colors. Curiously enough, however, the two "fleets" never really met. The few exchanges that will be treated below notwithstanding, Ottoman slavery and the Ottoman slave trade were never seriously debated, either on the political or on the intellectual plane. It was as if one party barged in fully armed with moral, economic, social, and political arguments, imbued with a strong sense of justice, while the other timidly turned its back, refusing to engage in a dialogue, claiming that there was basically no common ground, no common language, no frame of reference through which a true discussion could take place.

The nondialogue on slavery characterized British-Ottoman contacts on the subject from the outset. It was best expressed in a famous report of Lord Ponsonby, Britain's ambassador in Istanbul, to the foreign secretary, Lord Palmerston. Strongly urged by the Anti-Slavery Society, Palmerston instructed Ponsonby in November 1840 to clarify to the Ottoman government that, because of public opinion, continued British support depended on some action against slavery and the slave trade. In response, Ponsonby wrote:

I have mentioned the subject and I have been heard with *extreme astonishment accompanied with a smile* at the proposition for destroying an institution closely interwoven with the frame of society in this country, and intimately connected with the law and with the habits and even the religion of all classes, from the Sultan himself down to the lowest peasant. . . . I think that all attempts to effect your Lordship's purpose will fail, and I fear they might give *offence* if urged forward with importunity. The Turks may believe us to be their superiors in the Sciences, in Arts, and in Arms, but they are *far from thinking our wisdom or our morality greater than their own*. (PRO, FO, Dec. 27, 1840; my emphasis)

Thus, when for much of the Tanzimat period European abolitionist arguments were either taken as an offense or met with smiling dismissal, no real discussion of the issues could ensue. Since the question was immediately conceived in moral terms and translated into a competition between two value systems, no true exchange was possible. Subsequently, as already noted, Britain revised its goal from the abolition of Ottoman slavery to the suppression of the slave trade into the Ottoman Empire. It is noteworthy, however, that for about a quarter of a century—from the 1840s to the 1860s—the Ottoman government, acting to accommodate its British ally, operated without an ideological support that would justify such a policy or endow it with meaning. For those who carried it out, this was change without genuine motivation, reform without conviction, a putting things right without accepting that they were indeed wrong.

Throughout their dealings with the Tanzimat reformers, British diplomats noted that some of them were more inclined to assist in the suppression of the slave trade. One such was the leading reformer Mustafa Reşit Paşa, who served as grand vizier several times during the 1840s and 1850s. Others showed no interest whatsoever in promoting the cause, like another major reformer, Ali Paşa, who was grand vizier and foreign minister for a number of terms from the 1840s to his death in 1871. British records attributed the most forceful condemnation of slavery to Sultan Abdülmecit (r. 1839–61), who reportedly told the first dragoman of the British embassy in Istanbul in 1851 that he hoped to abolish the institution in his dominions. "It is shameful and barbarous practice," the sultan continued, "for rational beings to buy and sell their fellow creatures. Though slaves in Turkey are treated better than elsewhere, yet are they sometimes ill-used. Are not these poor creatures

our equals before God? Why then should they be assimilated to animals?"
(PRO, FO, Canning to Palmerston, Jan. 24, 1841). Such evidence might
not indicate more than the fact that some Ottoman personages, and not others,
desired to impress their British interlocutors with their sincerity on this issue.

Nonetheless, Ottoman sources contain information suggesting that a few
high- and middle-level officeholders supported anti–slave trade measures and
even justified them in terms not entirely different from the language used
in British discourse. In 1854 the grand vizier Kıbrıslı Mehmet Emin Paşa
argued in cabinet in favor of the prohibition of the slave trade in Circassians
and Georgians during the Crimean War. In 1860 Pertev Efendi, then governor
of the Red Sea port of Massawa, strongly criticized slave raids in the Horn
of Africa and proposed tough measures to stop them. Midhat Paşa, a leading
reformer and twice grand vizier in the 1870s, made an unsuccessful attempt
in 1876 to include an anti–slave trade clause in the accession speech of Sultan
Abdülhamit II. In the 1880s Ârifi Bey, governor of the major slaving port
of Jidda, explicitly condemned the trade.

In almost all these cases, one can observe a fascinating cultural translation
of Western-phrased opposition to slavery into Ottoman, but indeed Islamic,
terms. Not unexpectedly, the common ground here was humanitarian concern
for the suffering of the slaves. This necessarily shifted the emphasis from
slavery to the slave trade, thereby circumventing the futile head-on collision
of values and mores which was practically inevitable when slavery itself was
touched. As we turn to Ottoman writers and intellectuals, we find additional
means of defusing the tension that any discussion of slavery seems to have
produced, even when it was conducted within Ottoman society. Conclusive
evidence of that debate comes only from the very late Tanzimat period, from
the mid-1870s onward, though it certainly is still part and parcel of the
phenomena generated by and associated with the Tanzimat.

The Young Ottomans were the leading group of writers, publicists, intellectuals, and activists who, from the 1860s to the late 1870s, opposed the Ottoman
government for being too slow to introduce political and social reforms. One
would intuitively expect such a group of socially aware people to espouse
a clear abolitionist stance. It is amazing, however, how little interested in
Ottoman slavery and the slave trade those men actually were. In his recent
study of the treatment of slavery in Tanzimat literature, İsmail Parlatır rightly
senses that opposition to slavery should follow naturally from support of political rights, liberty, equality, and civil and human rights, for all of which
Young Ottomans firmly stood (Mardin 1962; Parlatır 1987:23–27). The evidence he himself adduces to back the claim that abolitionism actually did
follow from these principles, however, is insufficient. In fact, the very few
statements that the subject of slavery elicited from leading Young Ottomans
like Şinasi, Ali Suâvi, Ziya, and even Namık Kemal point out only too clearly

how unenthusiastic they were about dealing with it or how marginal they considered it to the larger issues for which they were fighting.

Three elements underscore the Young Ottomans' pregnant whisper on slavery and distinguish it from mere indifference or insensitivity. First, the subject matter undoubtedly belonged well in the realm of their concern. Second, these men spent much time in European capitals, where they also published their journals. Hence, they could not be unaware of the currency of antislavery sentiments in Europe, nor were they constrained by censorship from printing their views on the matter, as perhaps they might have been within the Ottoman Empire. Third, they not infrequently used the idiom of slavery as a metaphor in their writings about political and social freedom. Even the name of Kemal and Ziya's journal, *Hürriyet* (Freedom), is the Islamic legal opposite of the condition of slavery (*rıkkıyet* and *esaret*).[7]

One hardly need go farther than to cite a few lines from a poem written in 1856 by the prominent Young Ottoman writer Şinasi for the great reformer and grand vizier Mustafa Reşit Paşa:

> You have made us free, who were slaves to tyranny
> Bound as if in chains by our own ignorance.
> Your law is an act of manumission for men.
> (Lewis 1969:137)

The slavery metaphor appears in other verses, such as one by Sadullah Paşa, "Amr is not Zeyd's slave, nor is Zeyd Amr's master," or in Namık Kemal's "Dream" (Rüyâ), where Kemal plays on the words slave (*esir*), slavery (*esaret*), and freedom (*hürriyet*).[8] One can also quote Kemal's attack on Sultan Abdülaziz' speech in 1868: "If the purpose is to imply that up to this day the people in the Ottoman Empire were the slaves of the sultan, who out of the goodness of his heart, confirmed their liberty, this is something to which we can never agree, because, according to our beliefs, the rights of the people, just like divine justice, are immutable" (Mardin 1962:119).

When it came to Ottoman slavery, however, even Namık Kemal was not nearly as forceful. Only in 1875 did he write the first of two plays in which slavery figures as a theme, although not as the main one. That play was not published until 1910. The second play was written in 1876, featuring the question of slavery in a secondary, though still noticeable, role. This surely fell short even of what another Young Ottoman, Ali Suâvi, might have had in mind when he suggested in an article in *Hürriyet* that the Young Ottomans "counsel" the nation to prevent the harm caused by slave trading in Istanbul.[9]

As against these, Parlatır cites some clear-cut condemnations of slavery and the slave trade by a number of celebrated Tanzimat writers. Such expressions, also dating from the mid-1870s onward, were written mainly by Ahmet

Midhat, who had fallen out with the Young Ottomans about that time, Abdül-
hak Hamit, and Sami Paşazade Sezâi. Perhaps not surprisingly, all three had
Circassian mothers brought to the empire as slaves, a phenomenon not uncommon among members of the Ottoman elite even during and after the Tanzimat
period. The linkage between political freedom and the abolition of slavery —
absent in the writing of leading Young Ottoman activists — is explicitly and
naturally made by these novelists and playwrights. Yet for them, too, Ottoman
slavery was not a simple topic. They approached it as carefully as if they
were treading on very thin ice.

Although the Tanzimat writers who deal in some measure with slavery
all criticize the practice, one feels that they are somehow reluctant fully to
own up to its existence. In itself, this indicates the change that was taking
place in the value system. It manifests itself most strikingly in their total
refusal to grant any resemblance between Western and Ottoman slavery. In
an article published in 1869, Ahmet Midhat, one of the most prolific of
nineteenth- and early twentieth-century Ottoman writers, states categorically
that "Europeans who do not know the manners and customs of the East think
that slaves in Istanbul are like American slaves." In his plays, he draws a
clear dichotomy between Ottoman slavery and slavery elsewhere.[10]

Accordingly, American slaves are described as beasts (*behaim*) tied together
to a wooden board, slaves in antiquity are said to have been regarded as
animals (*hayvanat*) and not counted as human beings, and the killing of a
Russian slave is alleged to have been considered no more than the killing
of a dog. On the most vulnerable point of sexual relations, Midhat deflects
Western insinuations embodied in the "harem fantasy" of European literary
fame. Here, he inverts the charge by stating that female slaves, in Russia,
for example, were sexually available (*istifraş edebilir*) to their masters even
if they were married, a travesty in Islamic and Ottoman terms.

Conversely, Ottoman slavery is described as humane, almost benign. The
human sensitivity of Ottoman society is taken for granted and appealed to
in order to mitigate the circumstances that surround slavery and the traffic
that feeds it. In clear contradistinction to the extrahuman status of slaves
in other societies, Tanzimat writers dwell mostly on harem slavery —
admittedly the most comfortable kind of female servitude. The implication
is that many of the slaves in Ottoman society were actual members of the
elite. Thus, Ahmet Midhat, for example, states that many female slaves became queen mothers (mothers of sultans, *valide sultan*s), that the overwhelming majority of the wives of Ottoman "noblemen" were of slave origin, that
slavery was, in fact, a way of choosing one's wife or lady of the house,
and that slavery did not debase any female slave (Parlatır 1987:42–45).

This strong defense of Ottoman, actually Islamic, slavery vis-à-vis Western
slavery comes from the same author who, in another play, warmly identifies

with the pains of separation brought about by Ottoman slavery. The heroine, a slave girl, exclaims at one point: "May the eyes of those who sold us [into slavery] be blinded!" Ahmet Midhat, as narrator, concludes by saying: "I vowed never to buy a slave again. I began cursing the sellers and buyers for thus separating the poor children from their mothers and fathers and for causing this and thousands of similar painful tragedies" (Midhat A.H. 1290, 1:73–74). This striking contradiction reflects a very real and honest inner conflict. In the 1870s patriotic, Westernized Ottomans found themselves torn between a growing rejection of slavery and a deep attachment to their own sociocultural heritage, of which they remained proud. This is a classic example of what literary historians call resistance to cultural interference.

That defensive attitude was by no means limited to the Istanbul-centered Ottoman elite of the time. Intellectuals everywhere across the Muslim world were grappling, inwardly and outwardly, with the inroads made by Western ideas and their effect on Islamic culture. With regard to slavery, this conflict is reflected in Ahmad Shafiq's *L'esclavage au point de vue musulman*, published in Cairo in 1891 in response to Cardinal Lavigerie, the famous French abolitionist, whom the author had heard in Paris. To counter the cardinal's criticism, Shafiq, a French-educated Egyptian, compiled an essay strongly defending Islam's humane attitude toward slavery. The book, which was translated into Arabic and debated in the foreign and Egyptian press, elicited a reaction from Karatodori Paşa, former Ottoman foreign minister, ambassador to Belgium, and the Porte's representative at the Brussels anti–slave trade conference in 1889–90. This non-Muslim high-ranking official commended the author on his endeavor and shared his own frustrations at trying in vain to convince the Europeans of how different Islam's attitude toward slavery really was.[11]

Setting Ottoman slavery apart from Western slavery was not the only device employed by Ottoman writers sensitized to the subject. In addition, when condemning Ottoman slavery and the slave trade, they also tried to distance the object of their criticism from their immediate "high Islamic" elite milieu. Thus, they preferred to direct their comments against slavery among "uncivilized" Muslim peoples, most readily and pertinently among the Circassians. For Sezâi, it is the old Asian savageness (*Asya vahşet-i kadimesi*) that enslaved young children, which he unequivocally denounces. But quite astonishingly, and contrary to any historical account, Sezâi states that "African traders" are to blame for the enslavement of the "noble people" of the Caucasus. As for Ahmet Midhat, he opposes Circassian slavery, no matter how benign it might be, while at the same time he questions and bemoans the very use of the term *slavery* with regard to the kind of servitude which exists in the Caucasus.[12]

Sezâi's play on slavery was published in the late 1880s, not long before the Ottoman government joined the Brussels Act against the slave trade. Although the mood had already changed by then, a zealous abolitionist movement did not emerge in the empire, nor did an active, mobilizing antislavery lobby come to be. The voices calling to end the practice came from literary rather than political figures, and more from second-stratum writers than from major authors. Even these voices were cautious and not too forceful. Nonetheless, there was no real difference between the sentiments which prevailed in literary, intellectual, and political circles on this issue. Scholars have usually given two reasons for this lack of enthusiasm, if not outright reluctance, to consider the abolition of slavery.

The first is the relatively mild nature of slavery in the Ottoman Empire and the obvious gap which lay between the prototype of American slavery and Ottoman realities. Members of the Ottoman elite could not but feel that what British and other European critics of the institution were talking about and what they themselves experienced in Ottoman society were two completely different phenomena. The fact that the horrors of the slave trade were quite similar in both cases was conveniently brushed aside, if not repressed, by the Ottoman elite's "collective mind." That only reinforced their view of the benign, if not benevolent, nature of Ottoman slavery. Most wealthy, urban, and urbane Ottomans came upon slaves in their own houses and in those of their friends and relatives. They could pretend that this was where the story actually began and make believe that what had happened before belonged to another world, one that was uncivilized, unruly, and beyond their control.

The second reason given for the want of abolitionist sentiments among even members of the elite who were sensitized to ideas of political freedom, equality, and human rights is that slavery enjoyed a high degree of legitimacy in Ottoman society. That legitimacy derived from Islamic sanction and the unshakable conviction that Islamic law (the Şeriat) was predicated on deep human concern (*insaniyet*) and could not possibly condone any practice which was not humane, caring, and cognizant of the suffering of the weak and poor members of society. Slavery was part and parcel of the Ottoman family, an institution scrupulously guarded against any outside interference. Since slavery was thus doubly shielded by social and religious practice, any attempt to impugn it as morally reprehensible was perceived as an indictment of the culture as a whole.

It is immediately noticeable that scholars do not provide an economic explication of the Ottomans' reluctance to give up slavery. Given the fact that slavery in the empire was, by and large, domestic and of the kul-harem type, this is hardly surprising, though economic historians, quite naturally, are unlikely to be fully satisfied with current explanations. Nevertheless, political and economic factors are relevant to the discussion of agricultural slavery as practiced among the Circassian immigrants who entered the empire from the mid-1850s onward. The direction which is offered here only further stresses the importance of the sociocultural approach for understanding the intricate history of slavery during the Tanzimat. The point to be explored here is the nexus between the two most prevalent types of slavery in the empire at the time, the kul-harem and the domestic.

The Force of the Kul-Harem Ideal

Historians of the Tanzimat devote little attention to the phenomenon of military-administrative or kul-type slavery, assuming perhaps that it was of no importance. What is sometimes overlooked, or just underestimated, however, is the fact that within the Ottoman elite, kul-type slavery was still very much alive in the second half of the nineteenth century. As noted above, the major change that occurred in the practice was that the central government, and more specifically the Ottoman court, abandoned the devşirme as a system of recruitment, and the "palace school" no longer served as a major agent of socialization. A number of its constituent elements, however, survived both in the central government and in the provinces. Slaves in high and middle ranks of the army and bureaucracy could be observed also in Egypt, Tunisia, Algeria, and Iraq. In all core provinces, slaves served in government, although their number was small and steadily decreasing.

As a readjustment to the changes that were occurring in the old kul system, there emerged in the center and in many provinces what can be described as a "mamluk-type pattern of recruitment and socialization." The phenomenon that Metin Kunt (1975) identified in the provincial administration as the recruitment of slaves by prominent slaves (*kulların kulları*) was common from the seventeenth century onward, forming an important component of the household of Ottoman grandees. In that system, dignitaries of state (*devlet adamları*) purchased through agents and dealers young male slaves, educated and trained them within the household, and socialized them into male elite roles. They would then attempt to place them into the army or the scribal service—later the bureaucracy—in the hope that they could accumulate power, attain influential positions, and eventually protect and promote their patron's interest. This career pattern coexisted with the recruitment of free men via *intisap* networks and socialization through the apprentice pattern (Piterberg 1990).

The cognate female pattern was embodied in the harem system. Similarly recruited, educated, and trained, these young slaves were socialized into elite female roles. Whereas the male slaves, heirs to the kul tradition, inhabited the public world of government life, female slaves moved in the social network of elite households. Products of the two systems often intermarried, for women socialized in elite harems were the natural—almost politically and economically required—brides for elite males of slave origins, as they also were for

free men of the elite. The currency, legitimacy, and respectability of kul-
and harem-type slavery in the Tanzimat period seem to have been somewhat
underrated. The phenomenon is properly noted, however, by Halil Inalcık
(1950) in his article about Husrev Paşa (1756?–1855).

Of Abaza (Abkhazian) tribal origins, Husrev himself was brought to Istanbul
as a slave and entered into the household of Sait Efendi, chief of the corps
of halberdiers in the sultan's bodyguard (çavus başı). He was later placed
in the palace service but began his rise to the top as the protégé of Kücük
Hüseyin Paşa, commander of the navy. During his long career, Husrev Paşa
purchased and trained in his household more than fifty slaves, of whom about
thirty attained the elevated rank of paşa. He also succeeded in marrying them
to daughters of sultans and members of top elite harems. Inalcık notes that
this central political personage, who served in a great number of high governmental posts including the grand vizierate, was the last representative of the
old system. The Ottoman biographer Mehmet Süreyya (n.d.) notes that two
of Husrev Paşa's slaves reached the highest office of grand vizier, one became
minister of war, four were appointed cabinet ministers, one rose to the rank
of field marshal, and many became generals.

One of the most prominent of Husrev Paşa's slaves was the grand vizier
Ibrahim Edhem Paşa. He was bought by one of the paşa's agents when he
was only one year old and was taken to the paşa's mansion. There, the boy
was adopted by Husrev's second wife and reared as her child, the paşa having
no children of his own. Edhem did not know much about his origins, save
for the scanty and dubious information related to him in his childhood. Hence,
his biographers can only cite a number of conflicting stories. Because of
the large number of orphans and abandoned children thus taken into Husrev's
house, teachers were in residence, and tutoring was done at home. When
Edhem was nine years old, in 1827, Husrev Paşa, then commander of the
navy, sent him with three other young slaves to Paris to be educated (Pakalin
1942:403ff.).

The phenomenon of slaves in high office was well known not only to members of the Ottoman elite but also to European observers who acquired any
familiarity with Ottoman society. Adolphus Slade, a British naval officer who
visited the empire many times during the 1830s, asserts that "four-fifths of
the ministers of the present Sultan [Mahmut II, r. 1808–39] were purchased
slaves. How many of the pashas who rule the provinces sprung from the
same origin I cannot say, probably great numbers" (Slade 1832:243). Captain
Charles White, a Briton who spent three years in Istanbul and knew Ottoman
society well, writes that "slavery is often the road to the highest honours."
He then names some of the highest dignitaries of the empire who were of
slave origin and claims that "hundreds of others might be added" (White

1846:305–6). Although the estimates given by these observers are clearly exaggerated, they do convey a notion that was familiar to members of the elite as well.

In provinces that gravitated toward some form of autonomy, like Egypt and Tunis, kul-type slavery was part and parcel of elite life. The Ottoman-Egyptian elite during the long Tanzimat period was Istanbul-oriented and still reflected the Ottoman elite at the center (Toledano 1990:pt. 1). Although its recruitment patterns were being gradually reoriented toward native, Arabo-phone, Egyptian sources, its high and middle ranks continued to flaunt a considerable presence of former slaves. Nassau Senior, a prominent British economist who visited Egypt in the mid-1850s, conversed on the subject with Yusuf Hekekyan Bey, a high-ranking official in the Egyptian administration. After pointing out the slave origins of some of the cabinet ministers of Sait Paşa (r. 1854–63), Hekekyan asserted that "in fact, Stephan Bey and Edhem Pasha are the only ministers that occur to me who have not been slaves—and I doubt their continuance in power. The *Liberti* will intrigue against the *Ingenui*, and drive them out" (Senior 1882:118–19). This is obviously an over-statement, but again, it reflects common views in elite circles about the impor-tance of former slaves and the esprit de corps among them.

The importance of slaves in the army and administration of Tunisia under the Husaynid dynasty is well documented and analyzed in L. Carl Brown's work *The Tunisia of Ahmad Bey, 1837–1855* (1974: esp. 41–65). The phenomenon was manifested in the group of mamluks imported and trained by the ruling family and in the households of its ministers. The importance of the mamluks within what Brown calls the political class was accentuated by the nineteenth-century decline of the military corps of the *kuloğulları*, the descendants of the Ottoman kul regiments that had occupied Tunisia in 1574. A mamluk-type recruitment cum socialization was apparent also in Ottoman Algeria until the French occupation of 1830 and in Iraq during the nineteenth century.

Alongside other tracks of joining *intisap* networks, kul-type slavery survived well into the Tanzimat period. The amazing resilience of the mamluk pattern not only ensured its survival over the centuries, long after the defeat of the Mamluk sultanate at the hands of the sultan's kuls in 1517, but it also rendered it attractive and viable even when competing against modern alternatives in the second half of the nineteenth century. Its counterpart, harem slavery, also weathered the changes of time as an efficient system of elite recruitment, marriage, and reproduction in a male-dominated world. Elite members acted as if kul-harem slavery differed in quality of kind from domestic slavery or Circassian agricultural slavery. They viewed the practice much in the same way as they did officeholding, with its servile components, namely as a privi-

leged position with certain inherent disabilities. Painful though they were
at times, such disabilities were greatly outweighed by the advantages which
accrued with office and elite status.

Nevertheless, there was a difference between the perception of officeholders'
servility and that of kul-harem slaves. Because of European condemnation
of all types of slavery in the Ottoman Empire, a bifurcated view of kul-harem
slaves evolved. Within Ottoman society, these were considered to be persons
of slave origins who had been socialized in a mamluk-type pattern, which
by definition assumed a patron-client relationship of the master-slave kind.
To have been reared under the shadow of slavery did not attach any stigma
to the kul-harem slaves, nor did it assimilate them into the group of domestic
slaves familiar to members of the elite from their own households. In all
senses, Ottoman society treated kul-harem slavery as one of the paths to patronage, like kin, marriage, adoption, and suckling. Therefore, the dichotomy
which Patterson (1982:309) draws between patronage and slavery, because
one is voluntary and the other not, is both artificial and alien to Ottoman
realities.

At the same time, however, and as a defense mechanism of sorts, the same
elite mind, when faced with Western criticism of Ottoman slavery, collapsed
the category of domestic slavery into that of kul-harem slavery. Consequently,
defense of Ottoman slavery was predicated on drawing a sharp distinction—
which obviously existed—between the lot of slaves in Western society and
the lot of Ottoman grand viziers and elite ladies. A more subtle version of
the argument claimed that the "rags-to-riches" track was open to all Ottoman
slaves. This unrealistic claim was most often put forth with regard to female
slaves.

A striking example of that can be found in Ahmet Midhat's *Âcaib-i Âlem*
(Wonders of the world) in a dialogue between one of the main characters,
Suphi, and a Russian princess. Suphi is trying to disabuse the princess of
the notion that female slaves in the empire were objects of sexual pleasure
for Ottoman men. He says to her: "They are not [intended] for pleasure,
but for general household chores. All our female slaves perform duties that
women do, from what are called in Europe maids of honor, or [just] maids,
to cooks. . . . If the master's wife dies, or falls into illness or old age,
[he] takes a female slave for a concubine, and there is no difference [then]
between her and a legal wife. The children of that woman are [considered]
legitimate" (Parlatır 1987:43).

There can be little doubt that the author himself knew that this was not
the normal course. The various categories within harem slavery were quite
familiar to all members of the Ottoman elite. As is vividly related in Fatma
Âliye Hanım's four-part novel *Muhadderat* (Ladies of virtue), the practice
had its unhappy, as well as happy, sides. There were three major types of

female slaves: the menial domestic (*cihaz halayiği*), the concubine (*odalık*, the odalisque of Western fame and fantasy), and the girl brought up in the household and later married off and set up in life (*çırak/çırağ*) and *besleme*). Fatma Âliye claims that customs limited concubinage to cases of infertility — which is inaccurate — and required the consent of both the wife and the intended concubine. If the concubine did not bear children, she was then treated as *çırak* and married off comfortably. Other writers point out that concubinage was often the stepping-stone to marriage as the first wife and was not necessarily related to infertility (Parlatır 1987:156–63, 183).

It is perhaps not surprising that, as a woman, Fatma Âliye displays greater empathy with the plight of even the most privileged of harem slaves, the odalıks. Thus, we can learn of the pain of the wife whose husband takes two concubines but still cannot beget children, because the infertility, naturally attributed to the wife, is probably his. Or we read about the anger and humiliation of the wife who attempts to prevent her husband from flirting with slaves of the family. We also get a more realistic picture of the hard work of the menial slaves in wealthy elite households. But even Fatma Âliye deals mostly with the better-off slaves, those populating the mansions of the great, who were usually Circassian or Georgian. Most Ottoman slaves during the Tanzimat were, however, black and brown (Ethiopian) women who served in less congenial circumstances. As for male slaves, the kul-type track was open only to a select group of almost exclusively white candidates.

Thus, although both Ahmet Midhat and Fatma Âliye imply that Ottoman slavery is actually kul-harem slavery, a difference between them still exists. Ahmet Midhat in *Âcaib-i Âlem* and other works, though certainly not in all, constantly addresses himself to Western criticism of Ottoman slavery. He therefore assimilates all types of slavery in the empire into the kul-harem type, which is the most easily defendable practice and does not resemble slavery as known in the West. Fatma Âliye, on the other hand, is not animated by the same polemical concern but instead writes about Ottoman gentlewomen and the world they inhabited. Slavery to her is just one of the experiences of womanhood. Nontheless, even in her work, a clear distinction is maintained between the status of the ladies of the house, bond or free, and the status of the domestic slaves, whether belonging to the household or working outside in less enviable dwellings.

The dualistic representation of kul-harem servility, indeed the dualism in the attitude to slavery in general, may have also prolonged the existence of servitude in Ottoman society beyond the Tanzimat period. As long as Western perceptions of Ottoman slavery were deemed by the Ottoman elite as fundamentally wrong, demands to abolish it on moral grounds could be easily deflected. If, according to leading statesmen and intellectuals, slavery in the inhuman form did not exist in Ottoman society, but only in ancient and modern

Européan or American history, then it was not an Ottoman problem. The strong attachment of elite members to this pillar of their sociocultural heritage—slavery of the kul-harem type—blinded them to the unpleasant fact that Ottoman slavery was not all that different from slavery elsewhere in two respects: the plight of black domestic slaves and the brutality of the slave trade.

The systemic cultural process here exemplifies amplification and deletion as a measure of resistance to extracultural interference. The unpleasant, negative, disturbing manifestations of slavery—the traffic and the lot of African menial slaves—were deleted from the representation of Ottoman slavery. At the same time, the realities of kul-harem slavery were amplified to serve in the intercultural exchange. This manipulation of representations constituted the resistance of Ottoman elite culture to the "conversion" of Western abolitionism.[13] Because of the unmitigated and uncompromising nature of Western abolitionism, no other Ottoman counterstrategies were developed. A campaign to abolish only domestic and agricultural slavery—indeed the predominant and most painful types—was never contemplated by Western proponents of abolition. That similar or other pragmatic alternatives were not put forth may be safely laid at the door of nineteenth-century European zeal, moralism, and inability to differentiate and empathize across cultural boundaries.

Conclusion

Although the Islamic legal concept of slavery, *grosso modo*, admits only the basic distinction between free and slave, pre-Ottoman and Ottoman practice accepted the usage of additional terms to accommodate phenomena such as military-administrative slavery (kul, *gulam*). After the changes that occurred in the kul system from the sixteenth century onward and the ensuing distinction that emerged between the notion of officeholders' servility and the concept of slavery, however, the once convenient terminological distinction ceased to reflect reality. Concomitantly, the terms *köle* and *cariye* gradually gained ascendancy, coming to denote all types of male and female slaves respectively. Other terms, most notably *esir* for male slave (pl. *üserâ*), were also in use, but in a clearly subordinate status (Toledano 1982:xiv–xv; Pipes 1981:195–98). The survival of kul-type slavery in the revised form of slave turned general or minister was only partially represented in Ottoman Turkish terminology.

The Islamic legal unity of the notion of slavery, the lack of ready-made terminology in Western languages to accommodate the phenomenon of military slavery, and the gradual readjustment of the kul system and terminology so that one term served to denote all types of Ottoman slaves yielded the uniform, undifferentiated use of "slave" terminology in European languages to convey the full scope of the Ottoman pheonmenon. Thus, we might wish to consider the following ahistorical hypothesis: if what was conceived in European discourse under the category of "slavery" had included all types of Ottoman slavery except the kul-harem type, and if the latter had then been conceived under some other category, then the Ottoman elite might have been more receptive to moral criticism of "slavery" and, consequently, perhaps more willing to give it up. Based on Ottoman readiness to accommodate the British with regard to the slave trade in Africans, this does not seem so unthinkable. Hypotheses aside, however, kul-harem slavery was lumped with all the rest, defense of it spilled over to shroud the institution as a whole, and a deep abolitionist sentiment, let alone an active abolitionist movement, did not emerge in the empire.

If conceived in images and prototypes, this problem receives an added dimension. Thus, on the Western-Ottoman intercultural level, the prototypes of slaves were quite different. The slave prototype in Western eyes was, more or less, that of the American slave, whereas the slave prototype which the Ottomans projected to the outside world was that of the kul-harem type. Intraculturally, however, the Ottoman slave prototype was that of the domestic and, to a lesser extent, the agricultural slave, while kul-harem slaves were practically indistinguishable from their free social peers. Such perceived contradictions or inconsistencies should not constitute an analytical impediment. They are only to be expected in a culture coping with internal and external challenges, responding to change, and adjusting to the transformation of the world around it.

The dynamic processes which took place during the Tanzimat in Ottoman elite thinking can also be interpreted within the framework of semiotic theories of culture. The formulation and reformulation of Ottoman attitudes to slavery can be seen as a result of "cultural interference."[14] The concept of slavery took about half a century to gradually infiltrate, or to be "converted" from, Western (source) culture into Ottoman (target) culture. In comparison with the appropriation of other, related components of Western culture, the conversion of Western ideas about slavery was slow and late. Ideas about the security of life and property became current in the empire during the 1830s, and by the 1850s a campaign for political and civil rights, liberty, and equality was under way. In spite of measures to suppress the slave trade from the mid-1850s onward, however, ideas about slavery began to change only in the mid-1870s.

Here, we have been dealing only with the center of canonized culture, that of the Istanbul-oriented Ottoman elite, physically located in all the major cities of the empire. With regard to slavery, the process of conversion involved three broadly and loosely defined groups of cultural producers-disseminators. In descending order of strata, from the center to the semiperiphery of the

Ottoman elite, these were Ottoman statesmen, Young Ottoman publicists and activists, and playwrights, novelists, and poets.[15] This is also the order in which the groups became exposed to European abolitionist demands over a period of more than half a century. It is, however, the reverse order as far as ideological reception, cultural conversion, and formulation of critical attitude toward Ottoman slavery was concerned. Thus, it may be said that Western abolitionism first interfered with a lower stratum of Ottoman elite culture. It then went over to other, higher and lower strata, partially as an internal Ottoman process of conversion from semiperiphery to center.

The first to be faced with the need to formulate an attitude to slavery were the statesmen, who from the 1840s onward had to deal with British pressure to suppress the slave trade. On the ideological level, they responded defensively, although they accepted the need to prevent the human suffering caused by the slave trade and issued edicts to effect such a change without touching slavery itself. The Young Ottomans were the next to address slavery, but they were so absorbed in their struggle for political rights that they dealt with it only superficially. The last group to confront the unpleasant subject was the group of writers. They came to slavery late in the day, during the mid-1870s, but made the most impressive effort to grapple with it. In spite of these differences, all three groups coped with the Western image of Ottoman slavery and the denunciation thereof by adopting a strategy of bifurcation.

The result was that they projected to the Western world that kul-harem slavery was the only type of Ottoman slavery, while simultaneously, at home, they treated domestic and agricultural slavery as the only type of Ottoman slavery. To be able to do so, they intuitively applied to the variegated reality of Ottoman slavery procedures of selection, deletion, and amplification. Since the economic value of slavery was not the issue, British abolitionism must have touched the very core of Ottoman elite culture, where the belief and value systems were most vulnerable to criticism. Otherwise it would be quite difficult to explain why cognate products of Western culture, such as ideas about political freedom, faced much less resistance and were converted relatively early, while abolitionism was rejected on the ideological, not merely the political, level. It was resisted for a fairly long time, and when finally converted in a diluted version, was not warmly greeted nor enthusiastically embraced.

As things turned out, the slave trade in Africans, and later in Circassians and Georgians, slowly died down, agricultural slavery among the Circassian immigrants was being phased out during the post-Tanzimat period, and domestic slavery was gradually being replaced by similar, though legally free, practices (of the *besleme*-type). As might have been expected, the last vestiges of Ottoman slavery, the last bastion to hold out, was kul-type slavery and, even more, its harem counterpart. With the end of empire and the dissolution of the imperial household, it too had to go.

Notes

1. This concept is borrowed from literary and cultural historians and applied to the processes by which abolitionism was transferred (converted) from Western (source) culture into Ottoman (target) culture. For an elaboration of the theory, see Even-Zohar 1990.

2. The establishments of all leading members of the elite, as well as most others, contained slaves in various capacities, including men and women who would in due course become full-fledged members of that elite and might even rise to the very top.

3. The term *abolitionism* is used throughout to denote the call for the abolition of slavery, in our case, in the Ottoman Empire from the 1840s onward. Abolitionism was the *idea* (cultural product) which Western, mostly British, culture tried to foist upon Ottoman elite culture.

4. A rudimentary account of the structure of the imperial harem can be found in Gibb and Bowen 1950: vol. 1, pt. 1, pp. 71–77. For a more recent and elaborate account in Turkish, see Uluçay 1971. Elite households emulated their sovereign's household as much as they could afford to do so.

5. The most thorough account of the impact of these developments on the scribal service and the emerging bureaucracy is Findley 1980. As will become evident, I take a different view on the nature of official servility.

6. Often just *the Porte*, the term *Sublime Porte* was used in Europe to denote the Ottoman government.

7. The *Şeri* principle which governs issues relating to slave status asserts that "freedom is the overriding consideration" (al-aṣl huwwa 'l- ḥurriya [hürriyet]).

8. The translation of Sadullah's verse is in Lewis 1969:134. The Turkish text is cited in Parlatır 1987:25. Kemal's verse is cited in Parlatır 1987:26: "Ne efsunkâr immişsin ah ey didâr-i hürriyet / Esiri aşkın olduk gerçi kurtulduk esaretten."

9. Namık Kemal's *Kara Bela* (1875) is discussed in Parlatır 1987:13–32, and his *Intibah veyahut Âli Bey'in Sergüzeşti* (1876) is discussed in Parlatır 1987:123–29. Ali Suâvi's appeal is cited in Parlatır 1987:28–29.

10. My interpretation in this and the following paragraph is based on a selection of Midhat's texts cited in Parlatır 1987:42–43. On Ahmet Midhat, see Lewis 1969:189–90.

11. Karatodori's letter appears in Shafıq A.H. 1290:130–33. The book is discussed in Baer 1969 and Toledano 1982.

12. Texts of Sezâi and Midhat are cited in Parlatır 1987:37–40. Writing about Recaizade Mahmut Ekrem's *Vuslat*, Mizancı Murat accuses female slave dealers of bringing upon society damages worse than those caused by murderers (Parlatır 1987:41).

13. Conversions are the moves, or transfer processes, of cultural products (here Western abolitionism) from one cultural system to another, or from one stratum to another within a cultural system. See Even-Zohar 1990.

14. The theoretical framework used here is an elaboration of Russian Formalist and Czech Structuralist theories by Itamar Even-Zohar. The works of Jurij Tynajanov and Roman Jakobson form the basis for Even-Zohar's theory. For the most recent formulation of polysystem theory, see Even-Zohar 1990. Especially relevant to our discussion are "polysystem theory" and "laws of literary interference."

15. Owing to the predominance of the Young Ottomans in intellectual circles from the 1860s to the late 1870s, there was some overlapping between the second and third groups. The case of Ahmet Midhat comes to mind, as he was close to the Young Ottomans until the second half of the 1870s, when he began to operate under the aegis of Abdülhamit II's government. For his career, see Lewis 1969:189–90.

References

Baer, Gabriel. 1969. *Studies in the Social History of Modern Egypt.* Chicago: University of Chicago Press.

Brown, L. Carl. 1974. *The Tunisia of Ahmad Bey, 1837–55.* Princeton: Princeton University Press.

Crone, Patricia. 1980. *Slaves on Horses.* Cambridge: Cambridge University Press.

Curtin, Philip. 1969. *The Atlantic slave trade: A census.* Madison: University of Wisconsin Press.

Curtin, Philip, Roger Anstey, and J. E. Inikori. 1976. Discussion: Measuring the Atlantic slave trade. *Journal of African History* 17:596–627.

Davis, David Brion. 1984. *Slavery and human progress.* New York: Oxford University Press.

Davison, Roderic H. 1963. *Reform in the Ottoman Empire, 1856–1876.* Princeton, N.J.: Princeton University Press.

Even-Zohar, Itamar. 1990. *Polysystem studies: Papers in historical poetics and semiotics of culture.* Special issue of *Poetics Today.* Durham, N.C.: Duke University Press.

Findley, Carter V. 1980. *Bureaucratic reform in the Ottoman Empire.* Princeton, N.J.: Princeton University Press.

Fogel, Robert William, and Stanley L. Engerman. 1974. *Time on the Cross: The economics of American Negro slavery.* Vol. 1. Boston: Little, Brown.

Gibb, H. A. R., and H. Bowen, 1950. *Islamic society and the West.* Vol. 1. Oxford: Clarendon.

Inalcık, Halil. 1950. Husrev Paşa. In *Islam Ansiklopedisi* 5:613. Istanbul.

Inikori, J. E. 1976. Measuring the Atlantic slave trade: An assessment of Curtin and Anstey. *Journal of African History* 27:197–225.

Kemal, Namık. 1875. *Kara Bela.* Istanbul: Mehmed Edib Matbaasi.

Kemal, Namık. 1876. *Intibah veyahut Âli Bey'in Sergüzeşti.* Istanbul.

Kunt, Metin. 1975. Kulların kulları. *Boğaziçi Üniversitesi Dergisi, Hümaniter Bilimler* 3:27–42.

Lewis, Bernard. 1969. *The emergence of modern Turkey.* Oxford: Clarendon.

Mardin, Şerif. 1962. *The genesis of Young Ottoman thought.* Princeton, N.J.: Princeton University Press.

Midhat, Ahmet. A.H. 1290. *Letaif-i Rivayat.* Istanbul.

Pakalın, Mehmet Zeki. 1942. *Son sadrazamlar ve başvekiller.* Istanbul: Ahmet Sait Matbaasi.

Parlatır, İsmail. 1987. *Tanzimat edebiyatında kölelik.* Ankara: Atatürk Kültür Dil ve Tarih Yüksek Kurumu.

Patterson, Orlando. 1982. *Slavery and social death.* Cambridge, Mass.: Harvard University Press.

Pipes, Daniel. 1981. *Slave soldiers and Islam.* New Haven: Yale University Press.

Piterberg, Gabriel. 1990. The formation of an Ottoman Egyptian elite in the 18th century. *International Journal of Middle Eastern Studies* 22:275–89.

PRO, FO: British Public Record Office, Foreign Office. London.

Senior, Nassau W. 1882. *Conversations and journal in Egypt and Malta.* London.

Shafıq, Ahmad A.H. 1290. *L'esclavage au point de vue musulman.* Cairo.

Slade, Adolphus. 1832. *Record of travels in Turkey, Greece and of a cruise in the Black Sea in the years 1829, 1830, and 1831.* London: Saunders and Otley.

Süreyya, Mehmet. n.d. *Sicill-i Osmani* 2:276–77.

Toledano, Ehud R. 1980. Slave dealers, women, pregnancy, and abortion: The story of a Circassian slave-girl in mid-nineteenth century Cairo. *Slavery and Abolition* 2:53–68.

Toledano, Ehud R. 1982. *The Ottoman slave trade and its suppression, 1840–1890.* Princeton, N.J.: Princeton University Press.

Toledano, Ehud R. 1984. The imperial eunuchs of Istanbul: From Africa to the heart of Islam. *Middle Eastern Studies* 20:379–90.

Toledano, Ehud R. 1990. *State and society in mid-nineteenth century Egypt.* Cambridge: Cambridge University Press.

Uluçay, Çağatay. 1971. *Harem.* Ankara: Türk Tarih Kurumu Basımevi.

White, Charles. 1846. *Three years in Constantinople; or, domestic manners of the Turks in 1844.* London: H. Colburn.

Willis, John Ralph. 1985. *Slaves and slavery in Muslim Africa.* 2 vols. London: Cass.

2 *Anthony Reid*

The Decline of Slavery in Nineteenth-Century Indonesia

Slavery in Southeast Asia is not a remote historical phenomenon. Laws certainly have prohibited private ownership of persons for a century or more, yet in more remote hills and islands of the region one still encounters people who admit to being slaves or the children of slaves. Much more widespread are people who work without payment for a patron to whom they feel bound — by tradition, by monetary debt, or in return for past favor or protection. The centrality of such relations of obligation in Southeast Asian social structure lends importance to any investigation of slavery but also renders it sensitive and problematic. The pejorative connotations given to the term *slavery* by liberal and Marxist discourse remain, even though the clear-eyed recent literature (Davis 1966, 1984; Fogel and Engerman 1974; Patterson 1982) has made abundantly clear that the conjunction between slavery and periods of economic and intellectual progress in most cultures was not accidental. It is difficult to use the term without appearing to denigrate Southeast Asian cultural traditions which still have force and value.

Some Southeast Asian scholars (Aung Thwin 1983; Andaya 1988) have opted to avoid using such a powerful comparative concept at least until the indigenous social realities are better understood. There are a number of problems with this position. First, slavery was one of the most important means of interaction between ethnolinguistic groups. A Visayan woman of the eighteenth century, for example, might have been taken captive by a Samal raider from Balangingi, sold by him to a Tausug dealer in Sulu, and resold to a Bugis trader who took her to the great emporium of Batavia, where she was sold to a Dutch or Chinese merchant who may have had children by her and eventually freed her. Less dramatically, stronger lowland communities everywhere incorporated men and women from divided hill tribes through capture and temporary slavery. One group's perception of these transactions may have differed from another's, but the historian has need of terminology which is outside any particular culture.

Second, a refusal to use a broadly comparative term is often based on an association-laden stereotype rather than a clear definition. Recent work by Finley, Davis, and Patterson has certainly reemphasized the extraordinary diversity of the social forms of slavery, including the exceptional power exerted by some eunuchs and other royal slaves. The slave always represents a paradox: he is a commodity and yet human, exploited and yet loyal, inferior and yet intimate. That paradox is nowhere clearer than in Southeast Asia, and we learn more from confronting it than from trying to explain it away.

Finally, the growing literatures on slavery and on Southeast Asia have need of each other. To the great pioneer of the cross-cultural study of slavery, H. J. Nieboer (1910), and to some of his precursors such as Montesquieu (1949:239), La Loubère (1691, 1:296–98, and Marini (1663:445), it was apparent that Southeast Asian societies offered important evidence on the origins and variations of slavery, particularly in a "mild," domestic form. Since Nieboer, none of the great theorists of slavery have had access to the early Dutch ethnographic literature on Indonesia, and Southeast Asian specialists have been reluctant to help them by synthesizing the rich source material on this subject. In consequence, Southeast Asia remains the weakest area in a survey as comprehensive as Patterson's remarkable book *Slavery and Social Death* (1982).

In a recent study of the subject (Reid 1983), I therefore opted to retain the word *slave* for a salable person regarded as the property of another, of explicitly lower social status, and performing compulsory labor. At the same time it is necessary to have a broader term, for which I use *bondage*, to cover the related but more extensive system of obligation to labor for a patron without direct recompense. A number of features of Southeast Asia in general, and of Indonesia in particular, determined the character of bondage at least during the four centuries before 1900.

First, a relatively low population density made control of population always more important than control of land. Second, vertical bonding was the crucial system of social organization. Its centrality was emphasized, for example, by the necessity of using pronouns expressing superiority or inferiority in

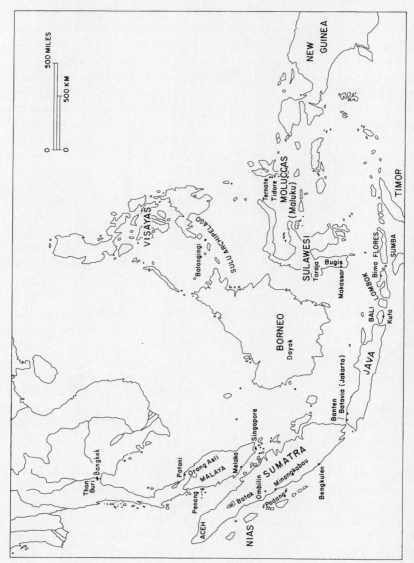

2.1 Indonesia and Thailand

66

order to establish a comfortable and intimate pattern of speech. In the languages of the region the most common first-person pronoun is frequently the word for slave: *saya* in Malay or *kawula* in Javanese.

Third, debt was important as a source of bondage, including forms which should be considered slavery. Indonesian texts often describe the routes which led to slavery: inheritance, incapacity to pay one's debts, capture in war, or condemnation by a court. Except for capture in war, all could be interpreted as a form of debt, since most crimes were punished by fines and the nonpayment of these fines led to enslavement. While some societies distinguished between debt bondsmen and captured slaves, most did not. Europeans emphasized this distinction in a quest to identify an "acceptable" form of bondage.

Fourth, a concept of wage labor was absent until quite recent times. Of seven examples of "wage rates" paid by Europeans in the great cities of Southeast Asia in the sixteenth and seventeenth centuries, six of them varied between eleven and six hundred times the value of a daily rice ration. The seventh was only twice this basic subsistence rate, but it was a food allowance paid by the Portuguese to their own slaves (Reid 1988:130). The other cases appear all to have been very high rates paid to masters for the privilege of hiring their bondsmen. A Persian traveler pointed to a common feature of Muslim Aceh, in northern Sumatra, and Buddhist Siam: "It is their custom to rent slaves. They pay the slave a sum of money, which he gives to his master, and then they use the slave that day for whatever work they wish" (Ibrahim 1972: 177–78). The only sources of free wage labor for several centuries were Chinese settlers or Indian sailors. Indigenous Indonesians, at least in the towns, identified manual labor with servility and were very reluctant to perform it for anyone not regarded as their legitimate lord.[1] "Free" wage labor became important in Java in the nineteenth century, in step with overpopulation and landlessness (Elson 1986), but elsewhere not until the twentieth.

Finally, the "mild" character of Southeast Asian "slavery" was often remarked by early European sources. Since a slave could be beaten, sold, or sacrificed for a ritual need—at least in Borneo, Sulawesi, and Nias—the word *mild* hardly seems appropriate. More to the point was the lack of strict legal definition of slave status (except under exceptionally strong Indian, Islamic, or European influence) or of a strong state anxious to enforce it. The Indonesian words used (*hamba, kawula, ata, hulun*) could be variously defined as "slave," "subject," or "retainer," because the imperative question was whose bondsman one was rather than the precise legal quality of that bondage. Consequently, the slaves most fully assimilated into a household were free to seek their own livelihood, to marry, and to possess their own houses, property, and other slaves.

Even European slave owners in Indonesia gradually adapted themselves to a type of slavery more flexible than their own. Two very practical considerations motivated them to do so: Indonesian slaves had a reputation for revenging themselves violently against masters who humiliated them, and before the rise of the modern state it was relatively easy to flee from an oppressive master. Pierre-Yves Manguin cited the complaint of one of the first European masters of Southeast Asian slaves, a Portuguese captain of Malacca: "Malacca is a place like no other. . . . One has to take care of everything: of the slave, to rear his son; to provide him with clothes for his wife and for himself; one has to pamper him so that he does not run away" (1983:209).

Examples could be found in the literature of the seventeenth and eighteenth centuries of people described as slaves filling almost every conceivable function. They included agriculturalists, miners, traders large and small, textile workers, domestics, concubines, prostitutes, construction workers, dock laborers, soldiers, surgeons, and entertainers. There are many instances of captured or bought slaves being put to work on the land: bought eastern Indonesians worked the pepper estates of southern Borneo, bought Indians cultivated rice in Aceh, and captured Filipinos produced the food crops of Sulu. In the absence of centrally managed latifundia, however, the slave character of these agriculturalists quickly dissolved with the second generation into a kind of serfdom or sharecropping (Reid 1983:22–24). In the affluent trading cities of the sixteenth century, bondage retained its servile and salable character longer, with most if not all urban labor bonded either to a powerful individual or to the king.

The most characteristic role of the slave in Southeast Asia was as a retainer of an urban aristocrat. Numerous sources of the sixteenth and seventeenth centuries attest the importance for those of high status to be surrounded whenever they went out by a retinue of umbrella carriers, betel carriers, guards, and other followers. The upper class invested in slaves predominantly for status, but also for protection—slaves were armed—and to assist their productive enterprises in trade, textile manufacture, and agriculture. Able slaves were trusted with great responsibilities, and some rose to become ministers or local governors.

The Dutch East India Company, which by the second half of the seventeenth century dominated the long-distance trade of the archipelago, introduced a new rigidity into the concept of slavery. The Dutch brought with them a legally enforced concept of the slave as servile outsider which was only partially modified by the more flexible pattern of bondage prevailing in the archipelago. Slaves, mostly of Balinese, Bugis, and other eastern Indonesian origin, became the indispensable labor source of all the Dutch enclave cities, with twenty-five thousand or more in Batavia alone over most of the period 1680–1770 (Reid 1983:14–18, 29). The only true latifundia in the region were introduced by the Dutch Company in the tiny Banda Islands, which produced all the world's nutmeg until the monopoly was broken in the mid-eighteenth century. Of the 3,842 inhabitants of the islands in 1638, 2,190 were slaves (835 men, 881 women, and 474 children), and the nutmeg was grown and harvested entirely with their labor (Hanna 1978:66).

Before turning to the decline of slavery, it will be useful to give some indications of the dimensions of its most visible and measurable aspect: the movement of slaves between regions or across ethnolinguistic boundaries. The largest such movements are probably the hardest on which to find concrete data: those whereby stateless hill peoples such as the Orang Asli of Malaya (Endicott 1983:221–36), the Batak of Sumatra (Anderson [1826] 1971:297, 315), the Toraja of Sulawesi, and various Dayak groups of Borneo lost population through capture or sale to the more powerful Islamic coastal peoples adjacent to them. It is probable that the majority of the urban population of such flourishing commercial centers as Malacca, Aceh, Banten, Patani, and Makassar in the sixteenth and seventeenth centuries were unfree people brought there as captives, in the retinue of the powerful men who settled there, or as cargo in commercial voyages. This was certainly the case with the Dutch enclaves of Batavia, Malacca (after 1641) and Makassar (after 1669) (Blussé 1982; Sutherland 1983).

H. G. Schulte Nordholt (1980:40) estimated that Bali exported one hundred thousand of its people, primarily to Dutch Batavia, in the period 1620–1830. Bugis and Makassar slaves from southern Sulawesi were being taken to Batavia at the rate of about two hundred a year in the late seventeenth century and about three thousand a year in the middle of the eighteenth. In the whole period of this trade, 1660 to 1810, southern Sulawesi must have lost over a hundred thousand of its people. The small island of Nias was even more profligate with its people, losing about 0.5 percent each year as slaves, or 20 percent in total for the period 1790–1830 (Reid 1983:29–32). In the few decades before 1905, when the slave trade was making heavy inroads on the Sa'dan Toraja population of Sulawesi, the region may have lost 10–15 percent of its population (Bigalke 1983:347).

The Decline of Slavery

The more we know about nineteenth-century slavery, especially in Southeast Asia, the less appropriate it seems to refer to its "abolition" by enlightened legislation. Certainly that legislation under pressure from European reformers ended overt slaveholding in the towns, removed legal sanctions, and discouraged the trade. But slavery had already become much less important long before it was legally abolished, and it survived long after the legislation. More important factors in the decline of slavery were profound but gradual changes in the nature of Indonesian society.

Impoverishment was undoubtedly one of these factors. Acquiring and maintaining slaves was expensive. It is no accident that slavery was most central an institution in societies at the peak of their urban florescence: classical Greece, imperial Rome, the Abbasid caliphate, the Italian city-states of the fourteenth and fifteenth centuries. In Southeast Asia too, slavery was most marked a feature of the social and economic system during the sixteenth and seventeenth centuries, when indigenous maritime cities were at their commercial peak. These cities were all in decline or total eclipse by the end of the seventeenth century. Dutch Batavia, which replaced them in many respects, including in the large-scale importation of slaves, was itself in decline a century later. Slaves ceased to be captured or bought on the same scale, and patrons encouraged their dependents to find their own livelihoods when they could no longer afford to maintain them. The growth of an impoverished population provided cheaper ways to acquire labor, particularly in Java. Crawfurd commented that "the numbers and servility of the population in Java have, among them, rendered slaves of little value" (1820, 1:248). Even Europeans, as soon as they gained a working relationship with the Indonesians around them, found they could acquire bonded labor more cheaply through debt bondage or corvée. A German in Semarang in 1772 was delighted to find he could buy a debt slave for only 25 rijksdaalders, whereas a "true" (i.e., exportable) slave would have cost him 150 (de Haan 1910, 3:208–9; also Nagtegaal 1988:68–69).

The advance of two universalist religious systems, Islam and Christianity, also tended to restrict the scope of slavery. Both religions brought clearer legal concepts of the category of slave and opposed the sale of slaves to those of a different religion. When Malay legal codes incorporated from Islamic law different punishments for crimes involving slaves or free men, they tended to use the Arabic-derived term *abdi*, which implied a more precise slave category than the Malay *hamba*. Islam, even more explicitly than Christianity, forbade the enslavement of coreligionists. When in the seventeenth century Islam spread to southern Sulawesi, where slavery was a central institution, this doctrine became a major point of conflict. The initial compromise, as recorded in a Bugis chronicle, was that "God would reward those who freed their [fellow Muslim] slaves" but that debt bondsmen should be defined as outside even this mild provision. When one zealous ruler of Bone tried to release all slaves in the name of Islam in the 1640s, he was overpowered by his neighbors (Reid 1983:169). Slavery remained a factor here as in other Muslim states, but the growing pressure of orthodoxy tended to redefine "true slaves" (*abdi*) as those taken from non-Islamic societies in the hills or in islands such as Nias, Bali, Sumba, and Flores. As such slaves became converted and assimilated, the quality of their bondage softened.

Dutch and English Christians had a narrower and more negative concept of slavery. They preferred not to Christianize their slaves, except in the case of favored concubines, because this allowed them to retain the social distance they felt appropriate on grounds of both race and status. Moreover, there was always pressure to free Christian slaves, and in 1770 this became a legal requirement for the Dutch in the East Indies. In practice, the majority of slaves of the Dutch and the English eventually assimilated to Islam rather than to Christianity.

Finally, the most fundamental reason for the decline of slavery was the rise in power of the absolutist state. Divided or stateless regions readily exported labor, but the strongest states never did so. Southern Sulawesi, for example, was one of the region's greatest providers of slaves in the sixteenth century and again in the eighteenth, when it was divided into numerous competitive states. But between 1610 and 1669, when the Sultans of Makassar succeeded in unifying the Makassar and Bugis states under their control, they forbade the sale of their subjects to outsiders. In general, it has been shown for Southeast Asia as for Europe that an increase in the power of the king in relation to the nobility brought about a decline of private slavery in favor of direct obligations to the Crown. Akin Rabibhadana (1969:110) has shown this for Siam, as Lieberman (1984:107-9, 163) has for Burma. It is equally true for Aceh (Reid 1975:47-54). In the nineteenth century the relentless growth in power of the colonial state was undoubtedly the most important reason for the retreat of the institution of slavery.

The United Kingdom banned the traffic in slaves in 1807 and imposed a similar ban at the Congress of Vienna in 1815. In consequence, the restored kingdom of the Netherlands also prohibited the slave trade throughout its colonies in 1818. Nevertheless, the purchase of slaves from Bali, Nias, the Batak area of Sumatra, Flores, Timor, and the slave-raiding center of Sulu continued. In fact, the impossibility of buying slaves from older established areas now under colonial control increased the traffic in many of these still independent corners of Indonesia. The slave exports of Nias peaked after the ban of 1807, supplying the Dutch ports of Padang and Priaman, British Bengkulen and Penang, and Aceh with laborers and the Chinese population of the colonial cities with wives (Raffles 1835, 2:175-85; Lyman 1856:368-77; Bock [1881] 1985:260). Batak slaves from the east coast of Sumatra, as well as Balinese, Bugis, and east Indonesians, were also exported in large numbers to supply Penang and Singapore, especially the overwhelmingly male Chinese population (Abdullah 1955:161-62).

The Dutch justified their continuing purchase of Nias slaves up to the 1840s by claiming them to be *pandelingen* (debt bondsmen). "The Dutch gravely talk of 'debtors', of 'sending to Nias for debtors.' But here [Nias] things go by their right names. It is selling slaves. They are brought down to the beach corded, and while the trade is going on, are bound to a post . . . and on board are fettered, and carried to a foreign land. . . . I have never yet . . . met with any one who has seen these people return to their native

land, or who has known them to be liberated" (Lyman 1856:368). The British
turned a blind eye to the importation of the predominantly female slaves,
since it "was of immense advantage in procuring a female population for
Penang . . . the condition of the slaves who were brought to the British
Settlements was materially improved, and . . . they contributed so much
to the happiness of the male population and the general prosperity of the
settlement" (Anderson [1826] 1971:298).

Most of this traffic was conducted in small Chinese or Indonesian craft.
The only large-scale shippers of Indonesian slaves after 1820 were French
and other vessels supplying the sugar planters of Mauritius and Réunion.
Deprived of older sources of supply in India and Africa, these islands took
over the role of Batavia as principal destination for slaves from Bali and
Nias between 1815 and 1830. In the latter year the French began seriously
to discourage the importation, which had taken place clandestinely through
their colony of Réunion. Only when slavery itself was finally abolished in
Mauritius in 1835 and Réunion in 1848 did the flow of Indonesian slaves
cease entirely (van der Kraan 1983:332–34; Lyman 1856:377).

In the second half of the nineteenth century, therefore, the slave trade was
continued only in small Indonesian *prahu*, which might carry a handful of
Florenese or Sumbanese to Lombok or Bima, of Batak or Nias to the Straits
Settlements or Aceh, of Balinese to the neighboring islands or to Singapore.
Local Dutch authorities often used the official rhetoric of horror at this small-
scale trade as the justification for a forward step against those Indonesian
rulers who remained independent. Though they were less purist once they
were in control, the trade retreated steadily as Dutch power advanced.

Colonial Labor Needs

The Dutch East India Company had been the largest slave owner in the archipelago in the seventeenth and eighteenth centuries. Its successor in the
nineteenth century, the government of Netherlands India, had far more extensive needs for labor. Having denied itself the option of continuing to buy
slaves, it nevertheless continued for some time to recruit its labor in ways
which differed only in details from the old ones. We have seen how Nias
slaves were redefined as debtors but bought through exactly the same channels
as before, for use in mining, port labor, and domestic service on Sumatra's
west coast. In the same way, the Dutch government in Java returned to traditional sources of Balinese slaves in 1826 when it needed manpower to help
fight the Javanese rebel Diponegoro. An agreement was made to pay the
raja of Badung, in southern Bali, five Spanish dollars for every "recruit" delivered to the Dutch through traditional slave dealers. About four hundred such
involuntary recruits were delivered to Dutch ships at Kuta each year between

1827 and the end of the Java War in 1830. The force required to take these men away from their homes was most graphically illustrated in 1828, when eighty-five Balinese "recruits" rebelled on board the Dutch warship *Anna Palowna*, leading to the deaths of seventy-two of them as well as of two Dutch soldiers (van der Kraan 1983:333–37).

The primary source of unpaid labor for the colonial government in the nineteenth century, however, was corvée. In the period 1830–60, when the system was at its peak, the Dutch required Javanese to labor for up to two-fifths of their time on export crops of Dutch choosing. This was the *cultuurstelsel* (cultivation system), probably the most systematic exploitation of labor as tribute ever imposed by a colonial power. Several million Javanese each year were mobilized through their chiefs to cultivate coffee, sugar, indigo, and other crops, delivered to Dutch overseers at such negligible costs that the sugar could compete with slave-produced sugar from the West Indies (Ricklefs 1981:115–16; Gonggrijp 1957:90–91).

Whereas the East India Company had been a private slave-owning corporation in a pluralistic archipelago, Netherlands India after 1830 was a state which claimed as a sovereign right the labor of its subjects. Having made the *cultuurstelsel* work so profitably for export crops, the colonial government found the use of corvée irresistible for all other public works.

Government corvée [*herendiensten*], usually unpaid, was demanded for the construction and maintenance of roads, bridges, irrigation ditches, dams, weirs, canals, fortifications; for the building of houses for European and native officials, *pasangrahans* [rest houses for traveling officials], and post houses; for delivering mail and parcels in the interior; the transport of convicts; the guarding of public buildings and the houses of officials; the cutting of grass for the government post-horses; and the provision and maintenance of so-called freemen's horses, which spared the government the required expenditure for the post-horses; for the carriage of government travelers and goods; for the transport of the considerable quantity of copper coins which were received from the land tax and the provision of the carts and draft animals. Corvée was, in a word, required to provide for all possible needs of the government and its servants. Indeed, it was often promoted to satisfy the whims, the vanity, the desires, and the ambition of officials. (Gonggrijp 1957:98; see also Elson 1984:39–40)

Contemporary critics estimated that the effect of the *cultuurstelsel* was to increase the burden of corvée between ten- and a hundredfold over the indigenous Javanese system and that about a quarter of total working time of all Javanese was occupied with it (Day [1904] 1966:284).

As opposition mounted to the *cultuurstelsel* from both idealistic reformers and private Dutch entrepreneurs who wanted a share of the action, the system was gradually dismantled, beginning in the 1860s. Forced labor was abandoned first for the crops for which it proved least profitable. For coffee, the most profitable, it was not finally terminated until 1919 (Ricklefs 1981:

118). The first use of wage labor for public works occurred in the cities of Java in the liberal "spring" after 1848. From 1857 official policy provided that wage labor should be used for all public works, but this was not effective in rural areas for another half century (Furnivall [1944] 1967:184–85).

As corvée was being abolished in Java, where desperate landless peasants first became available as cheap wage labor, the system was making its greatest gains in the outer islands of Sumatra, Borneo, Sulawesi, and the Lesser Sundas. In most of these areas Dutch intervention had been minimal before 1870, but thereafter the rapid expansion of the infrastructure of a modern state required the building of roads, prisons, and public buildings all over the archipelago. Between 1870 and 1910 onerous labor obligations were imposed on diverse peoples, many of whom had never known anything of the kind, and resistance to these demands was responsible for many of the outbreaks of rebellion in this period. The epic poem *Hikayat Perang Sabil*, a clarion call to holy war against the Dutch in Aceh (northern Sumatra), complained bitterly that one day in seven had to be worked for the requirements of the hated Kompeni (the Dutch government). "Such are the laws they make up: women and men, chiefs and people, old and young, even small children and the sick — as soon as they are strong enough, make them come out" (Damsté 1928:595). Although these demands were modified in the 1920s, notably by allowing people to commute their labor obligation into a money tax, in the outer islands of Indonesia the Dutch could never do without corvée altogether.

Subjects obligated to labor for their colonial government were far cheaper and more abundant than the slaves of the former East India Company. Their only disadvantage was that they could not be sent far from home to open up the frontiers of the colony. For this purpose the Netherlands Indian government made use of convicts.

The Napoleonic ruler of Java, Daendels, ended mutilation such as the chopping off of a hand or a foot as a penal measure in the Dutch possessions. The English, who defeated Daendels in 1811, in turn repudiated the more Southeast Asian practice of condemning criminals to slavery. After the Dutch restoration, forced labor (*dwangarbeid*) became overwhelmingly dominant as a form of punishment for every type of crime. An 1828 decree regulating punishments in Netherlands India put into practice "the express will of the king, that forced labor should as far as possible replace all other punishments, so that the state could make use of the labor of the criminals" (Louwes 1921:133). Offenders in Java were sentenced to varying terms in one of four categories, in descending order of severity: a chain gang at a specified place outside Java; a chain gang somewhere in Java; labor without chains, either with or without payment, at a specified place outside Java; labor without chains in Java. A fifth category for prominent aristocratic rebels was simple banishment from Java.

The number of laborers made available by this system rose far beyond the eighteenth-century slaveholdings of the East India Company. In the 1850s about two thousand Indonesians in Java were sentenced to forced labor each year, for terms which averaged three to four years (*Koloniaal Verslag* 1860: app. A, p. 43). The numbers increased steadily, passing four thousand in 1862 and six thousand in 1865. At the beginning of 1866 there were 9,335 convict laborers in Netherlands India, of whom 3,692 were in chains (2,346 of them outside Java). Of the total, 622 died in captivity during the year, while about half were released and replaced by newly sentenced convicts (*Koloniaal Verslag* 1868:88–9, app. G). In the period 1880–1900, the number of convict laborers appears to have reached its peak, averaging about twenty-six thousand at any one time, of whom between a third and a half were available to be sent anywhere (*Koloniaal Verslag* 1889:67, 1900:72).

The convicts sentenced to labor outside Java were particularly valuable to the colonial government for heavy work in dangerously disease-affected areas. The coal mines opened up in the nineteenth century relied heavily on convict labor. More than four hundred convicts were working at the southern Borneo coal mines in the 1860s (*Koloniaal Verslag* 1868:193). The much bigger mines at Ombilin in western Sumatra began to be exploited in 1892, and between two and three thousand convicts were required for the mine and the railway which served it. Their health was appalling. In 1898 the Ombilin mines had an average work force of 2,453 convicts, of whom about 500 were always hospitalized with fevers or chest and eye problems, while 1,748 had to be evacuated because they were too ill to work (*Koloniaal Verslag* 1900:72–73; Angoulvant 1926, 1:204–5). In the twentieth century an increasing proportion of the Ombilin work force comprised selected former convicts who had behaved well and were offered contracts as "free" laborers once their penal terms expired. Yet in 1922 there were still 4,822 convicts, now paid a small allowance, alongside 4,574 contract laborers at Ombilin (Angoulvant 1926, 2:561).

The other major employers of convicts sentenced to be sent away were the Dutch expeditionary forces. For the whole period 1873–1903 Dutch military resources were overextended in the attempt to conquer or contain Aceh, and the army constantly asked for more convict labor to build fortifications and railways and to carry supplies. Between five hundred and a thousand men were sent to Aceh in most of these years, and again they suffered heavily from illness. As against 625 convicts sent to Aceh in 1887, 57 died there, and 435 had to be evacuated because of illness (*Koloniaal Verslag* 1889:67). There was a big buildup in 1898 for Van Heutsz's strategy to bring the war to an end. Almost 3,800 men were sent to Aceh in that year, consuming all the available convict labor and depleting the labor force in Ombilin (*Koloniaal Verslag* 1899:79). After the submission of the major Acehnese

resistance leaders in 1903, however, the supply of convict labor for the army
there returned to about seven hundred per year for the remainder of the colonial
period (Angoulvant 1926, 1:204).

These convicts far from home were the closest in function to earlier East
India Company slaves, but they were by no means the most numerous source
of unpaid labor. A far larger number of Indonesians, close to a hundred
thousand per year in the second half of the nineteenth century, was sentenced
at the lowest-level police courts (*politierol*), where the local Dutch official
advised by Javanese subordinates gave quick, rough justice on the veranda
of his residence at a twice-weekly sitting. Dutch officials in the field valued
the system precisely because of its lack of formal safeguards. "Its defenders
argued that the public exercise of arbitrary authority was important to the
protection of Dutch interests and to the maintenance of a strong presence"
(Rush 1990:114). Anything could be construed as an offense against public
order or the interests of Dutch and Javanese officials. Although the great
majority of convictions were simply listed as "other offenses," those recorded
included such items as "selling charms, 'insanity,' sleeping under the trees,
seduction, overtaking the Resident's carriage, and wizardry" (Rush 1990:113).
After 1866, when whipping was in principle (though not always in practice)
abolished, forced labor for up to three months was the routine punishment
for all *politierol* offenses. At any one time almost as many of these short-term
minor offenders were at work on local projects (around fifteen thousand on
average in the 1880s) as there were long-term convicts condemned by higher
courts.

The economic value of the convict laborers was the principal reason that
the Indies government resisted attempts in The Hague to reform the system.
In 1880 Batavia could still protest that it was unwise to carry out the reforms
ordered thirteen years earlier because of the need for labor on public works
(Mailrapporten 1872/634, 1880/265). Even the long-debated new penal code
which became effective in 1918 continued forced labor as the cornerstone
of the penal system, though now with payment of a small allowance (Louwes
1921:147).

The determination of liberal reformers in the years after 1860 to end the
system of unpaid forced labor for the government had something to do with
humanitarian ideals, but much also to do with the rising influence of private
capital in Holland and its need for a different kind of labor system. Free
wage labor was the goal of liberal rhetoric, but while wages were paid by
private estates, a free labor market remained elusive. In Java, private European
planters continued to use local headmen, as the government had, to force
villagers to surrender their land and their labor to the sugar and coffee estates
(Elson 1986). Outside Java, the new plantations opened up after 1870, notably
in East Sumatra, found it impossible to recruit local labor at the rates they

were prepared to pay. A system of contracts quickly developed on the model of British indenture—the "new system of slavery" (Tinker 1974)—which took millions of Indians to labor on estates in the British colonies. Until 1900 the largest number of "contract coolies" came from China; thereafter the recruits from Java were far more numerous. By 1916 150,000 Javanese were already at work on the tobacco and rubber estates of East Sumatra under three-year contracts (Reid 1970:319). In the pioneering phase of transforming the jungle into a vast tropical estate, these coolies suffered many of the horrors that had marked slavery in its cruelest form: transportation far from home, miserable health, unremitting toil, the constant threat of violence, the disruption of families, obligatory prostitution or concubinage for women, and no possibility of escape or redress from the actions of cruel overseers.[2] Of course contract labor differed from slavery in that it was voluntary and temporary. Migrant workers were recruited in Java with substantial advances, which were often used to repay pressing debts or obligations there. Ideally, they had worked off this debt in time to be repatriated after three years, though a high percentage never succeeded in doing so. In one respect, however, the system was harsher than most Southeast Asian forms of slavery: there was no physical means of escape. The planters were supported by a strong, centralized colonial government which fined or imprisoned any coolie who attempted to flee. The whole plantation region resembled an outdoor prison, as its critics alleged. Although the welfare of coolies was far better protected by the 1920s, it was only in 1929, when the United States Congress voted to ban imports of tobacco produced under duress, that the penal sanction attaching to labor contracts was abolished.

The Abolition of Slavery

Although the Netherlands banned the slave trade in 1818, it did not prohibit the ownership of slaves until 1860, long after Britain and France did so. Even then the prohibition was interpreted as applying only to slaves owned by Europeans and Chinese in the areas under direct Dutch control. Despite the efforts of reformers in Holland, the 1860s were still marked by great hesitation regarding Indonesian-owned slaves in the outer islands. Not until 1874 did Batavia require that regional officials propose measures for liberating all the slaves under the direct authority of the colonial government and report the situation of slaves in indirectly ruled areas.

The governor of Sumatra's West Coast reported that it would cost 1.8 million guilders to buy the freedom of all those servants (presumably about twenty thousand) "who before 1860 would have been called slaves." Batavia characteristically refused to pay such a sum, but the local officials had nevertheless to persuade the Minangkabau elite that all their *kemanakan dibawah lutut* (literally "nephews below the knees") were now of free status as *kemanakan kandong* (Mailrapport 1875/338). At the end of 1876 the Resident of the Minangkabau area reported optimistically that these former slaves were now admitted to village rituals and allowed to marry as free people, even though "the majority of them have continued to live with their former owners" (Canne, Dec. 19, 1876, Mailrapport 1877/11). Elsewhere Dutch officials held elaborate festivities to announce the liberation of slaves, whose owners were compensated at about fifty guilders per slave. At Jembrana (northern Bali) in 1877 and in Ternate (northern Moluccas) in 1879, for example, there were speeches, the reading of a proclamation, a ball at the palace, and entertainments for the people (Blokzeijl, Dec. 22, 1877, and de Munniek, Sept. 22, 1877, Mailrapport 1878/23, 1879/626).

Without such public fanfare, the officials undoubtedly feared that the "liberation" would be unnoticed by the population. In the northern Moluccas, after all, the Dutch had ruled for more than two centuries, and both sides had long accustomed themselves to circumventing official disapproval of slavery. In 1877 a new and zealous Resident reported that the sultan of Tidore still expected an annual tribute of slaves from New Guinea, while the sultan of Ternate sent his theoretically free subjects to serve as guarantees for his debts to the merchants of the town. These people worked for the merchants as virtual slaves (Laging Tobias, Dec. 15, 1876, and Jan. 1, 1877, Mailrapport 1877/75, 1877/142). Undoubtedly it took more than proclamations to change the way people perceived these obligations, but some steps were at last being taken in the 1870s.

Where Dutch authority was less well established, the local officials did not even pretend to carry out the antislavery policy. The assistant Resident of Sintang (West Borneo) pointed out that "according to the contracts the Dayaks are free, but the chiefs who signed these contracts have never understood these noble aims, or they would never have signed the contracts." Unless colonial authority was vastly strengthened it would take more than a century of persuasion for the Dayak chiefs to accept the loss of their slaves. Moreover, most of the slaves "have no desire for their freedom," even if some of them were sacrificed at the burials of their chiefs (Gijsberts, Apr. 4, 1877, Mailrapport 1877/423). In independent southern Bali the Resident reported that even the most enlightened chiefs refused to consider giving up their slaves, no matter how gradually. The hundreds of slaves in their palaces were considered crucial to both their status and their wealth (Blokzeijl, June 8, 1877, Mailrapport 1877/434). The government therefore accepted that nothing effective would be done. Similarly for the rajas of Sumba and Flores, "the possession of slaves is a question of 'to be or not to be,' and their strength . . . is in the number of their slaves." The Resident based in Kupang had given up his earlier attempts to buy the liberty of the slaves he encountered on tour, since new slaves could easily be created to replace them and, moreover, the slaves themselves tended to fear "that in buying them the 'Company' [the Dutch] will use them for still harder labor than they now suffer from" (Versteege, June 4, 1877, Mailrapport 1877/456).

The slaves probably had good reason for this attitude. Corvée had for many Southeast Asians been more demanding than private slavery, particularly so when exacted by a government with the unprecedented power of that of Netherlands India. Reports on the situation of slaves continued to reach Batavia into the twentieth century, and they made clear that slavery could only be ended as the whole social structure changed. Some of the reports pointed to the heart of the problem, like this one from northern Sulawesi in 1896: "The slaves and debt slaves were not always attracted to their so-called freedom. They enjoyed certain rights: they performed no corvée and paid no tax—and this for the simple reason that they were considered not free to dispose of either their labor or their property. It has often happened that slaves refused to be made free [*mardika*]; that debt bondsmen, immediately after having been redeemed, again borrowed money from someone else and place themselves in debt bondage to him" (de Kanter, Oct. 5, 1896, Mailrapport 1897/438). When in eastern Lombok in 1902 the government took steps to buy out the last registered slaves, it found that the masters so identified with their slaves that they preferred to liberate them than to "sell them to the government" for a sum of money. The officials congratulated themselves on having saved the money, even though they appear to have realized that without it a kind of bondage would continue. "The bond between many masters and former slaves is undoubtly not wholly broken after their freeing; they will in many cases continue to help each other when this is necessary and help is asked for, but when this occurs by free will on both sides no objection can be made to it" (Gryzen, Jan. 1, 1902, Mailrapporten 1902/236).

It was possible to abolish slavery only in the sense of denying it any legal validity in the eyes of the state. In reality the bonds of obligation from one individual to another in Southeast Asia were slowly loosened over a period of more than a century. Three related processes were at work, in addition to formal legislation. First, the absolutist state became ever stronger and ever more intolerant that any agency but itself should demand from its subjects their money in taxes, their labor in corvée, or their service on the battlefield. Second, the spread of money, the growth of a national market, and above all the growing numbers of landless poor made wage labor cheaply and widely available. Finally and most gradually, the spirit of individual liberty gained ground in people's minds. These processes were still at work when the Dutch empire collapsed in 1942. Though greatly stimulated by Indonesian independence, they are not in sole command of the field today. The sense of obligation

to serve a patron or a creditor, which was at the heart of the precolonial
bondage system, still leaves its mark in many of the cultures which make
up contemporary Indonesia.

Notes

An earlier version of this essay was given as a lecture in the Ecole des Hautes
Etudes en Sciences Sociales, Paris, and will appear in French in a volume of essays
in honor of Philippe Groslier and Georges Condominas. I am grateful for the valuable
comments made by Robert Elson and Martin Klein on drafts of the essay.

1. In many areas of Indonesia the phrase *makan gaji* (eat wages) still has the
pejorative ring which *hireling* had for the English translators of the Bible.

2. The literature on this robust phase of plantation development is extensive, color-
ful, and often polemical. The liveliest account is the semiautobiographical novel of
Ladislao Szekely, *Tropic Fever* (London, 1937: Kuala Lumpur: Oxford University
Press, 1979). Scholarly accounts are Breman 1987: Pelzer 1978; Stoler 1985; and
Reid 1970.

References

Abdullah, Munshi. 1955. The Hikayat Abdullah [1849]. Trans. A. H. Hill. *Journal
of the Malayan Branch, Royal Asiatic Society* 28, pt. 3.

Akin Rabibhadana, M. R. 1969. *The organization of Thai society in the early Bangkok
period, 1782–1873.* Ithaca, N.Y.: Southeast Asia Program, Cornell University.

Andaya, Leonard Y. 1988. Man as rare as flowers. In *Glimpses of Indonesian history:
The 1987 MacMillan Brown lectures*, by Leonard Y. Andaya and Barbara Andaya.
Auckland: Auckland University.

Anderson, John. [1826] 1971. *Mission to the East Coast of Sumatra in 1823.* Kuala
Lumpur: Oxford University Press.

Angoulvant, G. 1926. *Les Indes Néerlandais: Leur rôle dans l'economie internationale.*
2 vols. Paris: Le Monde Nouveau.

Aung Thwin, Michael. 1983. *Athi, Kyun Taw, Hpayà-Kyun*: Varieties of commendation and dependence in pre-colonial Burma. In *Slavery, bondage and dependency
in Southeast Asia. See* Reid 1983.

Bigalke, Terence. 1983. Dynamics of the Torajan slave trade in South Sulawesi. In
Slavery, bondage and dependency in Southeast Asia. See Reid 1983.

Blussé, Leonard. 1982. An insane administration and an unsanitary town: The Dutch
East India Company and Batavia (1619–1799). In *Colonial cities*, ed. R. Ross and
G. J. Telkampe. The Hague: Nijhoff.

Bock, Carl. [1881] 1985. *Head-hunters of Borneo*. Singapore: Oxford University
Press.

Breman, Jan. 1987. *Koelies, planters en koloniale politiek: Het arbeidsregime op
de grootlandbouwondernemingen aan Sumatra's Oostkust in het begin van de twin-
tigste eeuw.* Dordrecht: Foris.

Crawfurd, John. 1820. *History of the Indian Archipelago*. 3 vols. Edinburgh: A. Constable.

Damsté, H. T. 1928. Hikajat Perang Sabi. *Bijdragen tot de Taal-, Land- en Volkenkunde van Nederlandsch-Indië* 84:545–608.

Day, Clive. [1904] 1966. *The policy and administration of the Dutch in Java*. Kuala Lumpur: Oxford University Press.

Davis, David Brion. 1966. *The problem of slavery in Western culture*. Ithaca, N.Y.: Cornell University Press.

Davis, David Brion. 1984. *Slavery and human progress*. New York: Oxford University Press.

Elson, R. E. 1984. *Javanese peasants and the colonial sugar industry: Impact and change in an East Java residency, 1830–1940*. Singapore: Oxford University Press.

Elson, R. E. 1986. Sugar factory workers and the emergence of "free labour" in nineteenth-century Java. *Modern Asian Studies* 20, no. 1:139–74.

Endicott, Kirk. 1983. The effects of slave raiding on the aborigines of the Malay Peninsula. In *Slavery, bondage and dependency in Southeast Asia. See* Reid 1983.

Finley, Moses. 1980. *Ancient slavery and modern ideology*. London: Chatto and Windus.

Fogel, Robert William, and Stanley L. Engerman. 1974. *Time on the Cross: The economics of American Negro slavery*. Vol. 1. Boston: Little, Brown.

Furnivall, J. S. [1944] 1967. *Netherlands India*. Cambridge: Cambridge University Press.

Gonggrijp, G. F. 1957. *Schets ener economische geschiedenis van Indonesië*. 4th ed. Haarlem: De Erven F. Bohn.

Haan, E. de. 1910. *Priangan*. 4 vols. Batavia: Kolff.

Hanna, Willard A. 1978. *Indonesian Banda: Colonialism and its aftermath in the Nutmeg Islands*. Philadelphia: Institute for the Study of Human Issues.

Ibrahim, ibn Muhammad. 1972. *The ship of Sulaiman* [1688]. Trans. J. O'Kane. London: Routledge and Kegan Paul.

Koloniaal Verslag: Bijlage van het Verslag der Handelingen van de Tweede Kamer der Staten-Generaal. 1860–1900. The Hague: Ministerie van Kolonien.

Kraan, A. van der. 1983. Bali: Slavery and the slave trade. In *Slavery, bondage and dependency in Southeast Asia. See* Reid 1983.

La Loubère, S. de. 1691. *Du royaume de Siam*. 2 vols. Paris: Jean Baptiste Coignard.

Lieberman, Victor. 1984. *Burmese administrative cycles: Anarchy and conquest, c. 1580–1760*. Princeton, N.J.: Princeton University Press.

Louwes, L. S. 1921. Strafrecht. In *Encyclopedie van Nederlandsch-Indië*, 2d ed. 4:119–71. The Hague: Nijhoff.

Lyman, Henry. 1856. *The martyr of Sumatra: A memoir of Henry Lyman*. New York: Robert Carter and Brothers.

Mailrapporten. 1872–1902. From Batavia to Ministry of Colonies in The Hague. Algemene Rijksarchief, The Hague.

Manguin, P.-Y. 1983. Manpower and labour categories in early sixteenth-century Malacca. In *Slavery, bondage and dependency in Southeast Asia. See* Reid 1983.

Marini, G. F. de. 1663. *Delle missione de Padri della Compagnia de Giesu nella Provincia di Giappone, e particolarmente di quelle de Tumkino.* Rome: Nicolo Angelo Tinassi.

Montesquieu, Baron de. 1949. *The spirit of the laws.* Trans. T. Nugent. New York: Hafner.

Nagtegaal, Luc. 1988. Rijden op een Hollandse tijger: De noordkust van Java en de V.O.C., 1680–1743. Ph.D. diss., Rijksuniversiteit te Utrecht.

Nieboer, Herman J. 1910. *Slavery as an industrial system: Ethnological researches.* 2d ed. The Hague: Nijhoff.

Patterson, Orlando. 1982. *Slavery and social death.* Cambridge Mass.: Harvard University Press.

Pelzer, Karl. 1978. *Planter and peasant: Colonial policy and the agrarian struggle in East Sumatra, 1863–1947.* The Hague: Nijhoff.

Raffles, Sophia. 1835. *Memoir of the life and public services of Sir Thomas Stamford Raffles.* 2 vols. London: James Duncan.

Reid, Anthony. 1970. Early Chinese migration into North Sumatra. In *Studies in the social history of China and South-east Asia,* ed. Jerome Ch'en and Nicholas Tarling. Cambridge: Cambridge University Press.

Reid, Anthony. 1975. Trade and the problem of royal power in Aceh, c. 1550–1700. In *Pre-colonial state systems in Southeast Asia,* ed. Anthony Reid and Lance Castles. Kuala Lumpur: Malaysian Branch, Royal Asiatic Society.

Reid, Anthony, ed. 1983. *Slavery, bondage and dependency in Southeast Asia.* St. Lucia: University of Queensland Press.

Reid, Anthony. 1988. *Southeast Asia in the age of commerce,* vol. 1, *The lands below the winds.* New Haven: Yale University Press.

Ricklefs, M. C. 1981. *A history of modern Indonesia.* London: Macmillan.

Rush, James R. 1990. *Opium to Java: Revenue farming and Chinese enterprise in colonial Indonesia, 1860–1910.* Ithaca, N.Y.: Cornell University Press.

Schulte Nordholt, H. G. 1980. Macht, mensen en middelen: Patronen van dynamiek in de Balische politiek, 1700–1840. Ph.D. diss., Vrije Universiteit, Amsterdam.

Stoler, Ann. 1985. *Capitalism and confrontation in Sumatra's plantation belt.* New Haven: Yale University Press.

Sutherland, Heather. 1983. Slavery and the slave trade in south Sulawesi, 1660s–1800s. In *Slavery, bondage and dependency in Southeast Asia. See* Reid 1983.

Tinker, Hugh. 1974. *A new system of slavery: The export of Indian labour overseas, 1830–1920.* London: Oxford University Press.

Warren, James Francis. 1981. *The Sulu Zone, 1768–1898: The dynamics of external trade, slavery and ethnicity in the transformation of a Southeast Asian maritime state.* Singapore: Singapore University Press.

3 *David Feeny*

The Demise of Corvée and Slavery in Thailand, 1782–1913

During the nineteenth century Thailand underwent fundamental social and economic change. Prominent among the trends was a decline in property rights in man, including corvée and slavery, and development of more elaborate property rights in land. Change occurred in an increasingly monetized and commercialized economy in which both domestic and international trade became relatively more important. Major domestic political change included the rise of the power of the central government and, within that government, a rise in the power of the monarch. International political events included both the decline of warfare with neighboring states and the increasing threat and influence of the Western colonial powers. This chapter provides a narrative account and interpretation of the evolution of human property rights in Thailand.[1]

Generalizations on Property Rights in Man

The economic historical literature on preindustrial Europe and the Americas provides important generalizations about the origins and evolution of property rights in man. First, property rights in man are associated with land-abundant, labor-scarce economies (Boserup 1965:72–75; Domar 1970; Domar and Machina 1984; Engerman 1973; Millward 1984; North and Thomas 1973; Patterson 1977). Labor scarcity creates rents: the scarcity of labor makes

83

it relatively valuable. Property rights in man provide a mechanism for elites to appropriate part of the high value of human labor. In circumstances of abundant land and scarce labor, labor markets typically are thin: little labor is supplied to the market, and employers cannot rely on being able to hire workers. Thin labor markets pose difficulties for the recruitment and retention of labor, again providing incentives to create and maintain human property rights. Human property rights may emerge in economies characterized by low population density. Low density is a necessary, but not a sufficient, condition for human property rights.

Second, the choice of slavery versus serfdom depends upon the characteristics of the economy. Slavery is favored when a well-developed market economy exists, property rights in man are more readily enforced, and there is an economic activity for which the cost of supervision is not prohibitively expensive and for which there may be economies of scale. Serfdom is favored in situations in which markets for products and labor are poorly developed, implying that the cost of negotiating the consumption bundle for the lord is high, thus favoring the use of taxes paid in factor services (corvée). A system of payment of factor services may be especially attractive when one party has superior information about the production technology, favoring direction by the lord (Fenoaltea 1975a, b, 1976, 1984). Finally, Engerman (1973), Eltis (1987), Fogel and Engerman (1974:29–37), Drescher (1977), and North (1987) stress the importance of political factors in accounting for the abolition of property rights in man. Gradual emancipation was the rule, swift abolition the exception.

These generalizations based on experience in Europe and the Americas are not entirely consistent with evidence from other settings. In a number of African societies, for example, the category of slave was used for nonindigenous persons such as war captives. Nonetheless, the generalizations are useful, and the Thai case is in large part consistent with their broad interpretation. Corvée and slavery were found in an economy characterized by an abundance of land and scarcity of labor. Their abolition was largely influenced by political rather than strictly economic motives. The two major forms of property rights in man, however, experienced parallel evolutions over the nineteenth century. Slavery did not persist as the economy became more commercialized.

Induced Institutional Change

The evolution of human property rights in Thailand will be described within a heuristic framework of induced institutional change.[2] In the context of property rights, an appreciation in the value (relative price) of a factor of production creates the demand for a more precise specification of property rights in that factor. As its value goes up, it is more worthwhile to have secure ownership rights. Thus it is not surprising that land-abundant, labor-scarce economies frequently have well-developed systems of property rights in labor, which because of its scarcity is relatively expensive, while property rights in land are defined with much less precision.[3] The creation of new property rights depends on the capability and willingness of the political order. The expected net benefit to elite decision makers frequently has a profound effect on the nature and timing of such change.

Change in Thai property rights took place in the context of a rapidly changing economy. The expansion of the intra-Asian rice trade and then the development of a world market in grains (Latham and Neal 1983; Huff 1989) resulted in changes in relative commodity and factor prices in Thailand and greatly expanded the size of the market. Domestic and international political trends reinforced the incentives for changing property rights created by economic change and were further reinforced by an international moral climate which disapproved of slavery.

Economic Change in Nineteenth-Century Thailand

Thailand in the early nineteenth century had a predominantly subsistence rice economy. There were, however, important elements of international trade, especially the intra-Asian trade based on Chinese junk shipping in the South China Sea. Thai exports included high-value products from natural resources, such as sticklac (a resin), teak, birds' nests, hides, horns, and skins (Ingram 1971:22; see also Bowring 1857; Curtin 1984; Evers, Korff, and Pas-Ong 1987; Hong Lysa 1984; Sarasin 1977; Terwiel 1989). Increasingly, rice became an important export, based on a growing demand in rice-deficient southern China and changes in shipping technology which favored bulky cargoes. The advent of Western designs for square-rigged vessels and the steamship were to expand further the rice export industry. Imports consisted largely of luxury manufactured goods such as silk and cotton textiles, precious metals, and chinaware. The royal government played an active role in international trade, which represented an increasingly important source of revenue for the monarch (Hong Lysa 1984; Terwiel 1989; Wyatt 1986). The volume of international trade expanded considerably over the first half of the nineteenth century. Hong Lysa, citing observations by D. E. Malloch, a British merchant resident in Bangkok, notes that the number of junks arriving in port was 265 in 1825. By 1850 it had risen to 331 (Hong Lysa 1984:52).[4] Quantitative evidence on the rate of growth in the early period is, however, sketchy.

A major change in the international trade regime came with the signing of the Bowring Treaty in 1855. The treaty between the United Kingdom and Thailand established a system of free trade (similar treaties with other Western powers and with Japan followed during the nineteenth century). Export and import duties and trade taxes were specified at low levels. Limits on land taxes were also included. Another important provision of the treaty was extraterritoriality. Subjects of nations signing the treaty were not under the jurisdiction of Thai law. The increasing needs of the monarch for tax revenue and general constraint on the ability to raise taxes gave the Bangkok government the incentive to overhaul its system of public administration, in order both to find new sources of revenue and to collect existing taxes more efficiently. The imperialist threat to sovereignty symbolized by the trade treaties created further incentives to develop strong and effective government to avoid colonization. Public administration and military developments were favored. These needs in turn created a demand for strategic facilities for the infrastructure such as railroads (Holm 1977; Sompop 1989:176, 193). Finally, the provision of extraterritoriality created the demand for a legal system which would be acceptable to the Western powers, a necessary condition for the abrogation of extraterritoriality.

Although the rice export boom antedates the Bowring Treaty, the rate of growth increased markedly in the last half of the nineteenth century. Between 1850 and 1910 total imports grew by 4.70 percent per year; exports grew by 5.07 percent per year (Ingram 1971:332–35). The rice export boom was accompanied by a shift in the terms of trade in favor of rice with respect to the price of imported cloth, the import commodity which accounted for the largest share of the value of imports. In the period from 1865–67 to 1912 the ratio of rice export to cotton cloth import prices appreciated by 1.41 and 1.55 percent per year for white and gray shirting respectively. The increase in the relative price of rice underwrote a migration of labor from urban and domestic handicraft occupations into commercial rice farming. The area under cultivation expanded rapidly, and the price of rice land appreciated. For the nineteenth century the evidence for the land price trend is largely qualitative. For the early twentieth century quantitative evidence corroborates these conclusions (Feeny 1982, 1988a, c).[5]

While the price of rice land appreciated over the nineteenth century, real wages appear to have declined or stagnated. Nominal wage data are given in table 3.1; real wage trends are given in table 3.2. The wage data are for unskilled dock workers in Bangkok. It is likely that trends in Bangkok wages are reasonably representative of trends in rural wages, especially for the central plain. It should be noted, however, that for the early to mid-nineteenth century, it is likely that the labor market even in Bangkok was thin. Thus it is not clear that the data reported in table 3.1 for that period are representative of the entire central plain. Real wages measured in rice declined by 1.35 percent per year from 1850 to 1914; for 1864 to 1914 they declined by 0.70 percent per year. For 1865 to 1914 real wages measured

Table 3.1. Nominal wages for unskilled labor

Year	Unskilled wage (baht/day)
1837	0.370
1850	0.420
1864	0.700
1865	0.700
1889	0.750
1890	0.750
1896	0.500
1898	0.500
1901	0.833
1902	0.875
1905	0.500
1912	0.875
1914	0.750

Source: Feeny 1982:132.
Note: For 1850–79, 8 baht equals 1 pound sterling. See Ingram 1971:337.

in white and gray shirting declined by 0.06 percent per year and appreciated by 0.09 percent per year respectively. Given that rice, the main foodstuff, represented a much greater share of consumption expenditures than cloth (evidence for rural Thailand is cited in Feeny 1982:159), the real wage measured in rice offers a more meaningful value.

These trends when interpreted within the model of induced institutional change imply that the incentives for defining and enforcing property rights in man may have been weakening over the period, while the incentives to define more precise property rights in land were increasing.

The Nature of Thai Property Rights in Man, circa 1800

The control of people has long been viewed as the key to power in Thai society (Akin 1969, 1975; Brummelhuis 1983; Chatchai 1982; Cruikshank 1975; Evers, Korff, and Pas-Ong 1987; Feeny 1982; Hong Lysa 1984; Sharp and Hanks 1978; Terwiel 1983a, b, 1984; Turton 1980; Wilson 1970; Wyatt 1984). From 1351 through 1767, Ayuthia, a city in the central plain of the Chao Phraya River Valley, was the capital. In 1767 the Burmese sacked Ayuthia, carrying away gold, silver, art treasures, livestock, and people as the spoils of war. The Thai monarchy was reorganized with Thonburi as the capital from 1767 to 1782, and then in 1782 the current dynasty was founded in Bangkok. Taksin, who reigned during the Thonburi period, and subsequent kings of the Bangkok period were convinced that the weakness of the late Ayuthia period stemmed in large part from loss of control of

Table 3.2. Indices of real wages for unskilled labor (1914 = 100)

Year	Wage in kg rice	Wage in kg white shirting	Wage in kg gray shirting
1850	238.6	–	–
1864	142.3	–	–
1865	–	103.1	95.5
1889	163.5	211.1	–
1890	149.5	–	–
1896	69.6	108.3	134.4
1898	61.5	115.2	158.8
1901	98.4	135.3	148.5
1902	103.9	123.1	154.4
1905	54.1	66.7	64.7
1912	81.9	123.1	114.9
1914	100.0	100.0	100.0

Source: Feeny 1982:127–30, 132.

labor by the monarch. This perception significantly affected policies for re-
constructing the Thai polity during the late eighteenth and early nineteenth
centuries.

Thai society during this period could be divided into five categories: the
monarch, members of the royal family, the nobility, commoners, and slaves.[6]
Officials or nobles, the *nai*, were directly responsible for the control of commoners, the *phrai*. There were three categories of phrai: *phrai luang* (or
royal phrai), *phrai som*, and *phrai suai* (table 3.3). Phrai luang owned their
obligation to the monarch under the direction of their nai. Obligations were
originally expressed in months of labor services, but practice in the Thonburi
and Bangkok periods allowed for monetary payments in lieu of in-kind services. Phrai som owed their major obligation directly to their nai. In practice,
the nai both of phrai luang and phrai som were able to use the services of
the phrai for personal projects in agricultural and household production. Phrai
suai discharged their obligations in kind in products. Phrai suai tended to
live in outlying areas, and their obligations were for highly valued forestry
and other products for the support of the court or its international trading
activities. The nai-phrai system was based on personal ties and was not a
territorially based system of government. In general, obligations to the state
and nai were flexible and negotiable (Wilson 1990a). The competition among
the nai for phrai constrained the exactions of the nai.

The law recognized seven categories of slaves, based on Hindu legal tradition (Masao 1905b). It is clearer, however, to divide slaves into two groups,
war captives and debt slaves (see table 3.4). Slaves were the traditional booty
of war in mainland Southeast Asia. Typically, prisoners of war were settled

Table 3.3. Corvée obligations, circa 1800

Phrai luang	Obligation to monarch of 6 mos./yr. or 18–24 baht
Phrai som	Obligation to nai of 2 mos./yr.; obligation to monarch, 1 mo./yr. or 6 baht
Phrai suai	Obligation payable in kind
Slaves	Obligation of 8 days/yr. or 1.5 baht

Sources: Akin 1969:90–96; Chatchai 1982:142; Terwiel 1983a:124–25.
Note: Corvée obligations were owed by all males aged twenty to sixty or until they had three
    sons who were at least twenty years of age.

as whole communities on lands far from their point of capture. Sometimes
ownership was retained by the monarch. Frequently loyal officials who had
played important roles in the military expeditions which had led to capture
of the slaves were rewarded with grants of slaves and the land upon which
to settle them.

The degree of control of the labor services of debt slaves depended upon
the price the owners had paid for the slaves. Thai debt slavery might be
better understood as servitude or indenture in the European context.[7] Those
sold for the full legal price were nonredeemable. They were under the control
of their owner, and their children became the owner's chattel.[8] Redeemable
slaves were sold for less than the legal price and may have worked directly
for the master or independently, owing an annual payment to the master for
interest on the principal. In an economy with an abundance of land and usufructary property rights in land, people served as collateral on loans (Akin
1969:104–12). There was a strong link between the slave and credit markets.
Even nonredeemable slaves could change owners if they could find a new
owner to take over their debts.

The laws on slavery provided slaves some legal protection from abuse by
their masters. For instance, although children born to nonredeemable slaves
normally became the property of their master, children resulting from the
liaison of the owner and a female slave who had a husband did not. Penalties
of the master also included freedom for the female slave. There were also
restrictions on the master's right to punish slaves (Akin 1969: 104–12).

Corvée labor was used for a variety of civilian and military tasks. In times
of war, corvée was the primary method through which armies were raised.
In peacetime many corvée laborers were used in the construction of major
public works, forts, and canals. Many were employed as artisans, clerks,
scribes, and retainers, serving the households of the royalty and nobility.
Skilled artisans were especially prized by nai. As a result, Thai commoners
had little incentive to become artisans and have their labor services preyed
upon by officials (Thompson [1941] 1967:599–602, 677–79).

War-captive slaves were often engaged in agriculture, with the surplus sup-
porting the household of the owner. Communities of war-captive slaves ap-

Table 3.4. Existing system of slavery, circa 1800

Seven categories of slaves

Slaves in which owner had full title
Children born of slaves in master's household
Slaves received as gifts from their parents or inherited
Slaves received as gifts
Slaves rescued from peril or legal penalties
Slaves supported in times of famine
Slaves acquired through capture in war

Basic categories of slaves

A. War captives
B. Debt slaves
  1. Nonredeemable, sold for full fixed price
  2. Redeemable, sold for less than full fixed price; worked for master
  3. Redeemable, interest-bearing, worked independently

Full fixed price for slaves from Ayuthia period

Adult Male 218.75 baht
Adult Female 187.50 baht

Sources: Lingat 1931:41; Akin 1969:105; Cruikshank 1975:316; Feeny
1982:92; Terwiel 1983a:130.

peared to enjoy considerable autonomy in managing their own affairs, organizing their own religious and cultural lives, and providing for their own subsistence (Hanks 1967, 1972; Sharp and Hanks 1978; Sripraphai and Sripraphai 1984). Slave "owners" appear to have relied upon slave elites to run village affairs. There do not appear to have been plantation-type estates or gang-labor operations. Communities seem to have been kept intact. War-captive slaves do not appear to have been traded in the slave market. Debt slaves tended to be employed in the households of their owners in domestic and handicraft occupations. In general, production by slaves was not an important component of the production which entered domestic or international trade. Most traded goods were produced by phrai, primarily on a commercial basis (most rice exports) or as taxes in kind by the phrai suai.

The various categories of serfdom and slavery in Thailand reflect a fundamental characteristic of the society: the natural condition was one of inequality. Thai society has been described as a hierarchy of patron-client relationships (Hanks 1962, 1966, 1972; Bowring 1857, 1:124; Brummelhuis 1983; Cruikshank 1975; Jacobs 1971; Sharp and Hanks 1978; Terwiel 1984). Thus commoners depended on their nai, who in turn depended upon an official in a higher position in the hierarchy. Similarly, the slaves depended on their owners, who in turn depended upon their nai. Everyone had obligations to someone else (Lehman 1984). The extent of those obligations depended on one's status.

In contrast to the well-developed system of property rights in man, land rights were less precise. In principle, all land belonged to the king. In practice, usufructary private property rights prevailed. The use of labor to clear land and the subsequent use of that land conferred upon the cultivator the rights to exclude others from using the land, to sell the land, and to pass the land on to heirs. If, however, the land was left idle for three or more consecutive years, the original cultivator's rights lapsed, and the land become available to other users. By the early nineteenth century the system of land taxation provided a means for documenting private property rights in land. The accuracy of the documentation, however, left much to be desired, and the system was administratively overwhelmed by the land booms and disputes of the late nineteenth century (see table 3.5). The resulting system represented a compromise between the traditional practice of acquiring ownership by clearing and the precision and requirements of a modern cadastral survey system.

The Evolution of Thai Property Rights in Man, 1800–1913

Changes in the system of corvée and slavery must be understood within the context of four major concomitant trends: the commercialization of the economy, the decline of warfare between Thailand and neighboring states, the struggle for the control of labor between the nobles, royal princes, and the monarch, and the increasing centralization of political power in Bangkok. The growing importance of trade in the economy broadened and deepened both product and factor markets. Increasing links with southern China resulted in the immigration of large numbers of Chinese wageworkers and traders (Skinner 1957). Chinese workers were attracted to the high wages and commercial opportunities. Wages in Thailand were among the highest in Southeast Asia. Chinese immigrants played an important role both in the wage labor and commercial sectors. The proportion of the population that was Chinese and data on the net flow of Chinese immigrants therefore provide a rough indication of the size of the labor market in Thailand, especially before 1911, when it was uncommon for Chinese females to emigrate and the immigrant flows consisted almost exclusively of adult males. The Chinese became increasingly important over the nineteenth century, especially from the 1880s on, when regularly scheduled steamship service between Bangkok and southern China ports began to operate (see table 3.6).

Growing commercialization meant that monetary payments could increasingly be substituted for in-kind payments of services for corvée obligations. The development of an enlarged labor market meant that the government

Table 3.5. Major changes in the Thai system of property rights in land, 1800–1954

Period	Institutional change
Early nineteenth century	Usufructary rights
1811	Survey of landholdings, title deeds based on taxation of land
1836	Removal of tax exemption on rice lands held by nai
1851–68	Title deeds issued based on paddy land tax receipts
1861	Edict clarifying private property rights with provision for monarch's rights of eminent domain
1867–68	Title deeds issued based on the area harvested
1880s	Standardized forms and procedures prescribed in an effort to reduce land disputes
1882–83	Title deeds issued based on the area owned
1892	Comprehensive land law with provision for title deeds and use of land as collateral enacted
1901	A Torrens system of land registration instituted and cadastral surveys conducted
1936	Amendment to 1901 law allowed for ownership based on registration with the Land Department of claims on unsurveyed lands
1954	A new land law providing for a variety of documents and levels of security of land rights enacted

Sources: Feeny 1982:85–98; Feeny 1988c:285–86; Hong Lysa 1984:31.

could turn reliably to wageworkers for major public works projects rather than relying upon corvée labor, which in general had little incentive to perform tasks conscientiously. From the third reign (1824–51), the government increasingly used wage labor in lieu of corvée workers (Vella 1957; Wilson 1990a).[9] The objective of the monarch in this substitution was not solely based on the perception of the superior cost-effectiveness of wageworkers. By accepting monetary payments for corvée obligations, the monarch undercut the control over labor of the nobility and was able to capture a greater share of the effective tax burden. The substitution became increasingly feasible because of the growth of the commercial economy, which meant that commoners had the opportunity to earn the money with which to discharge their obligations and the government could hire workers instead of using forced labor.

Both King Taksin and the early monarchs of the Bangkok period recognized that their power depended on restricting the flow of commoners from phrai luang to phrai som status. In the immediate reconstruction period after the fall of Ayuthia, the government needed a great deal of corvée labor. In order to inhibit the ability of commoners and officials to convert luang to som, Taksin instituted the practice of tattooing free men with the name of their nai at the beginning of each reign (Terwiel 1983b; Wyatt 1984).[10]

The ability of monarchs or officials to exploit labor was constrained both by the competition among officials for the control of labor and by the proximity

Table 3.6. Indirect evidence on the development of a wage labor market in Thailand, 1825–1917

Year	Percentage of Chinese in population	Period	Average annual surplus of arrivals from China, arrivals from China minus departures to China, in thousands
1825	4.8		
1850	5.8		
1860	6.2		
1870	6.6		
1880	7.0	1882–92	7.1
1890	7.5	1893–05	14.9
1900	8.3	1906–17	15.0
1910	9.5		
1917	9.8		

Source: Skinner 1957:61, 79, 183.

of unsettled areas to which the oppressed could flee. Commoners provided labor services and other compensation to officials (patrons) in return for protection and safety. Commoners were ready to change nai if their current patron extracted too much. In extreme circumstances, commoners were willing to flee to the jungle and establish their own communities.

Nobles tried to attract labor by offering lower obligations under phrai som status than under phrai luang. In order to check the flow of labor from royal control once the major fortification and other public works of reconstruction had been completed, Rama I (1782–1809) moved to lower the corvée obligations of phrai luang from six to four months per year. In the second reign (1809–24) obligations were further reduced to three months per year (see table 3.7).

Large numbers of phrai and debt slaves were under the control of the royal princes. Members of the royal family were heavily involved in the registration and supervision of corvée labor. Labor sufficient to complete specific projects was raised by combining phrai and slave labor under the control of various royal princes and nobles until enough labor was available to complete a given task. The system was fluid and flexible. There was considerable variance in the fees paid for exemptions, in the nature and timing of obligations, and in the composition of the labor force used for particular public works projects. The system was also characterized by substantial regional variation (Wilson 1990a).

The second wave of major change in corvée came as part of the modernization program of the fifth reign (1868–1910). King Chulalongkorn acceded to the throne as a minor. During the Regency period (1868–73) Thailand was ruled by the head of the leading bureaucratic family, the Bunnags. The

Table 3.7. Chronology of major changes in property rights in man, 1767–1914: Corvée

Period	Institutional change
1773	Practice of tattooing free men at beginning of each reign initiated
First reign, 1782–1809	Corvée obligation for phrai luang lowered from 6 to 4 mos./yr. or 6 baht/mo.
1805	Three Seals Laws, codification of laws from Ayuthia period and edicts from Thonburi period and first reign
1810	Corvée obligation for phrai luang lowered from 4 to 3 mos./yr.
1870s	Evidence that phrai luang paid 9–12 baht/yr. for exemption
1897–98	Exemption fee lowered to 6 baht/yr.
1899	Corvée replaced with head tax
1900–1910	Corvée replaced with a system of conscription; edicts in 1902, 1905
1901	Decree establishing wage payment of 0.5 baht/day for corvée labor unless on local public works
1906	Decree prohibiting corvée during growing season
1909	Decree limiting corvée, paid or unpaid, to a maximum of 15 days/yr.

Sources: Akin 1969:96–100; Battye 1974:19, 429, 459; Chatchai 1982:134–37, 301; Feeny 1982:85–98; Terwiel 1983a:124–30, 1983b:214; Wyatt 1984:155, 210.

Bunnag family had held important bureaucratic positions during the Ayuthia period and retained prominent positions in the early Bangkok period. Members of the family held key ministerial positions in what were to become the ministries of defense, treasury, and land in the reorganization of the government in 1892. The Bunnags were primarily responsible for bringing King Mongkut (r. 1851–68) to the throne (Wyatt 1969:221). Chulalongkorn was determined to shift power from the provinces to Bangkok and, within Bangkok, from bureaucratic officials and especially the Bunnags and other key families to the court (Wyatt 1968, 1969, 1984, 1986). Wyatt notes that "the challenge which the Bunnags posed against the power of the throne in the Fourth and Fifth reigns was but an extreme variation on a long-term political problem which concerned the division of power between the Crown and the nobles" (1968:222). Chulalongkorn was too insecure to impose effective change until the 1880s. By this time many of the elder statesmen of the bureaucratic families had died and had been replaced by appointees, especially relatives, loyal to Chulalongkorn.

Chulalongkorn was also increasingly threatened by the Western powers, especially France and the United Kingdom. He patterned many of his administrative changes after the colonial system of administration in British India (Bunnag 1968, 1977). Chulalongkorn made liberal use of foreign experts from a variety of countries to provide technical expertise and advice on the modernization of his government. His efforts included conscious steps toward nation building, especially in education and the military (Battye 1974; Murashima 1988; Wyatt 1969, 1984). A major reorganization of the administrative structure of government was undertaken in 1892. Chulalongkorn installed his brothers and other loyal relatives in key ministerial posts, including Prince Damrong at the Ministry of Interior. In the 1890s the final steps to convert corvée obligations from labor services to monetary taxes were undertaken. The head tax replaced the fiscal functions of corvée. The function of corvée in requiring military service was replaced by a system of conscription, begun in 1900. Thus commoners with corvée obligations were converted over the course of the nineteenth century into taxpaying, draft-eligible citizens. The legislation of the 1890s and 1900s converting the legal obligation for corvée into a monetary tax liability recognized a practice which by that time had already become prevalent (Wilson 1990a).

The struggle between the monarch and the nobles resulted in a redistribution of the control of labor services from the monarch and the nobles to commoners. In order to prevail over the nobility, the monarch surrendered much of his own control over labor. An important implication was a shift from personal to territorial administration, especially after the reorganization of public administration and the Ministry of Interior in 1892. Territorially based administration made increasing sense in a frontier economy in which forests were being cleared and the area under cultivation was increasing rapidly (Wilson 1988). Concomitant with these important administrative changes was the development of a reliable market for wage labor.

Parallel with the gradual dismantling of corvée was the abolition of slavery (see table 3.8). Evidence on the role of slavery in early nineteenth-century Thailand is thin. Documentation of the laws governing slavery has survived much better than records on its actual conduct. The Three Seals Laws of 1805 provided the foundation for the practice of Thai slavery in the Bangkok period. This code summarized what was remembered of the legal system of the late Ayuthia period and substituted for the documents providing legal precedent which had been destroyed in the defeat of 1767.

The substantial amount of Thai law, edict, and legal decision on slavery indicates that slavery may have played an important role in Thai society. The number of edicts reveals that the provisions of the 1805 code required clarification and interpretation and that there was sufficient interest on the part of litigants to pursue cases to the highest levels.[11] In the early nineteenth century, when the Thai government was heavily engaged in military operations, war captives were perhaps the dominant source of slaves. Malays from the south were resettled in the lower central plain (Hanks 1967, 1972; Sharp and Hanks 1978; Takaya 1987:210). Lao and others from the east bank of the Mekong River were resettled both in northeastern Thailand and in the central plain (Hanks 1967, 1972; Mayoury and Pheuiphanh 1987, 1989; Snit

Table 3.8. Chronology of major changes in property rights in man, 1767–1914: Slavery

Period	Institutional change
1805	Rama I set prices for redemption of war-captive slaves: adult male, 64 baht; adult female, 56 baht
Mid–nineteenth century	Guesstimates that one-fourth to one-third of the population are slaves
1868	Edict requiring consent of wife before she or her children could be sold into slavery by husband
1874	Edict prescribing declining prices for slaves born after October 1868 until they are freed at age twenty-one; these former slaves cannot sell themselves; grandchildren of slaves are free at birth
1884	Proclamation to eastern provinces ordering children of slaves to be set free, reducing legal value of slaves, and forbidding freed slaves from selling themselves
1890	Law freeing children of redeemable slaves at age twenty-one
1897	Law decreeing that no individuals born after December 16, 1897, can be sold or can sell themselves into slavery
1900	Earlier decrees extended to the north
1905	Act to abolish slavery; forbid sales; slave prices to decline by 4 baht/mo.
1908	Trading in slaves made a criminal offense under 1908 penal code
1911–12	Extend geographic coverage of previous legislation
1913	Extend geographic coverage of previous legislation
1915	Abolition to be completed in the provinces

Sources: Chatchai 1982:54, 262, 301; Chatthip and Suthy 1977:57; Feeny 1982:85–98; Terwiel 1983a:132, 1984:32; Turton 1980:284; D. Wilson 1962:106.

and Breazeale 1988; Sripraphai and Sripraphai 1984). Bowring (1857, 1:123, 190) lists Lao, Peguans, Cochin Chinese, Malay, Burmese, Cambodians, and Siamese among the groups held as prisoner-of-war slaves. To promote the conversion of war-captive slaves into commoners, Rama I set prices for the redemption of such slaves in 1805 (Thompson [1941] 1967:678). As warfare became less endemic and neighboring states came under colonial rule, debt slavery began to dominate (Bowring 1857, 1:124). It was especially common in urban areas. The role of debt slavery in rural areas is unclear (Wilson 1989, 1990a, b). Pallegoix (1854, 1:235) estimates that at least one-quarter of the population comprised slaves.[12] It is likely that Pallegoix's residence in urban Bangkok led him to overestimate substantially the prevalence of slavery. Although there is evidence of the buying and selling of slaves, no evidence exists of a well-established auction market. Transactions appear to have involved a creditor who was willing to discharge the debt of the person who was to become the slave in return for full or partial rights to that person's labor. Similarly, slaves could arrange to change masters if they could find someone to pay off their original debt or to buy them outright.

Virtually no data on prices actually paid for slaves appear to have survived. Bowring (1857, 1:191, 455) does, however, provide some anecdotal evidence. He reports that prices varied from 80 to 160 baht for adult male slaves, from 60 to 100 baht for adult females, and from 40 to 60 baht for twelve to sixteen year olds. He also reports that many freed slaves sold themselves back into slavery (Bowring 1857, 1:193).

One popular avenue to debt slavery was gambling. The Thai government extracted considerable revenue from fees for licensing alcohol, opium, and gambling establishments, especially in urban areas. Gamblers pledged their wives, children, and selves as collateral on wagers, and when they were unsuccessful, they or members of their families became slaves.

Large numbers of slaves were owned by the nobility and royal princes (Wilson 1990a). The distribution of slave ownership within the nobility was, however, quite uneven. In order to escape the obligations of corvée, some commoners were willing to become slaves. Officials also had war-captive slaves. It was therefore in the interest of the monarch to reduce the prevalence of slavery in order to remove the control of labor from the nobility.

Changes aimed at making Thai slavery more humane were forthcoming in the fourth reign (1851–68). In order to combat the growth of slavery from gambling debts, King Mongkut issued an edict in 1868 which required that a wife consent to the sale before she or her children could be sold into slavery. Mongkut found it morally objectionable that under the old law "a woman is like a buffalo, a man a human being" (Chatthip and Suthy 1977:57). In addition, Mongkut thought that the abolition of slavery was important to provide sufficient labor mobility to take advantage of the opportunities afforded by the growing international economy.

Major changes occurred in the fifth reign. In 1874 King Chulalongkorn moved to abolish slavery gradually by decreeing that for slaves born after October 1868 the price of the child slave would decline according to a prescribed schedule, until by the age of twenty-one the slave would be freed. He hoped that the freed children would then work to buy the freedom of their parents (Wyatt 1969:51). Chulalongkorn objected to the fact that the offspring of nonredeemable slaves became slaves at birth. He argued that "the offspring of slaves are born innocent" (Chatthip and Suthy 1977:65) and should not suffer for the sins of their parents. Domestic political constraints, including the Front Palace incident of 1875, prevented King Chulalongkorn from pressing for more rapid change.[13] As a gesture, however, the king did contribute eight thousand baht for the freeing of forty-four slaves in 1877 (Terwiel 1984:31). An 1884 edict restricted slavery in the eastern provinces (Terwiel 1984:32). An edict of 1890 extended the provisions of 1874 to redeemable slaves. Legislation in 1897 closed off other loopholes. In 1905 slavery was abolished. The prices of existing slaves were to be reduced by

four baht per month until freedom resulted. Additional legislation extended
the geographic coverage of earlier edicts. Trading in slaves was made a
criminal offense under the new 1908 criminal code, which imposed stiff
penalties for this infraction (D. Wilson 1962:106). By 1915 slavery legally
ceased.

King Chulalongkorn adopted a gradual path of abolition. He was aware
of the difficulties experienced in Russia and the United States when human
property rights were abolished abruptly (Engel 1975:97–98). Further, he
thought that the removal of inequalities in tax liabilities under which slaves
paid less in taxes than commoners and the development of a labor market
upon which former slaves could depend for their subsistence would eliminate
the causes of slavery. Chulalongkorn also argued that in the long run, compulsory primary education would bring an end to slavery. The scheduled
decreases in the legal prices of slaves served to accomplish the goal of abolition
without generating a fiscal burden on the government to compensate former
owners. Gradual abolition also blunted the opposition of slave owners, who
were for the most part members of powerful bureaucratic families or members
of the royal family. The removal of labor from the control of bureaucratic
officials was indeed one of Chulalongkorn's motives (Wyatt 1969:51). Opposition from nobles was probably crucial in delaying additional vigorous moves
against slavery until the 1890s. The 1868 edict of King Mongkut and the
1874 edict of King Chulalongkorn made their opposition to slavery clear.
The final steps in abolition, however, were delayed until the 1890s and 1900s,
by which time many of the nobles whose power rivaled the monarch's had
died. Finally, gradualism reduced the incentives for masters to mistreat slaves
in the period before their manumission.

Humanitarian motives were also clearly evident in the actions of Mongkut
and Chulalongkorn (Prachoom Chomchai 1973; Seni and Kukrit n.d.; Chatthip and Suthy 1977; Wyatt 1969). The monarchs used moral judgments and
authority in their arguments for the abolition of slavery. The political motives
for abolition were not strictly domestic. The abolition of slavery was clearly
required if Thailand was to regain sovereignty (Engel 1975:97–98; Terwiel
1984:25; Thompson [1941] 1967:599–602). The conversion of prisoner-of-
war slaves into common subjects was important in order to prevent any claims
of jurisdiction over non-Thais by foreign powers. During the 1890s, fearing
that the French would assert jurisdiction over slaves from areas on the east
bank of the Mekong River, by then under French control, the Thai government
stopped labeling these people as Lao, Phuan, Cham, or Vietnamese slaves
in their official records (Snit and Breazeale 1988:127–30). Diplomatic motives
were important in the abolition of slavery. The abrogation of extraterritoriality
required that Thailand adopt criminal and civil codes which were acceptable

by international standards. The development of a modern legal system was among the major initiatives of the fifth reign, relying in part on French, Belgian, English, German, Italian, Indian, Japanese, and Swiss legal expertise (Kyaw 1986; Masao 1908a, b; Tanin 1967a, b). In the prevailing climate of international moral opinion and in the view of missionaries in Thailand (Bradley 1981), a country in which slavery was practiced could not be considered civilized (Terwiel 1984:25).

The domestic acceptability of the gradual abolition of slavery was enhanced by economic change. The rise in the relative price of land and the development of more secure property rights in land made it an increasingly attractive asset. Land was to supplant people as the major form of collateral in the formal credit market.

The development of reliable product and factor markets and increases in land values were not the only effects of the commercialization of the Thai economy. The appreciation of the terms of trade for rice exports created incentives for clearing land. The high value of improved land in turn gave commoners an incentive to stay in the areas they had cleared. This made territorial administration more attractive and personal administration less viable. Economic and political change were linked.

Concomitant with these trends was the creation of a modern commercial code to handle default on debts. Legislation creating more secure property rights in land included provisions for using land as collateral. The complementary changes in commercial law were formalized in the Civil and Commercial Code of 1926 (Thailand 1935:442–558.) Under its provisions, creditors could seize land and other property of debtors in the event of default (Tanin 1967b:16). The decline in real wages made the ownership of labor less attractive. Contemporaries were aware of these trends. One official urged a relative to get out of slaves and into rice land and rice milling (National Archives, Bangkok, fifth reign, r. 5 k. s. 9.2/25, Oct. 18, 1899).

Evidence about what became of freed slaves is fragmentary. The social history of a village in the lower central plain, however, provides rich insights (Hanks 1967, 1972; Sharp and Hanks 1978). Artisans and other urban workers who had been slaves or court retainers were among the early settlers of Bang Chan, at the time a rice-growing village on the frontiers of settlement. Other contingents included war-captive Malay and Lao slaves settled there by members of the Bunnag family. Although the experience of this village in the lower central plain in close proximity to Bangkok may overstate the role of the release of slave labor from activities in the capital city, the evidence does indicate that the abolition of corvée and slavery enhanced labor mobility and that mobility was translated into participation in the commercial rice export boom.

Conclusion

Domestic and international political motives rather than economic incentives appear to have played the most direct role in the dismantling of human property rights in Thailand in the nineteenth century.[14] Corvée was not discontinued because officials were no longer interested in extracting surplus from commoners. Slavery was not abolished because it became unprofitable. The role of economic forces was indirect. Economic change created the product and factor markets which made corvée and slavery less attractive. The erosion of these arrangements helped to fuel the factor mobility upon which further expansion of the commercial economy depended.

The decline of property rights in humans in Thailand was part of a fundamental change in the nature of Thai society. Economic change favored the creation of property rights in land, territorially based public administration, and the development of a reliable wage labor market. Political change favored the deliberate creation of a nation-state, a change motivated both by domestic and international political factors. In this sense the normative and ideological changes which played a prominent role in the decline of corvée and slavery were in turn part of a larger set of changes which accompanied the growing influences of international political and economic forces on Thailand.

Change in Thailand was part of an international trend favoring the abolition of property rights in man. That trend reflected both a normative judgment that slavery and bondage were immoral and an ideological position that only a society of free men would have the incentive to work hard and prosper (Eltis and Walvin 1981; Eltis 1987). The 1868 edict of King Mongkut echoes this view.

The initial steps in the creation of a Thai nation-state were in part a response to the Western imperialist threat. The colonization of neighboring states virtually eliminated the intermittent nature of warfare in mainland Southeast Asia and in the process cut off an important source of new slaves. While the colonization reduced warfare, it also posed a grave threat to national sovereignty.

In Thailand, the rise of the commercial economy was not accompanied by the persistence of slavery with respect to corvée. Rice cultivation as practiced in Thailand depended primarily on owner cultivators who supplemented their labor input with reciprocal arrangements with neighbors and the modest use of hired labor.[15] The system of rice farming created little scope for the economies of scale which might have favored the use of gang slave labor.

Even if the economic incentives to retain slavery had been stronger, it is unlikely that in the climate of the nineteenth century such an outcome would have been acceptable. Instead, the factors that underwrote the decline of corvée also led to the abolition of slavery. Ideological and normative factors were a key part of the decline in property rights in man and the rise of property rights in land. In the nineteenth century in the Western democracies voters expressing their distaste for human property rights were able to alter governmental policy on slavery both at home and in colonial dependencies. In Thailand the preferences of the monarch and of foreigners inspired a gradual dismantling of human property rights. Ideas matter, even in nonelectoral systems. The result of both the domestic and the international political struggles for Thailand was the redistribution of the control of labor services from traditional elites to commoners.

Notes

Earlier versions of this chapter were presented at the University of Western Ontario in April 1988, the forty-eighth annual meeting of the Economic History Association, Detroit, September 23–25, 1988, the Economic History Workshop, University of Toronto, October 23, 1989, and the forty-second annual meeting of the Association for Asian Studies, Chicago, April 5–8, 1990. Helpful comments were given by participants in those meetings. In addition, the author thanks Michael Aung Thwin, Jon Cohen, David Engel, Stanley Engerman, Stefano Fenoaltea, Alexander Field, Peter George, C. Knick Harley, Yujiro Hayami, Paul Hohenberg, F. K. Lehman, Wayne Lewchuk, Gary Libecap, John Munro, Douglass North, Peter Temin, Andrew Watson, David Wyatt, several anonymous referees, and especially Constance Wilson and Martin Klein for helpful comments. The assistance of Dr. Porntip Sa-nguanmitra and especially Dr. Somjai Wangsuphachart with translations is gratefully acknowledged.

1. A more condensed account of the Thai case focused on the testing of a model of induced institutional change is found in Feeny 1989.

2. For more on the approach, see Feeny 1988b, c. See also Feeny 1982; Boserup 1965; Davis and North 1971; Hayami and Kikuchi 1981; Hayami and Ruttan 1985; North 1981, 1990; Ruttan and Hayami 1984; and Schultz 1968.

3. Analyses of the economics of property rights can be found in Alchian and Demsetz 1973; Ault and Rutman 1979; Barzel 1977, 1989; Davis and North 1971; Demsetz 1967; Domar 1970; Domar and Machina 1984; Engerman 1973; Feder and Feeny 1991; Feder et al. 1988; Feeny 1982, 1988c; Hayami and Kikuchi 1981; Hicks 1969; La Croix and Roumasset 1984; Libecap 1986; North 1981; North and Thomas 1973; Pejovich 1972; Posner 1980; Pryor 1972, 1977; and Roumasset and La Croix 1988.

4. Sources on economic change in Thailand include Evers, Korff, and Pas-Ong 1987; Feeny 1982, 1988a; Hong Lysa 1984; Ingram 1964, 1971; Johnston 1975, 1976, 1981; Sarasin 1977; Siamwalla 1972, n.d.; Skinner 1957; Sompop 1989; Suebsaeng 1971; Takaya 1987; van der Heide 1906; and Wilson 1970, 1977, 1980, 1983, 1984, 1987, 1989, 1990a, b.

5. The conclusion is reinforced through an examination of the implications of the appreciation in the terms of trade for land rents within a simple general equilibrium model. See Feeny 1982.

6. Sources on property rights in Thailand include Akin 1969, 1975; Archer 1885, 1886; Bunnag 1968; Chatchai 1982; Chatthip and Suthy 1977; Cruikshank 1975; Engel

1975; Feeny 1982, 1988c; Kemp 1981; Lasker 1950; Lehman 1984; Lingat 1931; Low 1847; Masao 1905a, b; Pallegoix 1854; Prachoom 1965, 1973; Reid 1988; Sharp and Hanks 1978; Smith 1880; Terwiel 1983a, b; Thompson [1941] 1967; Tomosugi 1969, 1980; Turton 1980; van der Heide 1906; Vella 1955, 1957; Wales 1934; Wenk 1968; Wilson 1970, 1990a; and Yano 1968.

7. A related discussion on the nature of slavery in India is found in Naidis 1981.

8. The lower price for female slaves presumably reflects their lower marginal product in agricultural labor.

9. Takaya 1987:198 and Hubbard 1977:75 date this process from the second reign, 1809–24.

10. For translations of some of the relevant documents, see Chatthip and Suthy 1977:17–24. Additional sources on administrative and political history in Thailand include Brown 1975, 1978; Engel 1975; Hall 1968; Holm 1977; Hooker 1975; Jacobs 1971; Ramsay 1971; Terwiel 1984; Thompson [1941] 1967; Thornley 1923; Vella 1955, 1957; Wales 1934; C. Wilson 1970, 1977, 1980, 1984, 1987, 1990a; D. Wilson 1962; Wira 1961; Wood 1959; and Wright 1908.

11. There is an alternative interpretation in which edicts are important primarily as symbolic public statements and bear relatively little relationship to actual practice or to immediate changes in behavior. Clearly edicts may not mirror social reality. Nonetheless, the issuance of edicts does reveal that slavery was an important political issue.

12. Tomosugi (1969:287) estimates that one-third of the Thai population in the mid-nineteenth century were slaves. He may have taken this estimate from Bowring (1857, 1:455), who also reports a figure of one-third.

13. In 1875 a dispute between King Chulalongkorn and the second king erupted. The stability of the regime was threatened when the second king sought temporary asylum in the British consulate. In the end a settlement was negotiated without the interference of foreign powers. See Wyatt 1969:57–61, 1984:193–94.

14. Interpretations of the decline of slavery in other Asian and African countries include Caplan 1980; Eltis 1987; Goody 1980; Naidis 1981; and Reid 1983a, b, c. Also see Reid's contribution to this volume.

15. A major exception was the Rangsit area to the northeast of Bangkok, which was settled during the boom of the 1890s. Much of this land was owned by absentee landlords, Bangkok officials, who leased land to tenants. The scale of operation was, however, still small.

References

Akin Rabibhadana, M. R. 1969. *The organization of Thai society in the early Bangkok period, 1782–1873*. Data Paper 74. Ithaca, N.Y.: Southeast Asia Program, Cornell University.

Akin Rabibhadana, M. R. 1969. Clientship and class structure in early Bangkok period. In *Change and persistence in Thai society: Essays in Honor of Lauriston Sharp*, ed. G. William Skinner and A. Thomas Kirsch. Ithaca, N.Y.: Cornell University Press.

Alchian, Armen A., and Harold Demsetz. 1973. The property rights paradigm. *Journal of Economic History* 33, no. 1 (March):16–27.

Archer, William J. 1885. *The Siamese laws on debts.* Bangkok.)

Archer, William J. 1886. *The Siamese law on disputes and assault.* Bangkok.

Ault, David E., and Gilbert L. Rutman. 1979. The development of individual rights to property in tribal Africa. *Journal of Law and Economics* 22, no. 1 (April):163–82.

Barzel, Yoram. 1977. An economic analysis of slavery. *Journal of Law and Economics* 20, no. 1 (April):87–110.

Barzel, Yoram. 1989. *Economic analysis of property rights.* New York: Cambridge University Press.

Battye, Noel Alfred. 1974. The military, government and society in Siam, 1868–1910: Politics and military reform during the reign of King Chulalongkorn. Ph.D. diss., Cornell University.

Boserup, Ester. 1965. *The conditions of agriculture growth: The economics of agrarian change under population pressure.* Chicago: Aldine-Atherton.

Bowring, John. 1857. *The kingdom and people of Siam, with a narrative of the mission to that country in 1855.* 2 vols. London: John W. Parker and Son.

Bradley, William L. 1981. *Siam then: The foreign colony in Bangkok before and after Anna.* Pasadena: William Carey Library.

Brown, Ian G. 1975. The ministry of finance and the early development of modern financial administration in Siam, 1885–1910. Ph.D. diss., University of London.

Brown, Ian G. 1978. British financial advisers in Siam in the reign of King Chulalongkorn. *Modern Asian Studies* 12, pt. 2 (April):193–215.

Brummelhuis, Hans ten. 1983. Control of land and control of people: The case of "Thai feudalism." Working Paper no. 27. Amsterdam: Anthropologisch-Sociologisch Centrum, Universiteit van Amsterdam.

Bunnag, Tej. 1968. The provincial administration of Siam from 1892 to 1915: A study of the creation, the growth, the achievement, and the implications for modern Siam, of the ministry of interior under Prince Damrong Rachanuphap. Ph.D. diss., Oxford University, St. Anthony's College.

Bunnag, Tej. 1977. *The provincial administration of Siam, 1892–1915.* Kuala Lumpur: Oxford University Press.

Caplan, Lionel. 1980. Power and status in south Asian slavery. In *Asian and African systems of slavery. See* Watson 1980a.

Chatchai Panananon. 1982. Siamese "slavery": The institution and its abolition. Ph.D. diss., University of Michigan.

Chatthip Nartsupha and Suthy Prasartset, eds. 1977. *Socio-economic institutions and cultural change in Siam, 1851–1910: A documentary survey.* Singapore: Institute of Southeast Asian Studies.

Cruikshank, R. B. 1975. Slavery in nineteenth-century Siam. *Journal of the Siam Society* 63, pt. 2 (July):315–33.

Curtin, Philip. 1984. *Cross-cultural trade in world history.* Cambridge: Cambridge University Press.

Davis, Lance E., and Douglass C. North. 1971. *Institutional change and American economic growth.* London: Cambridge University Press.

Demsetz, Harold. 1967. Towards a theory of property rights. *American Economic Review* 57, no. 2 (May):347-59.

Domar, Evsey D. 1970. The causes of slavery or serfdom: A hypothesis. *Journal of Economic History* 30, no. 1 (March):18-32.

Domar, Evsey D., and Mark J. Machina. 1984. On the profitability of Russian serfdom. *Journal of Economic History* 44, no. 4 (December):919-55.

Drescher, Seymour. 1977. Capitalism and the decline of slavery: The British case in comparative perspective. In *Comparative perspectives on slavery in New World plantation societies*, ed. Vera Rubin and Arthur Tuden. New York: New York Academy of Sciences.

Eltis, David. 1987. *Economic growth and the ending of the transatlantic slave trade.* New York: Oxford University Press.

Eltis, David, and James Walvin, eds. 1981. *The abolition of the Atlantic slave trade.* Madison: University of Wisconsin Press.

Engel, David M. 1975. *Law and kingship in Thailand during the reign of King Chulalongkorn.* Michigan Papers on South and Southeast Asia no. 9. Ann Arbor: University of Michigan.

Engerman, Stanley. 1973. Some considerations relating to property rights in man. *Journal of Economic History* 33, No. 1 (March):43-65.

Evers, Hans-Dieter, Ruediger Korff, and Suparb Pas-Ong. 1987. Trade and state formation: Siam in the early Bangkok period. *Modern Asian Studies* 21, no. 4: 751-71.

Feder, Gershon, and David Feeny. 1991. Land tenure and property rights: Theory and implications for development policy. *World Bank Economic Review* 5, no. 1:135-53.

Feder, Gershon, Tongroj Onchan, Yongyuth Chalamwong, and Chira Hongladarom. 1988. *Land policies and farm productivity in Thailand.* Baltimore: Johns Hopkins University Press.

Feeny, David. 1982. *The political economy of productivity: Thai agricultural development, 1880-1975.* Vancouver: University of British Columbia Press.

Feeny, David. 1987. The exploration of economic change: The contribution of economic history to development economics. In *The future of economic history*, ed. Alexander J. Field. Boston: Kluwer Nijhoff.

Feeny, David. 1988a. Agricultural expansion and forest depletion in Thailand, 1900-1975. In *World deforestation in the twentieth century*, ed. John F. Richards and Richard P. Tucker. Durham, N.C.: Duke University Press.

Feeny, David. 1988b. The demand for and supply of institutional arrangements. In *Rethinking institutional analysis and development*; ed. Vincent Ostrom, David Feeny, and Hartmut Picht. San Francisco: Institute for Contemporary Studies Press.

Feeny, David. 1988c. The development of property rights in land: A comparative study. In *Toward a political economy of development: A rationalist perspective*, ed. Robert H. Bates. Berkeley: University of California Press.

Feeny, David. 1989. The decline of property rights in man in Thailand, 1800-1913. *Journal of Economic History* 49, no. 2 (June):285-96.

Fenoaltea, Stefano. 1975a. Authority, efficiency and agricultural organization in medieval England and beyond: A hypothesis. *Journal of Economic History* 35, no. 4 (December):693–718.

Fenoaltea, Stefano. 1975b. The rise and fall of a theoretical model: The manorial system. *Journal of Economic History* 35, no. 2 (June):386–409.

Fenoaltea, Stefano. 1976. Risk, transactions, costs, and the organization of medieval agriculture. *Explorations in Economic History* 13, no. 2 (April):129–51.

Fenoaltea, Stefano. 1984. Slavery and supervision in comparative perspective: A model. *Journal of Economic History* 44, no. 3 (September):635–88.

Field, Alexander J. 1979. On the explanation of rules using rational choice models. *Journal of Economic Issues* 13, no. 1 (March):49–72.

Field, Alexander J. 1981. What is wrong with neoclassical institutional economics: A critique with special reference to the North/Thomas model of pre-1500 Europe. *Explorations in Economic History* 18, no. 2 (April): 171–98.

Field, Alexander J. 1984. Microeconomics, norms, and rationality. *Economic Development and Cultural Change* 30, no. 4 (July):683–711.

Fogel, Robert William, and Stanley L. Engerman. 1974. *Time on the Cross: The economics of American Negro slavery.* Vol. 1. Boston: Little, Brown.

Goody, Jack. 1980. Slavery in time and space. In *Asian and African systems of slavery.* See Watson 1980a.

Hall, D. G. E. 1968. *A history of South-East Asia.* 3d ed. New York: St. Martin's.

Hanks, Lucien M. 1962. Merit and power in the Thai social order. *American Anthropologist* 64, no. 6 (December):1247–61.

Hanks, Lucien M. 1966. The corporation and the entourage: A comparison of Thai and American social organization. *Catalyst* (Summer):55–63.

Hanks, Lucien M. 1967. Bang Chan and Bangkok: Five perspectives on the relation of local to national history. *Journal of Southeast Asian History* 8, no. 2 (September):250–56.

Hanks, Lucien M. 1972. *Rice and man: Agricultural ecology in Southeast Asia.* Chicago: Aldine and Atherton.

Hayami, Yujiro, and Masao Kikuchi. 1981. *Asian village economy at the crossroads: An economic approach to institutional change.* Tokyo: University of Tokyo Press.

Hayami, Yujiro, and Vernon W. Ruttan. 1985. *Agricultural development: An international perspective.* Rev. ed. Baltimore: Johns Hopkins University Press.

Hicks, John. 1969. *A theory of economic history.* London: Oxford University Press.

Holm, David Frederick. 1977. The role of the state railways in Thai history, 1892–1932. Ph.D. diss., Yale University.

Hong Lysa. 1984. *Thailand in the nineteenth century: Evolution of the economy and society.* Singapore: Institute of Southeast Asian Studies.

Hooker, M. B. 1975. *Legal pluralism: An introduction to colonial and neo-colonial laws.* Oxford: Oxford University Press.

Hubbard, Robert V. 1977. Canal construction in the Chao Phraya River system, central Thailand. In *The history of inland waterway development in Thailand,* pt. 1. Department of Geography and Center for South and Southeast Asian Studies, University of Michigan, Transportation Series no. 1, Applied Scientific Research Corporation of Thailand. Ann Arbor: University of Michigan.

Huff, W. G. 1989. Bookkeeping barter, money, credit, and Singapore's international rice trade, 1870–1939. *Explorations in Economic History* 26, no. 2 (April): 161–89.

Ingram, James C. 1964. Thailand's rice trade and the allocation of resources. In *The economic development of Southeast Asia*, ed. C. D. Cowan. London: George Allen and Unwin.

Ingram, James C. 1971. *Economic change in Thailand, 1850–1970*. 2d ed. Stanford, Calif.: Stanford University Press.

Jacobs, Norman. 1971. *Modernization without development: Thailand as an Asian case study*. New York: Praeger.

Johnston, David B. 1975. Rural society and the rice economy in Thailand, 1880–1930. Ph.D. diss., Yale University.

Johnston, David B. 1976. Opening a frontier: The expansion of rice cultivation in central Thailand in the 1890's. *Contributions to Asian Studies* 9:27–44.

Johnston, David B. 1981. Rice cultivation in Thailand: The development of an export economy by indigenous capital and labor. *Modern Asian Studies* 15, pt. 1 (February):107–26.

Kemp, Jeremy H. 1981. Legal and informal land tenures in Thailand. *Modern Asian Studies* 15, pt. 1 (February):1–23.

Kyaw, Aye. 1986. The Western impact on the legal system and customary law of Burma and Thailand. In *Proceedings of the international conference on Thai studies*, vol. 1. Canberra: Australian National University.

La Croix, Sumner J., and James Roumasset. 1984. An economic theory of political change in premissionary Hawaii. *Explorations in Economic History* 21, no. 2 (April):151–68.

Lasker, Bruno. 1950. *Human bondage in Southeast Asia*. Chapel Hill: University of North Carolina Press.

Latham, A. J. H., and Larry Neal. 1983. The international market in rice and wheat, 1868–1914. *Economic History Review* 36, no. 2 (May):260–80.

Lehman, F. K. 1984. Freedom and bondage in traditional Burma and Thailand. *Journal of Southeast Asian Studies* 15, no. 2 (September):233–44.

Libecap, Gary D. 1986. Property rights in economic history: Implications for research. *Explorations in Economic History* 23, no. 3 (July):227–52.

Lingat, Robert. 1931. *L'esclavage prive dans le vieux droit Siamois*. Paris: Les Editions Domat-Montchrestien.

Low, James. 1847. On the laws of Muang Thai or Siam. *Journal of the Indian Archipelago and Eastern Asia* 1:328–429.

McCloskey, Donald N. 1983. The rhetoric of economics. *Journal of Economic Literature* 21, no. 2 (June):481–517.

Masao, Tokichi. 1905a. Researches into indigenous law of Siam as a study of comparative jurisprudence. *Journal of the Siam Society* 2:15–18.

Masao, Tokichi. 1905b. The sources of ancient Siamese law. *Yale Law Journal* 15 (November):28–32.

Masao, Tokichi. 1908a. The new penal code of Siam. *Journal of the Siam Society*, pp. 1–14.

Masao, Tokichi. 1908b. The new penal code of Siam. *Yale Law Journal* 18 (December):85–100.

Mayoury Ngaosyvathn and Pheuiphanh Ngaosyvathn. 1987. 160 years ago: Lao chronicles and annals on Siam and the Lao. In *Proceedings of the international conference on Thai studies*. vol. 3, pt. 2. Canberra: Australian National University.

Mayoury Ngaosyvathn and Pheuiphanh Ngaosyvathn. 1989. Lao historiography and historians: Case study of the war between Bangkok and the Lao in 1827. *Journal of Southeast Asian Studies* 20, no. 1 (March):55–69.

Millward, Robert. 1984. The early stages of European industrialization: Economic organization under serfdom. *Explorations in Economic History* 21, no. 4 (October):406–28.

Murashima, Eiji. 1988. The origin of modern official state ideology in Thailand. *Journal of Southeast Asian Studies* 19, no. 1 (March):80–96.

Naidis, Mark. 1981. The abolitionists and Indian slavery. *Journal of Asian History* 15, no. 2:146–58.

North, Douglass C. 1981. *Structure and change in economic history*. New York: Norton.

North, Douglass C. 1987. Institutions and economic growth: An historical introduction. Paper presented at the Conference on Knowledge and Institutional Change. November 13–15. University of Minnesota, Minneapolis–St. Paul.

North, Douglass C. 1990. *Institutions, institutional change and economic performance*. New York: Cambridge University Press.

North, Douglass C., and Robert Paul Thomas. 1973. *The rise of the Western world: A new economic history*. London: Cambridge University Press.

Pallegoix, Mgr. 1854. *Description du Royaume Thai ou Siam*. 2 vols. Paris: Lagny-Imprimerie de Vialat et Cie.

Patterson, Orlando. 1977. The structural origins of slavery: A critique of the Nieboer-Domar hypothesis from a comparative perspective. In *Comparative perspectives on slavery in New World plantation societies*, ed. Vera Rubin and Arthur Turden. New York: New York Academy of Sciences.

Pejovich, Svetozar. 1972. Toward an economic theory of the creation and specification of property rights. *Review of Social Economy* 30, no. 3 (September):309–25.

Posner, Richard A. 1980. A theory of primitive society with special reference to law. *Journal of Law and Economics* 23, no. 1 (April):1–53.

Prachoom Chomchai, ed. 1965. *Chulalongkorn the Great*. East Asian Cultural Studies Series no. 8. Tokyo: Centre for East Asian Cultural Studies.

Prachoom Chomchai. 1973. Development of human rights in Thailand. *East Asian Cultural Studies* 12, no. 1/4 (March):1–10.

Pryor, Frederick L. Property justifications and economic development: Some empirical tests. *Economic Development and Cultural Change* 20, no. 3 (April):406–37.

Pryor, Frederick L. 1977. *The origins of the economy: A comparative study of distribution in primitive and peasant economies*. New York: Academic Press.

Ramsay, James Ansil. 1971. The development of a bureaucratic polity: The case of northern Siam. Ph.D. diss., Cornell University.

Reid, Anthony. 1983a. "Closed" and "open" slave systems in pre-colonial Southeast Asia. In *Slavery, bondage and dependency in Southeast Asia. See* Reid 1983c.

Reid, Anthony. 1983b. Introduction: Slavery and bondage in Southeast Asian history. In *Slavery, bondage and dependency in Southeast Asia. See* Reid 1983c.

Reid, Anthony, ed. 1983c. *Slavery, bondage and dependency in Southeast Asia.* St. Lucia: University of Queensland Press.

Reid, Anthony, 1988. Female roles in pre-colonial Southeast Asia. *Modern Asian Studies* 22, pt. 3 (July):629–45.

Roumasset, James, and Sumner J. La Croix. 1988. The coevolution of property rights and political orders: An illustration from nineteenth-century Hawaii. In *Rethinking institutional analysis and development*, ed. Vincent Ostrom, David Feeny, and Hartmut Picht. San Francisco: Institute for Contemporary Studies Press.

Ruttan, Vernon W., and Yujiro Hayami. 1984. Toward a theory of induced institutional innovation. *Journal of Development Studies* 20, no. 4 (July):203–23.

Sarasin Viraphol. 1977. *Tribute and profit: Sino-Siamese trade, 1652–1853.* Cambridge, Mass.: Harvard University Press.

Schultz, Theodore W. 1968. Institutions and the rising economic value of man. *American Journal of Agricultural Economics* 50, no. 5 (December): 1113–22.

Seni Pramoj, M. R. and M. R. Kukrit Pramoj. N.d. King of Siam speaks. Unpublished.

Sharp, Lauriston, and Lucien M. Hanks. 1978. *Bang Chan: Social history of a rural community in Thailand.* Ithaca, N.Y.: Cornell University Press.

Siamwalla, Ammar. 1972. *Land, labour and capital in three rice-growing deltas of Southeast Asia, 1800–1940.* Discussion Paper no. 150. New Haven: Economic Growth Center, Yale University.

Siamwalla, Ammar. N.d. Foreign trade and domestic economy in Siam (1820–1855). Unpublished.

Skinner, George W. 1957. *Chinese society in Thailand: An analytical history.* Ithaca, N.Y.: Cornell University Press.

Smith, Samuel J. 1880. *Siamese domestic institutions: Old and new laws on slavery.* Bangkok.

Snit Smuckarn and Kennon Breazeale. 1988. *A culture in search of survival: The Phuan of Thailand and Laos.* Monograph Series no. 31. Southeast Asia Center, Yale University.

Sompop Manarungsan. 1989. Economic development of Thailand, 1850–1950: Response to the challenge of the world economy. Ph.D. diss., University of Groningen. Privately printed.

Sripraphai, Kathleen, and Phornchai Sripraphai. 1984. Sayan's dilemma: An analysis of migration decisions. In *Strategies and structures in Thai society*, ed. Hans ten Brummelhuis and Jeremy H. Kemp. Publikatieserie Zuid-en Zuidoost Azie, no. 31. Amsterdam: Anthropologisch-Sociologisch Centrum, Universiteit van Amsterdam.

Suebsaeng Promboon. 1971. Sino-siamese tributary relations, 1282–1853. Ph.D. diss., University of Wisconsin.

Takaya, Yoshikaza. 1987. *Agricultural development of a tropical delta: A study of the Chao Phraya delta.* Trans. Peter Hawkes. Honolulu: University of Hawaii Press.

Tanabe, Shigeharu. 1978. Land reclamation in the Chao Phraya delta. In *Thailand: A rice-growing society*, ed. Yoneo Ishii, trans. Peter Hawkes and Stephanie Hawkes. Hawaii: University of Hawaii Press.

Tanin Kraivixien. 1967a. The judiciary and the courts. In *The administration of justice in Thailand*, by the Thai Bar Association. Bangkok: Thai Bar Association.

Tanin Kraivixien. 1967b. The legal system. In *The administration of justice in Thailand* by the Thai Bar Association. Bangkok: Thai Bar Association.

Terwiel, Barend. 1983a. Bondage and slavery in early nineteenth-century Siam. In *Slavery, bondage and dependency in Southeast Asia*. See Reid 1983c.

Terwiel, Barend. 1983b. *A history of modern Thailand, 1767–1942*. St. Lucia: University of Queensland Press.

Terwiel, Barend J. 1984. Formal structure and informal rules: An historical perspective on hierarchy, bondage, and patron-client relationship. In *Strategies and structures in Thai society*, ed. Hans ten Brummelhuis and Jeremy H. Kemp. Publikatieserie Zuid-en Zuidoost Azie, no. 31. Amsterdam: Anthropologisch-Sociologisch Centrum, Universiteit van Amsterdam.

Terwiel, Barend J. 1989. The Bowring Treaty: Imperialism and the indigenous perspective. Paper presented at the ASAA, CAS, ISEAS Conference. February 1–3. Singapore.

Thailand. 1935. Prachum Kotmai Pracham Sok. Vol. 38 for 1925–26. Bangkok. (Thailand, collected laws, arranged chronologically.)

Thailand. National Archives, Bankok. Fifth reign, r. 5 k. s. 9.2/25.

Thompson, Virginia. [1941] 1967. *Thailand: The new Siam*. 2d ed. New York: Paragon.

Thornley, P. W. 1923. *The history of a transition*. Bangkok: Siam Observer Press.

Tomosugi, Takashi. 1969. The land system in central Thailand: A methodological inquiry aimed at a dynamic grasp of social change in a Thai village. *Developing Economies* 7, no. 3 (September):284–309.

Tomosugi, Takashi. 1980. *A structural analysis of Thai economic history: Case study of a northern Chao Phraya delta village*. Tokyo: Institute of Developing Economies.

Turton, Andrew. 1980. Thai institutions of slavery. In *Asian and African systems of slavery*. See Watson 1980a.

van der Heide, J. Homan. 1906. The economic development of Siam during the last half century. *Journal of the Siam Society* 3:74–101.

Vella, Walter F. 1955. The impact of the West on government in Thailand. University of California Publications in Political Science 4, no. 3. i–iv, 317–410. Berkeley.

Vella, Walter F. 1957. *Siam under Rama III: 1824–1851*. Locust Valley, N.Y.: J. J. Augustin.

Wales, H. G. Quaritch. 1934. *Ancient Siamese government and administration*. London: Bernard Quaritch.

Watson, James L. ed. 1980a. *Asian and African systems of slavery*. Oxford: Basil Blackwell.

Watson, James L. 1980b. Introduction: Slavery as an institution: Open and closed systems. In *Asian and African systems of slavery*. See Watson 1980a.

Wenk, Klaus. 1968. *The restoration of Thailand under Rama I, 1782-1809*. Tucson: University of Arizona Press.

Wilson, Constance M. 1970. State and society in the reign of Mongkut, 1851-1868: Thailand on the eve of modernization. Ph.D. diss. Cornell University.

Wilson, Constance M. 1977. Ethnic participation in the export of Thai rice, 1885-1890. In *Economic exchange and social interaction in Southeast Asia: Perspectives from prehistory, history and ethnography*, ed. Karl L. Hutterer. Michigan Papers on South and Southeast Asia no. 13. Ann Arbor: University of Michigan.

Wilson, Constance M. 1980. Political and economic centers under Krom Mahatthai, Thailand, 1827-1868. In *Proceedings of the second international symposium on Asian studies*. Hong Kong: Asian Research Services.

Wilson, Constance M. 1983. *Thailand: A handbook of historical statistics*. Boston: G. K. Hall.

Wilson, Constance M. 1984. The geographical distribution of tax farms in Thailand, 1850-1890. In *Rural Thai society and the development of Thai economy*. Bangkok.

Wilson, Constance M. 1987. The Northeast and the Middle Mekong Valley in the Thai economy: 1830-1870. In *Proceedings of the third international conference on Thai studies*, vol. 3, pt. 1. Canberra: Australian National University.

Wilson, Constance M. 1988. Economic change and revenue administration in nineteenth-century Thailand. Paper presented at the Twenty-fifth Anniversary Conference, Center for Southeast Asian Studies, Northern Illinois University, Biennial Burma Studies Group Conference, Annual Council on Thai Studies Conference. October 14-16. DeKalb, Illinois.

Wilson, Constance M. 1989. Bangkok in 1883: An economic and social profile. *Journal of the Siam Society* 77, pt. 2:49-58.

Wilson, Constance M. 1990a. Corvée in Thailand: Organization, structure and duties. Paper presented at the forty-second annual meeting of the Association for Asian Studies. April 6. Chicago.

Wilson, Constance M. 1990b. Economic activities of women in Bangkok, 1881. *Journal of the Siam Society* 78, pt. 1:84-87.

Wilson, David A. 1962. *Politics in Thailand*. Ithaca, N.Y.: Cornell University Press.

Wira Wimoniti. 1961. Historical patterns of tax administration in Thailand. Bangkok: Institute of Public Administration.

Wood, W. A. R. 1959. *A history of Siam from the earliest times to the year A.D. 1781, with a supplement dealing with more recent events*. Bangkok: Charlermnit Book Shop.

Wright, Arnold. 1908. History. In *Twentieth-Century impressions of Siam: Its history, people, commerce, industries and resources*, ed. Arnold Wright and Oliver T. Breakspear. London: Lloyd's Greater Britain Co.

Wyatt, David K. 1968. Family politics in nineteenth-century Thailand. *Journal of Southeast Asian History* 9, no. 2 (September): 208-28.

Wyatt, David K. 1969. *The politics of reform in Thailand: Education in the reign of King Chulalongkorn*. New Haven: Yale University Press.

Wyatt, David K. 1984. *Thailand: A short history*. New Haven: Yale University Press.

Wyatt, David K. 1986. Family politics in seventeenth-and eighteenth-century Siam. In *Papers from a conference on Thai studies in honor of William J. Gedney*, ed. Robert J. Bickner, Thomas J. Hudak, and Patcharin Peyasantiwong. Michigan Papers on South and Southeast Asia No. 25. Ann Arbor: University of Michigan.
Yano, Toru. 1968. Land tenure in Thailand. *Asian Survey* 8, no. 10 (October): 853–63.

4 *Dharma Kumar*

Colonialism, Bondage, and Caste in British India

Writing on Africa, Miers and Kopytoff (1977) propose the phase *delegalization of slavery* for the situation in which the legal status of slavery was abolished but the social institutions of slavery continued. The term is applicable to India in that a long period of time intervened between legislation and social changes. On the other hand, the term *slavery* does not accurately describe many forms of traditional bondage in India. Above all, there was India's own peculiar institution, the caste system. The British did in fact bring profound changes in the social structure. Their intended instruments of change, such as laws abolishing slavery, however, were less effective than policies with other objectives or indeed than wider forces which owed little to deliberate governmental policies. In large part, this reflected the complexity of traditional social structures in India.

In pre-British India, as in many other complex premodern societies, there was a great range of unfree status, from chattel slavery to debt peonage. The classical Hindu and Muslim systems of law both recognized forms of servitude, and local customs legitimated others. Kings, temples, landlords – all had unfree laborers, and in addition, corvée labor was levied for public works. But personal freedom was also restricted by the caste system, which in its continuity, extensiveness, and degree of organization was unique to India. It is necessary first to consider the caste system, without which the institutions of bondage, the limits to legal emancipation, and the working of other factors

112

of change in the British period cannot be understood.[1] One need only add
that bonded laborers almost always came from the lower castes.

Caste and Servitude in Pre-British India

The caste system in fact consists of two classificatory schemes. The first,
the *varna* system, very loosely divides caste society into four orders, or varnas,
often called castes. At the top of the hierarchy came the Brahmans, the priests
and religious teachers; next came the Kshatriyas or warriors; and third came
the Vaishyas, farmers or traders. These three upper castes were "twice-born"
or "clean." Below them came the fourth varna, the Sudras, artisans and
laborers, whose function was to serve the three higher varnas. These people
were considered impure and polluting but still within caste society. Still lower
came a category that was considered extremely polluting. The last group
is of particular relevance here, and I shall use the term *untouchables* in general
for the group, or, occasionally, for the modern period, *Scheduled Castes*.[2]

Moreover, the operative units of social life were much smaller groups called
jatis. Since these too, like the varnas, were mutually exclusive, determined
by birth, endogamous, and hierarchically ranked (though not as unambigu-
ously as the varnas), the jatis formed a caste system. Some social anthropolo-
gists translate *varna* as "caste" and *jati* as "subcaste," but most prefer to use
caste for the jatis. Theoretical attempts to fit all the existing jatis into the
varna scheme have proven unsuccessful.

The caste system restricted social and economic mobility, but one must
not exaggerate the degree of rigidity. The system evolved and changed over
time; new castes were constantly created by fission, by fusion, and in other
ways. Moreover, a particular caste could raise itself in the hierarchy. Mobility
was in theory and almost certainly in practice severely limited for the untouchables. They were forbidden to do work of higher status or to own land. They
lived in separate hamlets, drank from separate wells, had to dress meanly
and behave humbly, and were denied education. These prohibitions were
zealously enforced by the upper castes, the community, and the ruler. Indeed,
although they are illegal today, occasional attempts by the upper castes to
enforce them still provoke violent altercation.

Caste was correlated with occupation, but not uniquely. Certain occupations
were too high for the low castes, and others were too low for the high castes.
Scavengers, leather workers, and those who handled the dead were considered
extremely polluting, and people who followed these occupations were untouchables. Occupation was not the sole criterion of status, however, and
certain occupations, notably agricultural ones, were in fact open to all castes,
or nearly all. In some areas, Brahmans were forbidden to touch the plow.

Similarly, caste and servile status were closely connected, but not uniquely.

Apart from the categories of the caste system, separate legal categories differentiated those of unfree status. The classical legal texts enumerate several categories of *dasas*, often loosely translated as "slaves." The classical Hindu legal texts are neither codes of formal laws nor mere descriptions of customary laws but are both normative and descriptive, in unknown proportions (Lingat 1973). The dasas were differentiated by origin: conquest, sale by parents or oneself (as in famines), birth to a female slave, enslavement to work off a fine or judicial decree, and so on (Kane 1974:184). Different disabilities and rules for manumission affected different types of dasas. According to some writers, no section of the population was exempt from bondage: Brahmans and warriors could sell themselves or be sold into slavery, and enslavement was a punishment from which none were exempt. According to one classical text, the *Arthashatra*, sinful Brahmans could be sent as slave labor to the mines (Chanana 1960:60).

I shall refer to these as types of "servile status" to differentiate them from low castes, though this usage has problems, as indeed any system of differentiation using only English terms has. We must bear in mind, first, that there are two distinct principles of status differentiation: a dasa could belong to any caste, although few were Brahmans, and a member of even the lowest castes was not necessarily a dasa. Second, the two systems were closely linked: members of the high castes were much less likely to become dasas than were members of the low castes, and an individual could not be held as a slave by a member of a lower caste. Third, low caste in itself entailed the lack of many kinds of personal freedom. Caste and other principles of differentiation overlapped and interacted in complex ways. Finally, although the ideology of caste had been attacked even within the Hindu fold, most notably by the medieval religious reformers known as the *bhakti* school, one could not escape from one's caste except by renouncing the world or by managing to deceive it: for instance, one might migrate and pass oneself off as a member of a higher caste. Hindu rulers believed that one of their main duties was to punish infringements of caste rules. The bhakti reformers also preached that caste was irrelevant in the eyes of God, but not on earth (Kumar 1991).

Private individuals, temples, and rulers might all own dasas or employ bondsmen of various sorts. The ruler could legitimately restrict the freedom of his subjects, for instance, by extracting forced labor for public works. Similarly, temples, landowners, and village magnates could exact unpaid labor, such as a day's plowing or porterage, from nominally free tenants and others. There were various local terms for this type of forced labor. All over northern India the term *begar* was used for unpaid labor as well as for payments in kind.

These generalizations apply to a very large area and to a very long period of time. Obviously, conditions varied enormously. Moreover, our knowledge of what actually prevailed is indistinct, derived as it is mostly from texts of uncertain provenance and age. The historians of ancient India consequently differ in their accounts of the extent and forms of servitude (Jha 1975). Nevertheless, it is clear that unfreedom of various degrees, from chattel slavery to debt peonage, was well established in ancient India. The general consensus, however, appears to be that the major part of the labor force did not consist of chattel slaves or of serfs of the European variety. The Mauryan empire of northern India is a possible exception. Sharma argues that "although we have no statistics for the Mauryan empire, the state sector of agricultural production was certainly run by slaves and agricultural labour, and in this sense dependent labour formed the backbone of the Mauryan state" (1958:183). Since the extent of state lands and the ratio of slave to other labor are not known, however, this remains a mere assertion. On the other hand, the so-called free laborers, and even tenants and small farmers, were constrained in various ways, because of the generally unequal distribution of land and wealth and the existence of the caste system.

From the seventh century onward, Islamic rulers brought Middle Eastern fiscal and administrative practices and Islamic jurisprudence to India. The numbers of chattel slaves increased sharply. These slaves were artisans, soldiers, and domestic servants (Kidwai 1985). We have descriptions of a large slave market in Delhi, and we know that Indian slaves were exported to other parts of the Islamic world.

This type of slavery declined after the fourteenth century (Habib 1982), but Kidwai (1985) argues that debt peonage increased, partly as a result of famines, which themselves partly resulted from the greatly increased revenue demanded in the Mughal period. Despite the Islamic prohibition of usury, apparently no law prohibited debt slavery. Hindu rulers tried periodically and in vain to limit the amount of repayment: one well-known rule was that the total of repayment and interest should not be more than twice the original loan. Older forms of bondage such as agrestic slavery or serfdom also continued. Again, Islamic rulers did not attempt to change the caste practices of the Hindus, and they may even have upheld them when they were appealed to. Our knowledge of the social policies of these regimes is lamentably limited.

The Colonial Regime

The British were understandably bewildered by the variety of statuses, the medley of schools of law and texts, unwritten customs and local practices, and untranslatable words in dozens of languages and dialects that they found in India. At first they were more concerned with collecting revenue than with addressing issues of personal freedom, but these were forced upon their attention in the early nineteenth century. Slaves were exported and bought and sold in local markets, some of the rich had domestic slaves, in some handicrafts industries artisans worked in bondage, and agrestic serfdom or slavery was widespread. Caplan (1980:182) is almost certainly wrong in asserting that with the possible exception of the south, "slaves were employed largely or predominantly in the domestic sphere." He states that agrestic slavery was found mainly in the south, and he only mentions Bengal Presidency and Kumaon as other areas where it was found. Severe servitude, however, prevailed in many other parts of India, including Bihar (Prakash 1990), Gujarat (Breman 1974), Assam, and Rajasthan. Perhaps evidence of servitude will come to light for other areas as their histories are written.

The British diligently codified laws and recorded customs. Our knowledge of Indian servitude takes a quantum leap for the colonial period, but even so it is deficient in three respects. First, our knowledge of servitude relates mostly to British India. The native states of Kerala have been studied (e.g., Jeffrey 1976), but the rest, a large number, have been relatively neglected by historians. The native states accounted for nearly one-fourth the population of undivided India. Social and economic conditions and state policies differed markedly in many of these states from those in British India. Knowledge of them would not only fill out our picture of the colonial period but would also throw light on the pre-British period, since historical continuity was stronger in the native states. Second, the tribal population has been little studied, but it is of specific relevance. Some tribes themselves practiced slavery, and more important, the steady conversion of forests into arable land was accompanied by the conversion of tribals into low-caste agricultural laborers.[3] Third, the official records which are our main source of information can sometimes be misleading. The initial impulse to inquire into slavery in India was transmitted by abolitionists in England. The answers of the local officials to parliamentary inquiries reflect the confusions of the officials, faced with a staggering variety of forms of servitude and with dozens of Indian words, whose meanings could alter from locality to locality. They were naturally not always successful in their attempts to describe these unfamiliar institutions. Native terms were often translated into terms drawn from European feudalism, such as *adscriptus glebae*, and the resulting confusion has lasted until today.

A significant form of error was that officials treated certain low-caste names as synonymous with *serf* or *slave* (Kumar 1965). Their reports make it clear that separate native terms existed for such statuses, but the confusion arose because these forms of hereditary bondage were confined to a few low castes. We will take southern India as an example since the connection between caste and bondage was particularly strong there, but elsewhere too, such as in Gujarat, hereditarily bonded agricultural laborers were drawn from the lowest castes (Breman 1974).

The *adima* of Kerala approached the condition of slavery. They were bought and sold, mortgaged and hired out, and the same terms were used to describe transfers in land and in human beings. They were given as gifts to temples or were part of a daughter's dowry. Local governments regarded them as their master's property and confiscated them as payment for arrears. Sometimes the master had practically unlimited powers over them: one deed of transfer for 1833 said, "You may sell or kill him or her." In some parts of Kerala, however, there were constraints on the master. For instance, he could not send the slave out of the district. These are the worst conditions of bondage known, though in Tamil areas to the southeast it was occasionally reported that laborers were bought, sold, and gifted, and there were even rules regarding the ownership of children. If a female *adimai* (the same word as in Kerala) married a free male or one belonging to a different master, on her husband's death she and her children were reclaimed by the former master. But on these matters our information is still dubious. For instance, there are conflicting reports on whether the agrestic laborer could be sold separately from the land he worked on, perhaps because in fact the rules varied from place to place (Kumar 1983a). These were matters of custom, not formal law, so conditions were not uniform and our knowledge of them is indistinct.

The rights and obligations of servants and masters and the sanctions by which they were enforced were not easy to grasp. The colonial government was tugged in different directions. Abolitionists in England, missionaries in India, and to some extent the colonial rulers' own consciences urged direct action. On the other hand, there was the danger that if long-standing agrarian arrangements were disturbed, government revenue, as well as agricultural exports, would fall. A southern Indian official expressed the dilemma well in the early nineteenth century: "There is something so revolting and abhorrent to an Englishman in the Idea of Slavery that the advocates of its continuance in any shape must ever labour under the disadvantage of prejudgment. Notwithstanding this, I shall endeavour to show that so far as it relates to the Revenue of the district (and I trust my opinion will not be supposed to extend further) any abolition of the Puller System would be attended with the most serious and ruinous consequences" (Kumar 1965:69). Puller, or, more correctly, Pallar, the name of an untouchable caste, was used by this official as a synonym for bonded labor.

The government of Madras and other provincial governments felt that reform should be slow and cautious, but at least they could immediately reform their own practices. The colonial governments themselves made use of unfree labor in two ways, both inherited from their predecessors. First, in the early nineteenth century in southern India slaves were sold to realize arrears of taxes from their masters. Such cases were always rare, and they were prohibited in 1819 (Kumar 1965:70). Far more important was the government's own employment of forced labor, mainly for public works. Laborers, generally from the lower castes, were impressed to repair roads and tanks, to dig channels, and to repair temple structures.

The East India Company used this kind of labor on canals and other public works, as well as for porterage for touring officials, especially in the hills. All economies in public expenditure were welcome, but the practice came to be seen as unethical. Proposals to give it up were mooted in the middle of the nineteenth century. This led to extensive official debate and strong protests from engineers and others who felt that the construction and maintenance of public works, especially roads and canals, would be seriously impeded if they did not have the power to impress labor at fixed rates of pay, often well below the market rates for free labor. There were various systems of employment. Government officials could force local landowners to send their laborers to work on public works, the workers being paid directly or through the landowners, or they could impress men directly. Even if laborers continued to get the same wages that they did for their normal agricultural work (and this was not necessarily the case), they were not indifferent to the arrangement. Digging roads or cleaning canals was hard, unpopular work and might entail staying away from home. One canal official in Sind reported that laborers were willing to pay substitutes much more than they received themselves to escape the work (Government of Bombay 1860). Civil engineers with tight budgets were reluctant to pay more, though, and in a few cases they argued that whatever the wages offered, force was absolutely necessary to carry on the public works. "It is doubtless desirable," Horsley, a civil engineer in Tinnevelly District in Madras, admitted in 1854, "that labor should, if possible, be voluntary, but such a thing as voluntary labor in Government works in the Talooks is quite new to the district and considering how little disposition for work is manifested by natives generally, and how small a sum suffices to give them their usual daily food, it is not to be wondered at that they do not come to the cotton Roads, except it may be at particular seasons when it suits their convenience" (Government of Madras 1855:10–11).

Regulations banning forced labor or establishing rules for paying market wages were passed in several provinces. The most forthright, perhaps, was the notice issued in Sind in 1856, which stated that statutory or forced labor was abolished in Sind: "Every man is at perfect liberty to work when, and at what rates, he pleases." Government servants who compelled labor could be dismissed or legally prosecuted (Government of Bombay 1860:9). Whether any were actually prosecuted is not known. Elsewhere, government servants were given limited powers to enforce work, as when a canal was breached.

Another parliamentary question in 1887 led to further inquiries by the government of India. From the answers of the local governments, the government of India concluded that the practice of forced labor was generally dying out. It was used in emergencies, for customary maintenance of public works, or in remote areas where labor was scarce. It was most prevalent in the Punjab. In two districts, Multan and Muzaffargh, tradition decreed that laborers were obliged to clean the canals (the cher system). The local government admitted that the system could be abused but was issuing orders to prevent this (IOL, L/PJ/6/205).

The use of forced labor by government was a survival from earlier regimes. Doubtless officials found it useful, but the practices ran counter to the basic principles of government, and it was steadily reduced. There is a marked contrast between Dutch and British colonial use of corvée labor. Moreover, forced labor for government was not officially abolished everywhere in the nineteenth century, and in at least one case it actually increased in the twentieth. In the hills, officials found labor in short supply for porterage, road building, and leveling sites, and finding it convenient to follow the practices of the hill chieftains who were their predecessors, they impressed labor. The villagers were supposed to be reimbursed, but this was not always done. In the nineteenth century the burden of compulsory labor in the hills was relatively light. It increased in the twentieth century as a result of the operations of the Forest Department. Moreover, the Forest Department reserved large areas of forest for governmental use. These two factors combined led to widespread protests and refusal to supply the labor. When the villagers were fined, they refused to pay the fines. The government ultimately gave in on the issue of forced labor, and the system was abolished in 1921. Thereafter, officials had to pay for transport (Guha 1989:99–111). But nothing in India dies out completely, with the exception, one hopes, of smallpox. Petty officials, such as forest guards, still force tribals to work for free (Kulkarni 1979).

Private Institutions of Servitude

The government could withdraw from its own use of bonded labor relatively easily. It was much more difficult for the government to transform the relationships between private masters and servants, including the extraction of forced labor by masters and landlords, which was extensive in some areas in India in the twentieth century.[4]

The East India Company indeed often supported the master. For instance, laborers sometimes tried to escape from an intolerable master by fleeing to another region, even though this often meant only an exchange of one master for another. If they went to a neighboring district in British India, however, their former master could appeal for official help in getting them back. Since the land revenue depended on agricultural output, the district officials often obliged the masters, and one zealous Collector of Tanjore suggested in 1800 that the police be empowered to force the "slaves" to work for the government and their masters. But such officials were reprimanded by higher authorities, and the practice of assisting masters in regaining their laborers ceased in the first half of the nineteenth century.

In the early nineteenth century the courts and officials generally upheld what they took to be the customary rights of the masters. Indeed, the forms officially sanctioned by an early administrator in southern India, Read, include form 38, a "Promissory Note to a Servant who engages to serve him for life": "If you serve me while you are able to work, I will maintain you while you live." Form 36 is also intriguing: "If you serve me five years from this date to the best of your ability, I will supply you with food and apparel, and at expiration of that period will give you my daughter in marriage" (Richards 1918). Can this form have been widely used? It would in any case have been restricted to debtors of the same caste as the creditor. Unfortunately, we do not know if such notes were actually executed or if the courts adjudicated on them. But governmental support to the masters did decline during the nineteenth century. The official pronouncements against it were effective to some extent, imperfectly obeyed though they may have been. Also, the power of the lower officials, often related to or of the same caste as the landlords, weakened as the bureaucracy became centralized (Breman 1974:77).

Even if officials did not actively support the masters, mere acquiescence was sometimes sufficient. The most notorious example was provided by the issues surrounding the cultivation of indigo in eastern India. Here most indigo was grown by small tenants of British planters or of Indian landlords (*zamindars*). The peasants, though, preferred to grow other crops, especially rice. One solution would have been to offer them higher prices for indigo, but the planters found a cheaper answer in Indian practices themselves. They advanced loans to the peasants and were not unhappy when they were not repaid, since, with the debt, their power to enforce the cultivation of indigo mounted. Their final instrument was force. All indigo factories had armies of musclemen who would beat up recalcitrant peasants. Neither the use of credit nor the use of private force was new—the zamindars too had their own armies—but the planters may have employed them on a greater scale and more vigorously. The planters tried to enforce contracts under which the peasants agreed to cultivate indigo without full awareness of the consequences. For a considerable time, the government did not suppress their manifestly illegal activities. Indeed, "government acquiescence had been the mainstay of the indigo system in Lower Bengal" (Kling 1966:84). This system was brought to an end in 1860 by peasant uprisings and governmental action to prevent illegal force. Moreover, the government rejected the demand by British cotton manufacturers for a permanent law which would have made the violation of a contract by a cultivator a criminal offense (Kling 1966:114).

Antislavery Laws

The government of India could not withstand the pressure by the abolitionists to impose a legal ban on "slavery," and finally, act 5 of 1843 was passed. This act attacked slavery in four ways: there were to be no more sales of slaves for arrears in revenue; no court should in the future enforce rights arising out of the alleged possession of slaves; no person was to be deprived of his property on the ground that he was alleged to be a slave; and any act which was a penal offense against a free person was to be equally an offense if committed against a person on the ground that he was a slave. The Indian Penal Code of 1860, which is still in force today, contained stronger provisions. Sections 370 to 372 of the code made trading in slaves, keeping slaves, and kidnapping and abduction for the purpose of slave trading criminal offenses, punishable by terms of imprisonment of up to seven to ten years. Buying or importing a girl with a view to marriage was not punishable under these sections, but buying her for domestic service was. In 1871 a man who had bought a Hindu girl, converted her to Islam, and kept her as a menial, giving her food and clothes but no wages, was found guilty (Ranchhoddas and Thakore 1987:352). Ranchhoddas and Thakore mention that a later judge found the decision "extraordinary" but give no further details.

Legislation had little direct effect. The laws did make it more difficult for officials and courts to support masters, but it was not official actions that kept alive the institutions of servitude. Nevertheless, as masters became aware of the official attitude, they sometimes changed old institutional forms without giving up the substance of dominance. Substantial change depended on the servants' becoming aware of their rights and being able to fight for them. That was more problematic.

Gyan Prakash (1990) has described these complex responses to legislation against debt peonage in Bihar. Similar legislation was enacted elsewhere, and there too laws were rarely enforced and in fact could do little so long as the laborer had no alternative sources of employment or of credit. In some cases, so-called debt bondage may have been a cloak for a hereditary relationship not based on a loan, but debt bondage in its true sense was found all over India and not just in agriculture. Men, and more rarely women, contracted a loan without security, frequently on the occasion of their marriage, and their labor was mortgaged until they repaid the loan. Since their wages were extremely low, they were frequently unable to do so. Parents could also mortgage the labor of their children against a loan, as parents doubtless do today, not only in India. The district gazetteers of the Bombay Presidency in the late nineteenth century generally state that debt bondage was not hereditary, but one case was reported in which a villager died leaving a debt of twenty rupees and his son had to work for twelve years to repay it (Fukuzawa 1983).

The Royal Commission on Labour found in 1930 that children, some only five years old, were bonded to pay off their parents' loans in artisanal industries, particularly carpet weaving and the making of cheap cigarettes, notorious employers of child labor to this day. The children worked very long hours, in wretched conditions, and under very harsh discipline (Government of India 1930: vol. 2, pt. 2, p. 92).

The difficulties of framing and enforcing legislation concerning debt peonage are well demonstrated by the yet unfinished chain of laws attempting to deal with it. As we have seen, the mortgage of labor at a subsistence wage against a loan could not always be repaid. Usually no written documents confirmed the transaction. The lender may well have found customary sanctions sufficient. Moreover, in remote or economically stagnant regions, default was difficult. If a laborer did manage to escape to some other part of India or abroad, legal action to bring him back would be futile. In some cases, however, the transaction was written down. Even in the early twentieth century promissory notes were occasionally presented for registration, of which the following is a sample: "I have received Rs. 37, and in lieu of interest I have employed my three sons under you for 15 years, on pay of Rs. 1–8–0 per annum, and 12 vallams of ragi [a coarse grain] per mensem. If my sons fail to work, I render myself liable to damages and punishments under the Acts of Government" (Richards 1918:246).

The government faced a dilemma. Were these arrangements normal commercial contracts, in which case the courts and the administration would have to punish or prevent breaches? This was what the landlords and masters urged. Or were the "contracts" so unequal and unfair that the government was under no obligation to enforce them? There was no clear way out of the dilemma, and in fact, the government took two sometimes contradictory types of measures. First, like other Indian rulers before them, they tried to restrict "usurious" lending, and acts restricting rates of interest were passed from time to time in different provinces. The usual effect was that credit dried up for a time after the law was passed and then the old conditions reasserted themselves.

On the other hand, other laws were passed in the nineteenth century reinforcing the master's powers. One act which is often cited as evidence of the colonial government's antilabor bias is the Workman's Breach of Contract Act of 1859. Under this act, if a workman obtained an advance of money from his employer and then refused to work, the employer could complain to the magistrate. If the magistrate was convinced that the complaint was justified, he could order the workman to work. If the workman still refused to work, he could be ordered to repay the money or could be sentenced to not more than three months at hard labor. The act was originally meant to apply to Presidency Towns, but it was extended to other areas. There is disappointingly little discussion of the act in the historical literature. To my knowledge, no detailed studies examine the working of this act. How many complaints were actually lodged under the act? How many workmen were punished? Was the knowledge that these sanctions were available to employers a sufficient deterrent to workmen wishing to break the terms of their loans? Perhaps the act, and other similar regulations, did in fact reinforce the powers of the masters in the unequal struggle between masters and laborers. This has been asserted, for example, to have been the case in part of Bihar (Schwerin 1978:32). The promissory notes from Madras cited earlier also suggest that laborers felt they could be punished under law for breach of their "contracts." Far more evidence is required, however, before one can agree that "bondage was cemented following the Workman's Breach of Contract Act of 1859, which made it impossible for bonded labourers to escape servitude unless the entire loan was repaid" (Sarkar 1985:110).

The law was repealed in 1926, and the general trend of legislation in the twentieth century moved away from support of the masters. This can also be shown by an analysis of the Assam tea industry, where the government once supported an indenture system officially described as "something in the nature of slavery" (Behl 1983:116–18, 147).

Pressure Groups and Other Reformers

Even in the colonial period, many outside the government, and some within it, saw that the law was an inadequate instrument of reform and that other direct measures were needed. In the latter part of the nineteenth century, nationalist critics of government drew attention to the miserable lot of bonded labor, and in the twentieth century the laborers themselves were able to exert some pressure, although economic stagnation and, perhaps, their own acceptance of their low status constrained them, though the strength of the latter factor is a matter of controversy (Moffat 1979).

Missionaries also constituted an important pressure group. In many parts of India, missionaries had at first concentrated on converting the upper castes, but they realized that the most promising converts were individuals of the lower castes, those worst affected by Hindu social inequality. Missionaries set up schools for the lower castes, for which they often received special government grants, and the literacy rate rose significantly in areas of missionary activity. The missionaries pressed the government to take other measures to improve the condition of the lowest castes, including the granting of land. In Madras Presidency, uncultivated lands were allotted through missionary societies and directly to "depressed classes," that is, the lowest castes, and agricultural laborers. By 1931 the lands thus allotted amounted to over 1 percent of the cultivated area (Kumar 1975:259). Most of it was almost certainly of poor quality, but the total amount is not insignificant. Madras was exceptional, however. Other provincial governments apparently did not do as much. But changes in governmental policies were less significant than the other effects of conversion to Christianity, notably the increased unwillingness of low-caste converts to put up with traditional restrictions and the increased mobility which literacy brought them (Frykenberg 1976 is only one example, but a particularly "thick" one, of various studies on conversion). Indeed, members of low castes sometimes found that it was sufficient merely to threaten to convert to Christianity to win some of their demands.

If the aim of official policy was social reform on some issues, on others it was the preservation of the status quo, and governmental efforts to preserve the rural social structure sometimes had the unintended effect of reducing the mobility of the lower castes. The best example is the Punjab Alienation of Land Act of 1900, which restricted the right to own land to a group of so-called agricultural castes, that is, those who had traditionally owned lands (Barrier 1966). The object was to prevent urban moneylenders from buying agricultural land, but the lower castes were also debarred. It is true that not many of them had the money to buy land and that they had sometimes been used as a front by moneylenders, but nonetheless, one escape route was closed to them (Bhattacharya 1985).

In the political arena, the government used Muslims and the lower castes to split the nationalist movement, for instance, by offering them separate electorates for the central and provincial assemblies. This was one of many factors leading to the growing organization and political consciousness, even militancy, of the lower castes. Unwillingness to accept social and economic disabilities showed itself in many ways, from a limited amount of unionization to the refusal to bear visible marks of lower status. The lower castes were once forbidden to wear shoes, for example, and their insistence on doing so often led to violent reprisals. The growing refusal of tribals and untouchables to acquiesce in the old restrictions was also demonstrated in the prevalence of religious and messianic movements (Juergensmeyer 1982; O'Hanlon 1985).

The southern Indian state of Kerala offers striking evidence of the importance of political awareness. In the nineteenth century agrestic servitude was at its worst here: slaves were bought, sold, and mortgaged, and the lowest castes were not merely untouchable but also unseeable, at least in theory. The rule was that they had to ring a bell as they walked along public roads so that Brahmans could avoid them. Today agricultural laborers in Kerala can dress as they please and go where they will. Kerala is not the richest and most industrial state in India, but missionaries and lower-caste social reformers have been active for a long time, and left-wing political parties are now very strong. Kerala has had a high rate of literacy for many years and may indeed eradicate illiteracy by the end of the century. One of the

great failures of the colonial regime was the abysmal growth of primary education, which undoubtedly held back laborers.

Economic Forces

Laws freeing bonded laborers had little significance when the workers had
no other means of subsistence, but economic change could bring a real improvement in status even without legal change. Thus K. Suresh Singh asserts
that while the system of bonded labor in Bihar survived laws meant to reform
it, it showed signs of disintegration when the construction of a dam in the
neighboring state of Uttar Pradesh in the 1950s provided alternative employment (1975:14). In the colonial period, the construction of railways and public
works, urbanization, and the growth of modern industries all provided avenues
of escape for individuals. Frequently the only way of escaping the burden
of debt and a master was to run away. Unfortunately, economic growth and
urbanization were slow. India lagged behind other developing countries even
in the half century or so before 1914, when the world economy expanded.
Moreover, it is possible that bonded laborers in some places were less aware
of and less able to take advantage of new opportunities than others.

Another escape route was emigration abroad. Soon after the abolition of
slavery in the British colonies, sugar cane planters tried to obtain Indian
laborers. Thereafter, they were in demand in other parts of the empire and
elsewhere for tea, coffee, and rubber plantations and on the railways. Laborers
went to free themselves from debt bondage and to escape miserable conditions
at home. The numbers of migrants frequently rose after famines or during
droughts. Between 1846 and 1932 some twenty-eight million Indians
emigrated, mainly to work in the tropics (Davis 1951). Conditions en route
and on plantations abroad were terrible, especially in the early years, and
the indenture system for emigrants, similar in many ways to indentures for
the tea plantations, has been described as a "new system of slavery" (Tinker
1974). But one must consider the conditions the emigrants were leaving behind
and the probability that they went willingly, though undoubtedly with insufficient knowledge (Emmer 1986). Moreover, conditions did improve, and
the indenture system itself was abolished in 1922.

The demand for labor outside agriculture rose slowly and fitfully, but the
supply began to rise after 1921, and this had a definite effect on institutions
of servitude. As the supply of labor increased, the employer's need to secure
labor with loans, or by other means, decreased. One study of a southern
district found a marked correlation between a decline in the length of labor
contracts and the growth of population (Reddy 1978). The laborer also lost
an appreciable degree of security, perquisites, and probably wages. On the

other hand, the length of the work day also declined, and whether it was voluntary or not, the increase in leisure was valued by the laborer. This fact is easily overlooked by historians who have never had to do twelve hours or more of hard labor, mostly in the sun. When computing the loss of welfare due to falling wages, the value of increased leisure, which may be less significant than the fall in income but is positive nonetheless, should be included. Jodha's finding from his field studies is also pertinent. Even when national income statistics showed no improvement in their incomes, the villagers he studied felt that they were in fact better off because of their freedom from debt bondage (Jodha 1988).

The improvement in the laborer's lot in India has been painfully slow in the last two centuries. Debt bondage and abject poverty are widespread, and servile status is reinforced by caste. The lack of change is striking in comparison with changes in many other countries in Asia, but compared with the preceding centuries of India's own past, the occurrence of change is equally striking. It has been greatest of all in precisely that part of the country where the worst conditions of "agrestic slavery" prevailed 150 years ago, Kerala.[5] In other parts of the country, too, the reduction of bondage is not a legal or political sham but a fact of experience for the laborers and the lower castes, imperfect but real.

Different, intertwined, sometimes mutually reinforcing, at other times opposed forces have contributed to this change. Colonial policies were often ineffective or had unintended effects. Legislation against debt peonage had little impact in the absence of sources of credit other than the employer. On the other hand, the growth of employment opportunities at home and abroad enabled the debtors to escape their bonds without the benefit of special legislation. These opportunities were limited, though, by the slow pace of growth in the colonial period (Heston 1983; Krishnamurty 1983). Moreover, the rapid growth of population after 1921 and the closing of avenues for emigration meant that the master found it less necessary to extend loans or to guarantee employment for long periods.

The social reform movements, the growth of political consciousness and political organization, and governmental policies to ameliorate the lot of the lower castes, whether in response to pressure from missionaries or in an effort to woo the laborers as allies against the Indian National Congress, all acted to strengthen laborers' bargaining powers. The legislation against "slavery" and bondage may have been less important in the long run than the various forces set in train in the colonial period weakening the constrictions of caste.

Notes

1. Patterson has a very interesting discussion of the distinction between caste and slavery (1982:49–51), but his treatment begs a number of questions, and the Indian experience is not sufficiently taken into account, for instance on the matter of sexual relations between "outcastes" (an ambiguous term) and others. Caplan (1980) discusses the relations between caste and slavery (or "power" and "status" in his terms) in Nepal and India from a comparative perspective. His focus is different from mine. In particular, colonial policy is not his main interest, as it is mine, though he does touch upon it.

2. The terms used for this group have changed over the years, to avoid giving offense, like the transition from *Negroes* to *blacks* in the United States. The term *Scheduled Castes* arose from the fact that these castes were listed in a special schedule of the Government of India Act of 1935, which gave them special electoral representation. They are also listed in the Constitution of India of 1951, along with the Scheduled Tribes. Galanter (1984) discusses the history of the various terms used for this group and the difficulties of defining the castes included in the schedules.

3. There is no tribe from India among the sixty slaveholding societies listed in Murdoch's *Ethnographic Atlas*, on which Patterson bases some of his generalizations, though there is one from Tibet (Patterson 1982:350–52). One Indian tribe practicing slavery is the Appa Tani (Furer-Haimendorf 1962).

4. The novels and short stories of the great Hindi novelist Premchand describe the various types of begar and the relations between the begar-takers and begar-givers in East United Provinces in northern India. In Premchand's writings the exactions of landlords are less resented than those of officials, possibly because the former are part of the community and begar is part of patron-client relations (Kohli 1990).

5. Kerala is not among the ten states found to have particularly large concentrations of bonded labor today, though other southern Indian states are. There is, however, some bonded labor in the Wynaad District in Kerala. The ten are Andrha Pradesh, Bihar, Gujarat, Karnataka, Madhya Pradesh, Maharashtra, Orissa, Rajasthan, Tamil Nadu, and Uttar Pradesh. A National Institute of Labour survey reports that 86.6 percent of the bonded laborers still belong to the Scheduled Castes and Tribes (Mala 1981:144). It must be stressed, however, that the definition of *bonded labor* adopted in the survey is questionable and the estimates are consequently exaggerated.

References

Barrier, N. G. 1966. *The Punjab Alienation of Land Bill of 1900*. Durham, N.C.: Duke University Program in Comparative Studies on South Asia.

Behl, Rana Partap. 1983. Some aspects of the growth of the tea plantation labour force and labour movements in Assam Valley districts (Lakhimpur, Sibsagar and Darrang), 1900–1947. Ph.D. diss., Jawaharlal Nehru University.

Bhattacharya, Neeladri. 1985. Agrarian change in Punjab, 1850–1950. Ph.D. diss., Jawaharlal Nehru University.

Breman, Jan. 1974. *Patronage and exploitation*. Berkeley: University of California Press.

Breman, Jan. 1985. *Of Peasants, migrants, and paupers*. Delhi: Oxford University Press.

Caplan, Lionel. 1980. Power and status in South Asian slavery. In *Asian and African systems of slavery*, ed. James L. Watson. Oxford: Basil Blackwell.

Chanana, Dev Raj. 1960. *Slavery in ancient India*. New Delhi: Peoples.

Davis, Kingsley. 1951. *The population of India and Pakistan*. Princeton, N.J.: Princeton University Press.

Emmer, Pieter C. 1986. The meek Hindu: The recruitment of Indian indentured labourers for service overseas, 1870–1916. In *Colonialism and migration: Indentured labour before and after slavery*, ed. Pieter C. Emmer, Dordrecht: Nijhoff.

Frykenberg, R. E. 1976. The impact of conversion and social reform upon society in south India during the late Company period: Questions concerning Hindu-Christian encounters with special reference to Tinnevelly. In *Indian society and the beginnings of modernisation, 1835–1850*, ed. C. H. Philips and Mary Doreen Wainwright. London: School of Oriental and African Studies.

Fukuzawa, H. 1983. Agrarian relations: Western India. In *The Cambridge economic history of India*. See Kumar 1983b.

Furer-Haimendorf, C. von. 1962. *The Apa Tanis and their neighbours*. New York: Free Press of Glencoe.

Galanter, Marc. 1984. *Competing equalities*. Delhi: Oxford University Press.

Government of Bombay. 1860. *Selections from the records of the Bombay government*, 7, n.s., *Correspondence on the subject of the effect produced by the abolition of statute labour in Sind on the prosecution of canal clearance in that province*. Bombay.

Government of India. 1930. *Report of the Royal Commission on Labour in India*. London: HMSO.

Government of Madras. 1855. *Selections from the records of the Madras government*, no. 6, *Correspondence relative to proposals for organising permanent corps of coolies for employment on road works*. Madras.

Gune, V. T. 1953. *The judicial system of the Mahrattas*. Poona: Deccan College Research and Post-Graduate Institute.

Guha, Ramachandra. 1989. *The unquiet woods*. Delhi: Oxford University Press.

Habib, Irfan. 1982. Northern India under the sultanate: Non-agricultural production and urban economy. In *The Cambridge Economic History of India*, vol. 1, ed. Tapan Raychaudhuri and Irfan Habib. Cambridge: Cambridge University Press.

Heston, A. 1983. National income. In *The Cambridge economic history of India*. See Kumar 1983b.

IOL: India Office Records and Library, London. L/PJ/6/205.

Jeffrey, R. 1976. *The decline of Nayar dominance*. New Delhi: Vikas Publishing House.

Jha, Vivekanand. 1975. Stages in the history of untouchables. *Indian Historical Review* 2, no. 1: 14–31.

Jodha, N. S. 1988. Poverty debate in India: A minority view. *Economic and Political Weekly*, special bulletin, 23 (November):2421–28.

Juergensmeyer, M. 1982. *Religion as social vision*. Berkeley: University of California Press.

Kane, P. V. 1974. *History of Dharmashastra*. Vol. 2, pt. 1. Pune: Bhandakar Oriental Research Institute.

Kidwai, Salim. 1985. Sultans, eunuchs and domestics: New forms of bondage in medieval India. In *Chains of servitude*. *See* Patnaik and Dingwaney 1985.

Kling, Blair. 1966. *The blue mutiny*. Philadelphia: University of Pennsylvania Press.

Kohli, Kartikeya. 1990. Premchand's writings and the institution of begar. M.A. thesis, Delhi School of Economics

Krishnamurty, J. 1983. The occupational structure. In *The Cambridge economic history of India*. *See* Kumar 1983b.

Kulkarni, S. D. 1979. Bonded labour and illicit money lending in Maharashtra. *Economic and Political Weekly* 14:561–64.

Kumar, Dharma. 1965. *Land and caste in south India*. Cambridge: Cambridge University Press.

Kumar, Dharma. 1975. Landownership and inequality in Madras Presidency, 1953–54 to 1946–47. *Indian Economic and Social History Review* 13:229–61.

Kumar, Dharma. 1983a. The agrarian history of South India. In *The Cambridge economic history of India*. *See* Kumar 1983b.

Kumar, Dharma. 1983b. *The Cambridge economic history of India*. Vol. 2. Cambridge: Cambridge University Press.

Kumar, Dharma. 1991. Attacking untouchability: The changing role of the state in India. In *Europa und die "Civil Society,"* ed. Krzysztof Michalski. Stuttgart: Klett-Lotta.

Lingat, Robert. 1973. *The classical law of India*. Trans. J. D. M. Derrett. Berkeley: University of California Press.

Mala, Sarla. 1981. *Bonded labour in India*. New Delhi: Biblia Impex Private.

Miers, Suzanne, and Igor Kopytoff, eds. 1977. *Slavery in Africa*. Madison: University of Wisconsin Press.

Moffat, Michael. 1979. *An untouchable community in south India*. Princeton, N. J.: Princeton University Press.

O'Hanlon, Rosalind. 1985. *Caste, conflict and ideology*. Cambridge: Cambridge University Press.

Patnaik, Utsa, and Manjari Dingwaney, eds. 1985. *Chains of servitude: Bondage and slavery in India*. Madras: Sangam.

Patterson, Orlando. 1982. *Slavery and social death*. Cambridge, Mass.: Harvard University Press.

Prakash, Gyan. 1990. *Bonded histories: Genealogies of labor servitude in colonial India*. Cambridge: Cambridge University Press.

Ranchhoddas, R., and D. K. Thakore. 1987. *The Indian Penal Code*. 26th ed. New Delhi: Wadhwa and Co.

Reddy, M. Atchi. 1978. The agrarian history of Nellore. Ph.D. diss., Delhi University.

Richards, F. J. 1918. *Gazetteer for Salem District*. Madras: Government of Madras.

Sarkar, Tanika. 1985. Bondage in the colonial context. In *Chains of servitude*. *See* Patnaik and Dingwaney 1985.

Schwerin, Detlef. 1978. The control of land and labour in Chota Nagpur, 1858–1908. In *Zamindars, mines and peasants*, ed. Dietmar Rothmund and D. C. Wadhwa. New Delhi: Manchar Publications.

Sharma, R. S. 1958. *Sudras in ancient India*. Delhi: Motilal Banarsidas.

Singh, K. Suresh. 1975. *The Indian famine, 1967*. New Delhi: Peoples.

Sundari, T. K. N.d. Caste and the agrarian structure: A study of Chingleput District. Ph.D. diss., Centre for Development Studies, Trivandrum.

Tinker, Hugh. 1974. *A new system of slavery: The export of Indian labour overseas, 1830–1920*. London: Oxford University Press.

5 *Gyan Prakash*

Terms of Servitude: The Colonial Discourse on Slavery and Bondage in India

Of all the ironies that characterized British rule in India, perhaps the most telling one lies in the effects of the colonial discourse of freedom. Enunciated initially at the discovery of slavery in India in the late eighteenth century, this discourse gained a fuller expression in the nineteenth-century pronouncements and actions of East India Company officials. As a range of different social relations, defined as unfreedom, was seen to be founded in the Hindu and Islamic texts compiled and authorized by the Orientalists, the British first enforced and regulated these religious laws on slavery; then they surrounded the supposed textual sanctions with legal protection guided by the principles of "equity and justice"; and finally, finding the denial of unfreedom contrary to their post-Enlightenment legacy, they abolished slavery in 1843. In fact, what the British actually did, although they were unaware of it, was abolish their own creations. After all, it was the colonial discourse that had both constituted India as an other and had found in the opposition to that otherness the affirmation of its self – a self that professed its identity in freedom and was constituted in antagonism to the unfreedom that India was seen to cradle. But if India was defined by unchanging traditions, unfreedom, and unreason, the colonial self-representation was that its project was to reclaim Indians for order, progress, and capitalist modernity. This meant that, notwithstanding their otherness, the Indians had to be subject to, and were capable of embodying, universal laws and truths. So the colonial discourse was called

131

upon to treat the Indians as subjected others while at the same time to appropriate them as part of the dominant self devoted to the "civilizing" project. The dialectic of the self and the other could not resolve this tension because the claim for freedom's universality rested upon its opposition to unfreedom. Consequently, while British rule installed the discourse of freedom and made free labor appear as a natural human condition, freedom remained haunted by unfreedom. The institution of freedom had to be proclaimed repeatedly, because each proclamation was followed by an awareness of failure. Thus, the 1843 abolition was followed by the discovery of new forms of unfreedom, such as debt bondage, requiring the enactment of new emancipatory legislations, the last of which was passed by the postcolonial government in 1976.

In this chapter my main concern is to show how the colonial texts, describing slavery and debt bondage in India, formulated and exemplified the discourse of freedom. Elsewhere I have described a range of arenas and activities in which this discourse was shaped, given an account of its effects, and depicted how the "bonded laborers" dealt with the official practices and produced their own accounts (Prakash 1990). Here I analyze official actions and texts that both reflected and constituted the post-Enlightenment language of freedom and argue that this language operated as a colonial discourse in India insofar as it sought to first subordinate indigenous social relations as unfree ties and then to reappropriate them as free labor relations. These features of the discourse, I suggest, urge us to look at its description of unfree social relations as political practices. To emphasize this point, I precede the reading of a classic colonial text (Grierson [1885] 1975) with a brief sketch of its pre-text, that is, the acts of the discovery, enforcement, regulation, and abolition of slavery and the constitution of debt bondage in this process. The bonded laborers I will investigate were called *kamias*. They inhabited mostly the southern part of the Bihar province in eastern India. The kamias were distinguished by their long-term ties, in most cases, to *maliks*, who were village landlords. For British observers in the early nineteenth century, the kamias' long-term relations made them no better than slaves. After the abolition of slavery in 1843, they were defined as bonded laborers. The following section turns to the official pronouncements, debates, and actions on slavery in order to sketch how the kamias came to be defined as debt-bonded unfree laborers.

From Slavery to Bondage

When the East India Company conquered eastern India in the mid-eighteenth century, it did not envision interfering in the indigenous traditions, so long as its trading and ruling interests remained secure. In fact, the senior officials of the Company took a keen interest and participated in the fascination with India and Sanskrit that was rapidly developing in Europe (Schwab 1984; Bernal 1987). But the commitment to respect native religions and customs also required that these be discovered. Officials made these discoveries as they set out to administer the newly conquered territories. It was thus that the existence of slavery was reported, as was its basis in native laws. The first expression of this process is provided by the 1774 declaration of the Provincial Council at Patna, issued under the direction of the governor-general, Warren Hastings (IOL, BRC, Aug. 16, 1774, no. 442). While stating that the right of masters over their slaves should not extend more than a generation, this declaration identified two forms of slavery: *moolzadeh* and *kahaar*. According to the Provincial Council, the first referred to Muslims who were war captives enslaved after military conquests, while the second identified Hindu palanquin bearers owned by their masters. The two were grouped together as slaves because both were seen as unfree. Indeed, any variation in their condition was intelligible only in relation to this condition of unfreedom. Thus, when the council found that, in spite of being the property of their masters, the palanquin bearers could marry and work at their own discretion, it concluded that these conditions made it appear "almost as if no bondage existed." In this phrase, "almost as if no bondage existed," we can see the suggestion of a continuum of conditions defined by the freedom-unfreedom opposition.

While the Provincial Council's declaration stands as the first pronouncement of the discourse of freedom, its accounts of the Hindu and Islamic laws on slavery were neither detailed nor complex. Both of these came from the Orientalists who established the Asiatic Society of Bengal in 1784. One of the most important results of the Orientalist efforts was the publication of *A Digest of Hindu Law on Contracts and Successions* (Colebrooke 1801). The work on this project was initiated by the eminent eighteenth-century Orientalist William Jones, who saw it as an effort to produce a body of Hindu laws modeled on the Justinian Code. It was compiled from various other digests, with commentaries by a Brahman theologian, and was translated by H. T. Colebrooke, a Company official and a prominent Orientalist. The *Digest* included a description of fifteen categories of *dasas*, or slaves, permitted by Hindu law. These included individuals born of a female slave, received in donation, or won in a stake, as well as apostates from a religious mendicancy. They were distinguished from another group, called servants. The principal distinction was that while slaves performed ritually polluting labor, the servants were required to do only "pure" work (Colebrooke 1801, 2:321-40). What is important to note is that, although the *Digest* was framed by Western conceptions of law and slavery, it did not distinguish the servants from the slaves according to the free-unfree opposition. This is how the text was subsequently read, however, as the Company government was increasingly drawn into the issue of slavery.

In the early nineteenth century, Company rulers were forced to respond to the powerful antislavery rhetoric of both the abolitionists in England and the official and nonofficial English opinion in India (Chattopadhyaya 1977: 156–214). An important catalyst in this context was a letter written by J. Richardson, a minor Company official (IOL, BJC, CJ, Mar. 15, 1816, no. 47). In this letter, written in 1808 to the civil court authorities in Calcutta, Richardson denounced the existence and the British tolerance of slavery in India on the grounds that slavery was contrary to "natural laws." Stating that the restoration of natural rights would inspire progress and prosperity in the region, he went on to argue that free labor would bring the benefits of a market economy and promote population growth and industriousness. Upon receiving Richardson's letter, the Court of Sudder Dewanny Adawlut (the supreme civil court) at Calcutta asked the Muslim mufti and the Hindu pundit attached to the court to reply to its questions on Islamic and Hindu laws on slavery (IOL, BJC, CJ, Mar. 15, 1816, nos. 48–50). The Muslim theologian stated that since "all men are by nature free and independent," only the infidels captured in war could be subjected to slavery. The Hindu pundit went on to list fifteen categories of slaves permitted by religious authorities. In these pronouncements of Muslim and Hindu "experts," we can discern the construction of an authoritative and indigenous basis for slavery. In the Hindu case, the fact that the pundit's enumeration of the fifteen classes of slavery had been mentioned in the *Digest* suggests an interesting pattern of collaboration between the Orientalists and the Hindu theologians in "inventing" a Brahmanic textual tradition as authentic Hinduism. In the Muslim case, I do not have any evidence that would suggest such collaboration, but the statement that "all men are by nature free" indicates that the codification of indigenous laws was already framed by the free-unfree opposition. It is true that the Hindu pundit had not defined slavery as unfreedom, but the context in which his opinion was solicited was marked by such a definition. Therefore, the dasas of the *Digest*, who were defined by their status as performers of ritually polluting tasks, became slaves with lost "natural rights" when the court sought the guidance of Hindu codes on slavery.

In furthering the process of seeking the "traditional" basis for unfreedom, Richardson's letter produced effects other than those he had sought. While he had hoped that the government would abolish slavery, the interpretations displacing the alterity of unfreedom in Hindu and Islamic otherness that his letter generated instead strengthened the case for noninterference. This was because, although it was considered contrary to "natural law," the existence of Hindu and Muslim religious provisions for unfreedom meant that these were indigenous practices that the government was pledged to leave alone. Thus, aside from forwarding the replies of the Hindu and Muslim clerics to Richardson and asking if in the light of these any reform was required, the judicial authorities did nothing. They did not even forward Richardson's letter to the governor-general until 1816, when these issues once again gained the government's attention. The renewed attention, however, did not advance the cause of abolition. J. H. Harington, the chief judge of the supreme criminal and civil courts at Calcutta, recommended the application of Hindu and Muslim laws (IOL, BJC, CJ, Dec. 29, 1826, no. 14). And in 1826 the governor-general, while justifying inaction, invoked the authority and cited the opinion of Colebrooke, who had said in 1812 that "great circumspection will be requisite to . . . meddle with so delicate a matter as the relation of master and slave in an Asiatic country, in any but extreme cases, where humanity indispensably requires the rescue of a fellow-creature from barbarity; and the interposition of the British Legislature is to be deprecated in a country among a people so peculiar as this" (IOL, BJC, CJ, Dec. 29, 1826, no. 15). The Company decided to treat Indians as the "peculiar" other, but in this apparent respect for cultural difference something more subtle happened. To appreciate this, one has only to recognize that the tolerated otherness was defined in relation to self: the freedom-loving colonizer's self, after all, was incestuously related to the enslaving Hindu and Muslim laws. So the decision to recognize Indians as "peculiar," the expression of respect for their otherness, was in fact an attempt to constitute their subjectivity, a generative exercise of power seeking to define Indian traditions.

This process occurred not only at the higher levels of colonial government in Calcutta but also at lower levels, in the districts. As a matter of fact, as the case of Richardson's letter has shown, the Company government at Calcutta became concerned with the issue of slavery partly because of initiatives from below. The official discussions at the higher level and the knowledge produced by Orientalist scholarship in turn spilled back on the districts. Away from Calcutta, without explicit guidance from above, local officials administered Hindu and Muslim laws derived from Orientalist ideas and from their own interpretations of customary practices. In doing so, however, they also applied principles of "equity and justice" to outlaw cruel punishments, or they reinterpreted religious laws to make room for such interventions. It is at this level, in the actions of local officers, that the kamias of southern Bihar began to make their appearance in relation to slavery. I offer two examples that illustrate this process and the strategy adopted by local officers. The first one comes from the judge of Patna District, who had adjudicated numerous disputes on property rights in slaves. Speaking of his experience, he stated that, in settling these cases, he dismissed the masters' suits against slaves when he found evidence of cruel punishments, because "Mahomedan law and practice, is simply to preserve life." The second example comes from another district, where 143 civil and criminal cases related to slavery were tried from 1825 to 1835. In these cases, the courts "recognized generally the rights of masters over their slaves, to the extent of enforcing any engagements voluntarily entered into by parties, according to the customs of these parts, and provided they be not repugnant to the feelings of a British judge."[1]

These official actions had three consequences: they helped entrench the notion that Hindu and Muslim laws provided for enslavement; they surrounded slavery with a regulatory economy of laws restricting the master's juridical control and cruel treatment of the slave's body; and they made space for the definition of the kamias' condition as "voluntarily entered" servitude as a position in the continuum extending from slavery to freedom.

The operation of these effects was visible in the abolition of slavery. When the government, following the recommendation of the *Report from the Indian Law Commissioners* (United Kingdom 1841), abolished slavery in 1843, it saw itself eliminating practices constituted by indigenous religious laws. Furthermore, the institution of freedom came stalked by "gentle" and "voluntary" unfreedom. So if the abolition gave precedence to the Indians' status as "fellow-creatures" over their "peculiarity," the reinstitution of unfreedom in the form of "voluntary" servitude cast a shadow on that discourse of the universal and free self. Some colonial officials had already recognized that "voluntary" servitude was not entirely alien to their discourse of freedom. They had noted that, even before the abolition of slavery in 1843, landlords had begun representing their relations with laborers as conditional leases based on loan transactions. As the report itself noted, government rules, such as Regulation X of 1811 banning slave imports, and court decisions had sent a signal to Indians that contractual servitude was legitimate. Judges ruled to enforce lease deeds stipulating that the laborers serve their employers for ninety years as provided in their contracts because such transactions were considered consistent with English laws on contractual obligation, and the report classified the kamias of Bihar, whose condition from earlier accounts suggested the existence of remarkable diversity, as conditional slaves. After 1843 these contracts, often recorded on stamped legal paper, were seen as evidence of creditor-debtor relations and were regularly enforced by the courts (Government of Bengal 1854:57, 1856:1–2; IOL, BJP, Mar. 17, 1859, no. 290). One official even issued a general notification in 1855 ordering the kamias to honor their contracts and asking the railway authorities to dismiss those workers whom landlords claimed as their kamias (IOL, BJP, Sept. 27, 1855, nos. 62–63). By the middle of the nineteenth century these actions shifted the official attention from slavery to debt bondage. The kamias began to appear increasingly in official texts as laborers whose freedom was suspended by their debts, and the notion that transactions of money had the power to bind people became self-evident in the colonial discourse.

Textual Constructions

Among the many colonial texts that articulate the belief—fostered by the history of the discourse of freedom in India—that debts suspended a person's "natural" freedom, *Bihar Peasant Life* (1885) by George Grierson, an eminent administrator-scholar of the late nineteenth century, is perhaps the most complex. A dictionary of agricultural terms remarkable for its attention to local context, it appears as a text written purely out of an antiquarian interest by someone who single-mindedly dug for facts, without any concern for interpretation. It is precisely this appearance that makes it close reading a rewarding task, because it reveals the most enduring and subtle elements of the colonial discourse.

Exhaustive in design, systematic in composition, and marked by an almost fanatical attention to local detail and variation, Grierson's work was presented as a discursive catalog that could "serve as a solid foundation for more elaborate disquisitions on the Bihar raiyat and his surroundings" ([1885] 1975:1). Thousands of native terms for agricultural implements, operations, and seasons, along with those for tools, cloth and clothing, ornaments, furniture, soils, insects, weeds, cattle, labor, land tenures, trade, moneylending, and rituals appear in the catalog. The obvious scholarship that went into its composition is impressive, and its formal structure has a striking effect: its encyclopedic scope, its excess, positions the work as an unmediated record, and the indigenous terms printed in the native (Devanagari) script help produce the notion that it is an imprint of reality, a true representation of the "original." Grierson's focus on language, on words, for producing descriptions of otherness and his later work with Indian languages resulting in multivolume linguistic surveys are not surprising in view of the fact, as Edward Said points out, that with the emergence of philology as a secularized and scientific discipline by the mid-nineteenth century, language provided a privileged realm for systematizing Orientalist knowledge (Said 1978:123–48). In keeping with this trend in Orientalism, *Bihar Peasant Life* concentrated on native terms in order to provide a systematic account of otherness. Short on elaborate commentaries and long on the cataloging of terms, the work relies on its appearance as an imprint of reality to yield ideas about what made the Indians, or, more specifically, the Bihari peasants, unique and different. Classification, trivia, minutiae, all serve to constitute the otherness of the Bihari peasants, depicting them in a world organized by an epistemology radically different from that of Europeans. The coherence of this native world, however, was not the result of native efforts but the product of the classificatory schemes that Grierson deployed, an outcome of knowledge that the power over the natives enabled. While designed to capture the otherness of Bihari peasants, his classification of native terms and their meanings made the agrarian society of Bihar appear not strange but familiar to Western categories.

In his work, Grierson notes *kamia* as only one of several terms for plowmen and agricultural laborers. In addition to *kamia*, he recorded terms such as *harwāhā, majurā, banihār, dopahariyā, agwār jan,* and *laguā jan* (Grierson

[1885] 1975:177–78, 313–14). Some of these terms were used more generally in some areas than others, but Grierson made it quite clear that just because a particular term was recorded in one particular area did not mean that it was not used in another. So more than regional variation lay at the basis of terminological multiplicity. Thus, having brought a variety of terms under the general heading of laborers, Grierson accounted for the difference between them through two principles: length of labor ties and the form of payment. Thus, majurā and banihār were agricultural laborers in general, without long-standing ties with the landholder, and were distinguished from kamias, laguā jan, and agwār jan, who were bound by debt to their landholders. Somewhere in the middle of these two extremes were the dopahariyās—plowmen who worked for half a day (i.e., for two *pahars*, with four constituting a full day)—and the harwāhās, or plowmen engaged for the year. Distinguishing these categories of laborers on the basis of payment, Grierson noted that the laborers paid in kind were *jan, uphangiyā*, and *bani*, while those paid in cash were *nokar* and *koranjā*.

Terms for landholders, unlike terms for laborers, show a remarkably limited range. Grierson does not provide a list of terms that applied to landholders in their capacity as employers of labor. Terms for landholders that find mention, such as *malik* and *sarkār*, are those that were used, according to Grierson, for the *zamindārs*, that is, for landholders designated as landowners by the British land revenue settlement ([1885] 1975:322). To *malik, zamindār*, and *sarkār*, we may also add the term *raiyat* (peasant) that other British administrators used in referring to the kamia's employers (Government of Bihar and Orissa 1928:63). Introduced by Muslim warriors and rulers, terms such as *malik, zamindār*, and *raiyat* received new legal definitions during British rule.

The basis for distinctions between different terms that Grierson laid out has a compelling ring of practicality: one laborer is different from another because different conditions are attached to the mode of payment and the length of ties; one landholder is different from another because different legal rights are involved. It is remarkable that the caste hierarchy appears to have no effect on the production of terminological differences. In mentioning caste, it is not my intention to resurrect the familiar but fruitless debate over caste versus class but rather to point out that Grierson's account cannot be treated simply as a document that we can mine for facts. Instead, we must interrogate its categories to reveal the classificatory scheme that represents and classifies facts in a certain manner. Thus seen, the omission of caste, something that colonial writers never tired of writing about in other contexts, needs an explanation.

By the late nineteenth century colonial writers came to see caste as the most pervasive and dominant institution in India. Drawing on their official experience, administrator-scholars wrote books cataloging castes and tracing their histories through legends and Hindu scriptures (Risley 1891; Crooke

1906; Thurston 1909). The census operations, which commenced at this time, made enumeration according to caste an important part of population classification and became deeply embroiled in the issue of ritual ranking of different castes. It is true that in giving caste a central place in their description and enumeration of Indian society, the British felt that they were taking note of Indian attachments to traditional beliefs and institutions. The picture of "traditional" India that thus emerged, however, with caste as its central subject, was the product of colonial classificatory schemes. Because the power to name, rank, classify, and represent lay with the British, it is they who constructed the coherence of the native world.[2] But if one impulse of this power was to represent Indians as the other who, steeped in caste and religion, required British rule, its other impulse was to assert the superiority of the colonial epistemology. While one might consider indigenous sentiments and beliefs about caste, Indian society could be analyzed and understood, ruled and administered, only by an epistemology that the British possessed. In doing so, even though Indians were treated as the other, universal categories were also made applicable to Indians. Thus, the census operations, while enumerating the population according to castes, set out to classify Indians according to age, sex, and occupation.[3] Similarly, although Grierson set out to understand the otherness of Bihar peasants, the very cataloging of indigenous terms according to supposedly universal classifications (such as soils, general agricultural operations, labor, advances, wages, and perquisites) denied difference. Terms for caste and religious practices, when mentioned at all, did not find a place in sections on land tenures or labor systems but in a section entitled "Ceremonies and Superstitions of Rural Life." In other words, contrary to the other impulse in contemporary colonial thinking which saw Indian social and economic life deeply immersed in caste and religion, Grierson's text separated the religious from the social and economic domains and listed terms according to a classification that had political and scientific legitimacy.

While the legal codification of land rights that the British enacted provided Grierson with a basis for drawing distinctions between landholders, the silence of the law in the realm of labor relations forced him to discover an alternative basis for understanding the terminology for laborers. Conditions of work and payment provided one such basis. Now, while the mode of payment and the length of ties may have imparted a certain meaning to a particular term in relation to other terms, surely economy does not exhaust the range of meanings articulated. To assume otherwise, as Grierson's classification did, oversimplifies the terminological issue but, more important, also represents agrarian groups and agrarian relations according to categories that capitalism regards as natural. While economic practice may have provided one way for distinguishing between different terms, to conclude that terminological distinctions mirrored the economy is to accept a particular kind of representation according to which the economy constitutes an independent domain. A brief discussion of the etymology of the word *kamia* will show that differences between terms may not necessarily reflect different economic conditions.

The term *kamia* appears to be related to the Sanskrit *karmakāra*, or the Pali *kammakāra*, which is defined in ancient Indian texts as a person who earns his livelihood working for *bhatta-vetana*, that is, for cooked rice and wages for fixed periods (Chanana 1960:129). While some kammakāras' positions may have been marked by debt relationships, the term as such denoted work for wages. The texts often speak of kammakāras as servants working for wages and distinguish them from the dasas.[4] Thus, at least initially, the notion of bondage was not associated with the term *kammakāra*. Nor was there a term for "free" laborer to which bondage could be opposed. Even the term *dasa*, usually glossed as "slave," referred to those non-Aryan peoples whose subjection to the self-defined Aryan ruling class approximated slavery. Even from the rather sketchy records of ancient India, however, it is clear that the bonded-free antinomy was irrelevant to the meanings articulated in the practical use of terms for labor. Indeed, in one text, the term *kammakāra* is opposed not to "free labor" but to a monk: Nanda, Buddha's cousin, is called *kammakāra* by other monks who accuse him of having become a monk in order to get, as a sort of wage, fairies in heaven (Chanana 1960:170). The important point to note is that *kammakāra* is distinguished from other terms not because of the mode of payment or by the economic relationship that exists between the laborer and his employer but by the fact that a kammakāra chose to place his economic relationship over all others, to work for wages rather than to offer service without any expectation of return. In ancient India, then, the term *kammakāra* represented the person, his status, and his character rather than the particular economic relationship that he may have had with his employer.

Moving on to the nineteenth century, Bihari landlords and laborers could also have defined the difference between kamias and, let us say, majurā and harwāhā according to notions of status and social obligations, unless it is argued that bourgeois political economy had come to constitute the social discourse. At first glance, this appears to be the case when we look at colonial records concerning the kamia's relations with his employers, the maliks. Translated usually as "owner," the term *malik* appeared in the fourteenth century to define those local magnates who combined their high ritual status with control over land and people. The Mughal emperors frequently gave zamindāri rights, that is, the responsibility for collecting the imperial land revenue, to many maliks. Under British rule, maliks holding zamindāri rights were declared landowners over all lands for which they paid land revenue.

So while it is true that maliks clearly witnessed considerable change in their legal responsibilities to the state, they remained powerful magnates ruling over peasants and labor in the localities for a long period. It is to these powerful maliks that kamias were related as their dependent servants.

In most historical records, the term *kamia*, among all others for laborers, comes across as particularly well defined. The reason was that the kamia was bound to his employer, usually the malik. The kamia's bondage rested, as Grierson and several other sources tell us, on the *kamiauti* transaction (Grierson [1885] 1975:315; Government of Bibar and Orissa 1928:63) The malik provided money, grain, and sometimes a small plot of land, and in return the kamia agreed to work on the malik's land until such time as the sum advanced was repaid. In practice, this meant never, and thus bondage became hereditary. *Bihar Peasant Life* calls these advances of pay, but almost all observers, including Grierson in another work (1893:114), have translated these transactions as "loans" (NAI, GOI, RAD, Feb. 1920; BSA, GOBO, RD, Nov. 1919). The kamia-malik relationship has thus always been seen as a debt relationship, and the kamias as bond servants. When one equates terms for social groups to their economic functions and conditions (kamias as laborers with long-term ties and maliks as landlords), the transactions and relations between them naturally appear as economic. So advances became debts which tied laborers to landlords. Thus, in distinguishing *kamia* from other terms for a laborer such as *jan* and *banihār*, Grierson mentions debt as the major difference, and debt also appears as the basis of the kamia's bondage.

Once again, as in the case of terminology for agrarian groups, Grierson's account of terms for servitude bear the mark of categories that appear natural under capitalism. If free individuality that included ownership of one's own labor was the natural condition of people, what accounted for the bondage of kamias? Grierson's answer was debt. Once his classificatory scheme construed *kamia, jan*, and *majurā* as terms reflecting different modes of payment and lengths of service, it followed that advances of money and grain, represented as loans, explained why kamias were bound the longest to their employers: money was the glue that bonded kamias to maliks. Why is it that a thing, money or grain, is considered to have power to bind people? Here, Marx's discussion of money in *Grundrisse* is relevant:

People place in a thing (money) the faith which they do not place in each other. But why do they have faith in the thing? Obviously only because that thing is an objectified relation between persons; because it is objectified exchange value, and exchange value is nothing more than a mutual relation between people's productive activities. Every other collateral may serve the holder directly in that function: money serves him only as the "dead pledge of society," but it serves as such only because

of its social (symbolic) property; and it can have a social property only because individuals have alienated their own social relationship from themselves so that it takes
the form of a thing. (1973:160)

Marx here was referring to the phenomenon he called commodity fetishism,
that is, the appearance of social relations between persons as relations between
things which, he argued, capitalism naturalizes. It is precisely such a construction of Indian social reality that Grierson's text advanced, while naturalizing
the constitutive dimension of the text as a descriptive effort.

Freedom and Servitude: The Genealogy of the Colonial Discourse

An objection to the reading I have proposed above may be made on the ground
that as debt bondage predates capitalism, Grierson's characterization of transactions between kamias and maliks as an exchange based on debt may be
an accurate description of reality rather than merely a representation according
to emergent capitalism. After all, one may argue, the ancient societies of
Rome, Greece, and even India knew debt bondage. Indeed, debt relationships
have a long history. So, what is objectionable about Grierson's view that
kamia-malik ties were based on debt?

It is true that severe punishment for the nonpayment of one's debts is of
great antiquity. In Greek law, outstanding debts became thefts, and the debtors
were punished as robbers (Finley 1981:152). We are all too familiar with
the debtor prisons in the Middle Ages. But debt bondage, according to Moses
Finley, referring to ancient Greece, was imposed not as a punishment for
default in repaying the loan but to create relations of dependence between
unequals: "Save in exceptional cases, it was only between classes, between
rich and poor, to put it in loose and simple terms, that debt led to bondage
in practice" (1981:153). If servitude was not a punishment for default but
a condition that followed a loan transaction between classes, then it was not
the power of money that bonded people but the fact that persons advancing
and receiving money were of unequal ranks. But as long as people were
legally recognized as unequal to begin with, the juridical representation of
power had to deal only with different conditions of service, not with servitude
in general. Because power did not constitute people as "naturally" free and
equal, it represented debt servitude not as a general category opposed to freedom but as one particular condition of dependency that the laborer's low
rank required when he took a "loan" from a person of superior rank. Recogniz-
ing unequal ranks as "natural," premodern discourses could think of bondage
only as a particular condition that applied only to certain classes. Thus, the
Greeks had no term for what we call debt bondage or bondage (Finley
1981:150–51), nor is there a term in Sanskrit for bondage as a general cate-

gory, even though both Greeks and Indians deployed the juridical notion of debt to represent certain conditions of service.

Servitude as a general category is the product of the post-Enlightenment discourse that discovered humanity, and liberty as the essence of humanity. True, as David Brion Davis shows, the record of the Enlightenment philosophes was mixed. While speaking of natural rights, many of them used some notion of public good to justify slavery. It is also true that while Europe was celebrating the emergence of man with natural rights, it was busy enslaving Africans in America (Davis 1966:391–421). But what is pertinent for our discussion is the fact that the Enlightenment established freedom as man's natural condition and reconstituted slavery as its opposite. Whatever its record in extending or curbing slavery, it is significant that both proslavery and antislavery positions incorporated the premise that slavery was the negation of man's natural being. Rousseau's clear antislavery stance carried this notion, as did Montesquieu's tortuous defense of slavery on the grounds that Africans were not quite human and that people from tropical lands required coercion because the climate made them slothful. If only Africans were fully human and hardworking, the natural rights of man would apply to them as well. From this point of view, anything other than the natural condition of man could be explained, understood, and even justified only as a modification, negation, and suppression of man's being. In fact, once liberty was regarded as the natural condition of man, slavery could be attacked on the grounds that it stifled progress, as Adam Smith did when he argued that slavery was a system of restraints, that it made slaves more expensive than free labor and thus stifled the slaves' desire to advance their self-interests ([1776] 1937:80, 364–67). Insofar as this discourse established slavery as the negation of freedom, we can argue, as Foucault has in the context of sexuality, that power represented itself and represented its effect—servitude—as a thing "that only has the force of the negative on its side, a power to say no; in no condition to produce, capable only of posting limits, it is basically anti-energy" (1980:85).

Thus was born the general notion of servitude as suppression of freedom, the subjection of an anterior human essence, as a restriction on freedom to move, choose employers, and practice religion. Striving to rescue this human essence and reflecting the antislavery sentiment that the British began to express in the early nineteenth century, colonial officials in India constituted servitude as the object of power and knowledge. Inquiries and reports represented bondage as a denial of freedom, a perversion of the natural state of man that, originating in traditional ties and assisted by poverty and hardship, rested on sales and debts. It was thus that colonial practice allowed power to reveal itself only in servitude, constituting social relations other than servitude as free—free from and external to power, as if, banished from everywhere, it found refuge only in servitude—and established debt bondage as a point somewhere in the middle of the movement from slavery to freedom. But only when servitude was posited as the repression of a transcendental human quality, once people were declared essentially equal because of their humanity, could money reveal its fantastic power. Debt bondage was one particular case of servitude caused by loans, just as slavery was another form of bondage caused by the buying and selling of "free" people. Thus, since the nineteenth century, the juridical representation of control over the persons of labor has been founded on the seductive power attributed to money. When the exercise of power appears to deny the fundamental equality of human beings, we attribute it to legal contracts that represent conditions of servility as a consequence of the use and abuse of money's magical power.

The juridical notion of debt servitude, however, serves an important function: by reconstituting servitude as a loss of the natural and free self caused by debt, it helps to reproduce the social relations of dependence. After all, once bondage is considered as a loss, servitude is attributed not to the social relations between landlords and laborers but to an act by which the laborer lost his free self. Similarly, when debt is considered to have caused bondage, freedom can be regained only by clearing the debt. The consequence of both these formulations is to represent the social relations between landlords and laborers as creditor-debtor relations. Thus represented, bondage can be reproduced until the debt is cleared. But the object of the whole transaction is to exclude repayment, because if the laborer repays the principal sum, social relations can no longer be represented juridically as creditor-debtor relations. For this reason, the notion of debt servitude can become literally applicable only when it also faces dissolution. When repayment is systemically part of the relationship, once repayment becomes a structural possibility in the relationship, then only the conditions of debt servitude apply. When the debtor seeks a way out by trying to repay the original sum and the creditor squeezes the noose tight through interest calculation to maintain the servitude, then only the conditions of debt are activated. Generally speaking, these conditions arise only when economic alternatives become possible and, much more important, when social relations can only be mediated through market exchange. This is so because only when social relations are no longer direct, when prior social hierarchies cease to bond people, only then can social relations be represented as products of monetary transactions. Is it any wonder that the cases of so-called debt bondage have historically always involved groups that were unequal before the bondage began?

Seeing individuals as owners of free will and commodities and drawing on categories derived from the separation of civil society from the state, the colonial discourse regarded kamias and maliks as equal and saw their relations only through the exchange relations of things. But bondage tainted exchange. How could there be equal exchange when laborers remained bound to their employers? From the fetishist vantage point of equal exchange between free owners of commodities, exchange between kamias and maliks appeared unequal. Thus, from Grierson on, nearly everyone has argued that labor bondage was a system of cheap labor. Freedom means equal exchange, and bondage means unequal exchange.

Grierson, sticking to the debt-servitude view, argued that the kamia received a wage that was lower than the ordinary laborer's because he was indebted. The difference in the daily wage rate accounted for the interest on the principal (Grierson 1893:113–14). The kamias were, therefore, exploited (denied equal exchange), according to Grierson, only because they were indebted. In this view, all other labor relations that did not involve debts and lower wage rates were exploitation-free equal exchanges. Even if we do not go all the way with Grierson, is it possible to argue that what debts allowed was not exploitation but superexploitation of labor? The difference in daily wage rates would appear to support this idea, but the matter did not end with the daily wages. The settlement officer of Gaya District, who noted that kamias were paid lower daily wages, reported that "curiously enough, at harvest time the kamia's wages exceed those of the ordinary labourer" (Government of Bihar and Orissa 1928:63). So when we calculate all the payments and consider the fact that the harvesttime was the busiest period of employment (hence, when laborers earned most of their annual income), the notion of debt servitude as an instrument of superexploitation becomes untenable, because the kamias' lower daily wages were offset by higher harvest receipts than those of the ordinary laborers.

For the colonial officials, however, the question was not superexploitation but exploitation, even though they did not use these terms to characterize their concerns. Unequal exchange, in their view, followed debt servitude, and about the existence of debt servitude they had no doubt. Legal bonds executed by kamias and maliks made the case for debt servitude even stronger, even though the British were aware that the maliks had taken to presenting the kamia-malik relationship as debt bondage because they were aware that the colonial authorities considered the labor relationship legitimate only when it was given the legal form of debt servitude. Otherwise, it was regarded as tantamount to slavery and thus illegitimate (BSA, GOB, RD, Sept. 1902). In 1920 the government moved to change the legal position. The Bihar and Orissa Kamiauti Agreement Act of 1920 provided that one year's labor was equal to the repayment of the money advanced and the interest on it and declared all labor engagements longer than a year illegal. While the act was successful in juridically representing the kamia-malik relationship as debt servitude, this was no original accomplishment. As I have argued above, the genealogy of juridical representation of the kamia-malik power relations as debt servitude can be traced back to the mid-nineteenth century, when the categories of the bourgeois political economy began to appear as natural in official documents. As a member of the Bihar Legislative Council pointed out when a draft of the act was brought up for discussion, it was legally redundant since judicial courts had already declared the system illegal (Government of Bihar and Orissa 1920:361–62). The legal bonds executed by the maliks and kamias showed that even the colonial subjects had learned the legal lesson well. The stated aim of the act, to abolish kamia-malik relations, however, was frustrated. The Royal Commission on Labour in its report in 1929 noted that the act had been unable to check the prevalence of kamia labor relations (Government of India 1931:362). Attempts to "rehabilitate" the kamias failed because the laborers did not appear to value freedom. This, the officials concluded, "was primarily a question of psychology" (BSA, GOB, RD, July 1941).

Conclusion

The moment of lapse into psychologism was also the point of recognition that the claim to self-identity through the subordination of otherness was a failed enterprise. For if the attachment of freedom was a matter of psychology that some had and others did not, then the universality of the freedom-embodied self was in doubt. However relentlessly the British rulers tried to constitute and rule India through the Manichaean opposition of the self and the other, these efforts were repeatedly marked by the frustration of their desires. Nowhere does this frustration speak more eloquently than in the realm of slavery. Because slavery denied and debt bondage suspended what was construed as the universal attribute of human beings—freedom—the colonial enterprise in this realm was perhaps one of the most important elements in its self-representation as the force of reason and progress. After all, it was in the advocacy of slavery's otherness, and in projecting Indians as the bearers of this deviance, that the ideology of liberal imperialism was forged. The legitimation of this ideology rested on the representation that slavery and freedom were not questions of political epistemologies but ontologies— questions of being and identity. Such a representation made it possible for the rulers to see their efforts in discovering, enforcing, and finally abolishing slavery as prepolitical matters that had to do with such questions as the identity of the Hindus and Muslims, the substance of their religious laws, and how these laws opposed the universal identity that the British embodied. When placed in the context of commodity fetishism fostered by capitalism, the deployment of the discourse of freedom also made possible such texts as Grierson's *Bihar Peasant Life*, which construed debt bondage as a state of suspended freedom brought on by the "natural" power of money to bind people. Insofar as the historiography of slavery in India has often seen freedom as a question of being, the colonial discourse has had far-reaching effects. One might even say that it has enjoyed hegemony. But that should not make us lose sight of the fact that it was always dogged by a sense of frustration, if not failure: the discourse of freedom has had to repeatedly assert itself by admitting the lingering presence of unfreedom.

Notes

1. These examples come from the many cited in United Kingdom 1841: app.
2. For a more detailed consideration of the evidence, see Prakash 1990:146–61.

2. Beginning with the first census in 1872, caste was adopted as a major category for enumeration. But because the initial censuses did not attempt any strict definition of caste, the result was "not satisfactory partly owing to the intrinsic difficulties of the subject, and partly to the absence of a uniform system of classification" (Waterfield 1875:21). Owing to the acknowledged absence of a consistent theory, the ranking of castes that the compilation of caste lists yielded did not follow a well-defined scheme: it only followed a well-understood system of employment." All this was considered too vague by H. H. Risley, who guided the 1901 census. Eliciting the opinion of literate Indians, collecting information on such practices as interdining, birth, and mortuary rites, he attempted to put the 1901 census on a more systematic track (Risley and Gait 1903:536–38). According to Risley, while the literate Indian opinion and the ethnographic reality described the order of castes, the principle behind such ordering lay in racial divisions (Risley 1908:32–33). Having already published the cranial, nasal, and stature measurements of different castes of Bengal in his earlier work (Risley 1891), he extended this methodology for the whole of British India in his later work (Risley 1908). In this way, even an institution regarded as the very essence of Indian otherness, the caste system, became amenable to mastery by a universalist epistemology.

3. To know India, the British were aware, was to rule and administer it. But to know it according to the political technology of universal statistical categories was additionally significant: it clearly illustrated the complementary relationship between knowledge and power. As Richard Saumarez Smith puts it, "Once society had been broken down to a group of individuals, by means of censuses and surveys, and had been pieced together again by means of statistics, it was no longer necessary to delegate the function of government contractually through privileged instruments of mediation" (1985:156). On this question, see also Bernard Cohn's brilliant study of census and objectification (1987).

4. Chanana notes that a kammakāra could be a wage laborer or a mortgaged person. When he was mortgaged by someone else—by his relatives, for example—his wages went to the person who had mortgaged him to the master. Otherwise, his wages served to redeem the sum advanced against his person (Chanana 1960:72–73, 131–32).

References

Unpublished Sources

BSA: Bihar State Archives, Patna
  GOB, RD: Government of Bengal, Revenue (Agriculture) Department Proceedings. September 1902, nos. 7–10.

GOB, RD: Government of Bihar, Revenue (Land Revenue) Department Proceedings. July 1941, nos. 1–4.
GOBO, RD: Government of Bihar and Orissa, Revenue (Land Revenue) Department Proceedings. November 1919, nos. 6–10.
IOL: India Office Records and Library, London
BJC, CJ: Bengal Judicial Consultations (Criminal Judicial). March 15, 1816, nos. 47–50; December 29, 1826, no. 14.
BJP: Bengal Judicial Proceedings. September 27, 1855, nos. 62–63; March 17, 1859, no. 290.
BRC: Bengal Revenue Consultations. August 16, 1774, no. 442.
NAI: National Archives of India, New Delhi
GOI, RAD: Government of India, Revenue and Agriculture Department (Land Revenue) Proceedings. February 1920, nos. 3–5.

Published Sources

Bernal, Martin. 1987. *Black Athena: The Afroasiatic roots of classical civilization.* New Brunswick, N.J.: Rutger University Press.
Chanana, Dev Raj. 1960. *Slavery in ancient India.* New Delhi: Peoples Publishing House.
Chattopadhyaya, Amal Kumar. 1977. *Slavery in Bengal Presidency, 1772–1843.* London: Golden Eagle Publishing House.
Cohn, Bernard S. 1987. The census, social structure and objectification in South Asia. In *An anthropologist among the historians and other essays*, by Bernard S. Cohn. Delhi: Oxford University Press.
Colebrooke, H. T., trans. 1801. *A digest of Hindu law on contracts and successions.* 3 vols. Calcutta: Honourable Company's Press.
Crooke, William. 1906. *Tribes and castes of north-western provinces and Oudh.* 4 vols. Calcutta: Superintendent of Government Printing.
Davis, David Brion. 1966. *The problem of slavery in Western culture.* Ithaca, N.Y.: Cornell University Press.
Finley, Moses. 1981. *Economy and society in ancient Greece.* Ed. Brent D. Shaw and Richard P. Saller. London: Chatto and Windus.
Foucault, Michel. 1980. *The history of sexuality.* Vol. 1, *An introduction.* Trans. Robert Hurley. New York: Pantheon.
Government of Bengal. Annual series. *Bengal Zillah court decisions, lower provinces.*
Government of Bihar and Orissa. 1928. *Final report on the survey and settlement operations in the district of Gaya, 1911–18.* Patna: Superintendent of Government Printing.
Government of Bihar and Orissa. Annual series. *Proceedings of the Bihar and Orissa Legislative Council.*
Government of India. 1931. *Report of the Royal Commission on Labour in India.* Vol. 1. London: HMSO.
Grierson, George A. [1885] 1975. *Bihar peasant life: Being a discursive catalogue of the surroundings of the people of that province.* Delhi: Cosmo Publications.

Grierson, George A. 1893. *Notes on the district of Gaya*. Calcutta: Bengal Secretariat Press.

Marx, Karl. 1973. *Grundrisse: Foundations of the critique of political economy*. Trans. Martin Nicolaus. New York: Vintage.

Prakash, Gyan. 1990. *Bonded histories: Genealogies of labor servitude in colonial India*. Cambridge: Cambridge University Press.

Risley, H. H. 1891. *Tribes and castes of Bengal*. 2 vols. Calcutta: Bengal Secretariat Press.

Risley, H. H. 1908. *People of India*. Calcutta: Thacker and Company.

Risley, H. H., and E. Gait. 1903. *Census of British India, 1901*. Calcutta: Superintendent of Government Printing.

Said, Edward. 1978. *Orientalism*. New York: Random House.

Schwab, Raymond. 1984. *The oriental renaissance*. Trans. G. Patterson-Black and V. Reinking. New York: Columbia University Press.

Smith, Adam. [1776] 1937. *The wealth of nations*. Modern Library edition. New York: Random House.

Smith, Richard Saumarez. 1985. Rule-by-records and rule-by-reports: Complementary aspects of British imperial rule of law. *Contributions to Indian Sociology*, n.s., 19, no. 1:153–76.

Thurston, Edgar. 1909. *Castes and tribes of southern India*. 6 vols. Madras: Government Press.

United Kingdom. Parliament. 1841. *Slavery (East Indies): Report from the Indian law commissioners*. 28 (262).

Waterfield, H. 1875. *Memorandum on the census of British India*. London: HMSO.

6 *William Gervase Clarence-Smith*

Cocoa Plantations and Coerced Labor in the Gulf of Guinea, 1870–1914

The employment of coerced African labor on privately owned plantations is usually associated with the New World, but Africa itself became the location for such forms of production from the mid-nineteenth century. Scholarly attention has focused on the clove plantations of Zanzibar (Cooper 1977), but the cocoa plantations of the Gulf of Guinea were of equal significance. For although cocoa is generally considered a peasant crop in an African context, the first great burst of cocoa cultivation took place on plantations in the Gulf of Guinea. The Portuguese formally abolished slavery in São Tomé and Príncipe, the largest cocoa producer, but the bulk of the laborers remained de facto slaves (Duffy 1967). The smaller producers had much less recourse to slave labor, but the workers on their cocoa plantations were nevertheless highly coerced. This was as true of the Spaniards in the island of Fernando Po (Bioko) as it was of the Germans around Kamerun Berg (Cameroon Mountain) (Sundiata 1974; Liniger-Goumaz 1979; Rüger 1960:162–68; Michel 1969). The purpose of this chapter is to explore the relationship between coerced labor and the rise and fall of cocoa plantations in the Gulf of Guinea.

The boom in the plantation sector was as intense as it was brief. By the onset of the First World War, peasant cocoa production in the Gold Coast was already surging ahead, and in the postwar years plantations stagnated and declined, unable to sustain peasant competition. Although several factors contributed to this boom-and-bust cycle, I will argue that the high real cost

150

of labor was the key factor. Coerced labor was cheap to the extent that wages were low or nonexistent, but productivity was poor, mortality rates were excessive, and the costs of recruitment were high. The advantage of coerced labor was that it provided an available work force to take immediate advantage of a combination of a bullish world market in cocoa and unusually fertile virgin volcanic soils. Once prices stabilized at lower levels and virgin lands were exhausted, however, the truly cheap labor at the disposal of peasant households settled the issue against the plantations.

A bullish cocoa market existed prior to 1914 because cocoa prices ran contrary to the general falling trend for tropical commodities from the 1880s. Whereas wholesale prices for tea in London roughly halved between 1870 and 1910, cocoa prices rose by nearly 50 percent in the 1870s and remained more or less steady thereafter (Othick 1976:77). This was due in turn to an overlapping set of technical improvements in the manufacture of cocoa products, coupled with changes in demand. Although the process for the separation of cocoa butter and cocoa powder had been known since 1828, only in the 1860s were alkaline products added to cocoa powder to make it more soluble and palatable. The temperance movement helped to spread the consumption of cocoa powder, marketed as a fortifying and healthy drink among the growing concentrations of urban workers. In the 1870s milk chocolate was invented, as well as new forms of chocolate with a higher content of cocoa butter and a higher melting point. Together with better machinery and a more effective international market in cocoa products, this allowed manufacturers to cut their costs and to diversify their markets. The supply of cocoa beans had some difficulty in following expanding world demand, however, for it took seven to eight years for trees to come into full production. This kept prices buoyant, as exports of cocoa around the world rose from around thirty-thousand metric tons a year in the 1870s to nearly three hundred thousand on the eve of the First World War (Van Hall 1932: table opp. 295; Othick 1976; Stollwerck 1907; Fincke 1936; Norero 1910).

Technical improvements and the democratization of consumption patterns had the further effect of increasing demand for inferior and cheaper kinds of cocoa. There was now a better market for the "ordinary," more bitter varieties of western Africa, northeastern Brazil, and Santo Domingo, which grew on trees that were hardier and more productive than those producing the "fine" cocoas of Ecuador, Venezuela, and Trinidad. In the long term, this was to give rise to the flourishing peasant cocoa farms of western Africa, but in the short term it stimulated rapid expansion in the output of the plantations of the Gulf of Guinea (Othick 1976:85; Urquhart 1956:156).

Cocoa planting on a major scale in the Gulf of Guinea was limited to the scarce but unusually fertile soils around the four volcanic massifs jutting into the Atlantic. The Creoles of the Portuguese islands, long involved in slaving

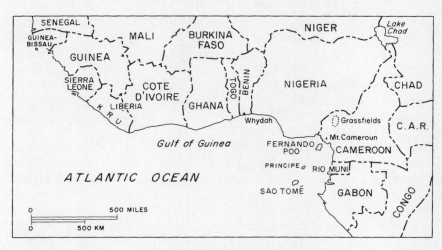

6.1 Gulf of Guinea

and more recently in coffee production, pioneered the cocoa boom, and São
Tomé and Príncipe dominated the cocoa plantation economy to 1914. By
the early 1900s the Portuguese colony was among the world's four largest
producers of cocoa, emerging as the front-runner in some years. From 1900
to 1913 São Tomé and Príncipe's contribution to world exports by weight
fluctuated between 14 and 18 percent (Mantero 1910:81; Galvão and Selvagem
1951:390; Urquhart 1956:174).

Cocoa was also the dominant plantation crop in the Spanish and German
zones, and although output remained considerably lower than that of the Portuguese islands, it was rising faster in the years just before the First World
War. In 1908 São Tomé and Príncipe produced some thirty thousand metric
tons a year, while Fernando Po and the plantation sector in Kamerun both
hovered around the three-thousand-ton mark (Mantero 1910: appendixes).
Just before the war, São Tomé and Príncipe employed about thirty-seven
thousand laborers, Fernando Po at least six thousand, and the plantations
in Kamerun around eighteen thousand. These figures are all rough and include
laborers employed outside the cocoa sector, especially in Kamerun, where
rubber and banana plantations were well developed (United Kingdom 1920b:4;
Liniger-Goumaz 1979:459; Rudin 1938:317).

The greater success of the Portuguese was due mainly to their access to
a plentiful supply of slave labor. It is true that they also had the advantage
of starting earlier and of having a local Creole elite with capital and a knowledge of local conditions. But the Fernandinos of the neighboring Spanish
island were not too dissimilar from the São Tomense Creoles (Mantero 1910;
Liniger-Goumaz 1979:123–24). The Germans, for their part, had the advan-

tages of plentiful capital and of the most advanced scientific research facilities (Rüger 1960:162–68). The planters themselves certainly saw the labor question as the crux of the matter. The endless lament of all employers was "shortage of labor," but the Portuguese were best able to deal with this, until they were obliged to put an end to the slave trade just before the First World War.

The root of the labor issue lay in an intractable demographic problem. Equatorial Africa was notorious for its virulent diseases, low population densities, and low fertility rates (Austen and Headrick 1983:32–38). The sparse local population could usually keep enough land to avoid proletarianization and to grow cash crops to pay their taxes. Imported labor was especially vulnerable to the diseases of the region, making repeated imports of fresh labor necessary. Every formula was tried—slavery, indentured labor, forced labor, tax-induced migration, and free wage labor—but nothing was truly successful. The numerous human tragedies of cocoa planting can be traced to a juxtaposition of unusually fertile land and an exceptionally unhealthy environment.

The issue was further complicated by irregularities in the need for labor. Intense work was required for clearing virgin forest and digging large holes in which to plant the young trees. Once the trees were planted, however, they were not given a great deal of attention. Some weeding was practiced, but manuring was very rare and pruning was not extensive. Labor was required for picking the pods, breaking them open, extracting the seeds, and fermenting, drying, and packing them for export. Cutting the pods from the tree was the most skilled job, for a messy cut could prevent pods from growing again in the future. This task was usually reserved for experienced male workers, whereas women and juveniles extracted the seeds. The picking season was quite lengthy, but the demand for harvesting labor was nonetheless not spread evenly through the year. Labor could be redeployed in food production or in working with other plantation crops, but it was not always easy to find either food or cash crops whose requirements fitted in easily with those of cocoa (Van Hall 1932:95–228).

The structure of the labor process may help to explain the ambiguities in the planters' attitudes toward the locally resident African population. On the one hand, planters frequently complained that local Africans were lazy parasites who should be obliged to work on the plantations (see Michel 1969:198–99). On the other hand, it is striking how little was actually done to achieve this aim. One can argue that this was because the local population was too small to meet the planters' overall labor needs but could be useful in meeting certain types of casual seasonal labor requirements.

São Tomé and Príncipe had no indigenous population at all prior to colonization by Portugal in the late fifteenth century. Over time, three kinds of free people had become established: Maroons in the inaccessible parts of the islands, freed slaves, and the more or less Africanized descendants of Portuguese settlers. None of these groups had the slightest intention of doing regular plantation labor if they could possibly help it. Creoles and some freed slaves had acquired land in freehold or leasehold from the Crown. The most recently freed slaves squatted on Crown lands or illegally on remote corners of plantations. In addition to subsistence crops, these lands provided some coffee, cocoa, and other cash crops with which to pay taxes. Baptized persons could claim to be full Portuguese citizens and could use legal processes to defend their rights. Thus, although some free persons were persuaded to sell or evacuate their lands, by fair means or foul, the majority of the Creoles and freed slaves clung tenaciously to their economic independence. The Maroons were in a slightly different situation. In São Tomé, the nucleus consisted of the descendants of a cargo of slaves shipwrecked in the sixteenth century who had kept their Mbundu language, were not Christians, and were organized in chieftaincies. Known as Angolares, they were not Portuguese citizens, and they inhabited the very rugged and isolated southern parts of the island. The chiefs grew a little cocoa themselves, but the major contribution of the Angolares to São Tomé's economy was in casual work, such as clearing the forest, fishing, or performing other maritime jobs, which fitted in with their traditional hunting and gathering. Regular plantation labor they would not touch, and the Portuguese feared guerrilla war by people superbly adapted to such warfare, if coercion were used to oblige them to work (Banco Nacional Ultramarino 1890:619, 663–65; Nogueira 1893:30–34; Tenreiro 1961:81, 87–88; United Kingdom 1920b:3–4, 7, 21).

In Fernando Po, an indigenous population, the Bubi, did exist, but the Spaniards had no greater success in harnessing them as regular plantation laborers. Indeed, fierce Bubi resistance had been one of the reasons that the Spaniards had found it impossible to occupy the island after the Portuguese ceded it to them in the late eighteenth century (Moreno Moreno 1952:16–17). The undoing of the Bubi was strong alcohol and diseases brought by traders, resulting in a population decrease of alarming proportions. When the British leased the island as an anti-slave trade base in the early nineteenth century, the Sierra Leoneans and other English-speaking black settlers pushed the enfeebled Bubi back toward the mountainous interior of the island (Sundiata 1974:97–102).

Spanish military expeditions in the 1880s and 1890s slowly subdued the Bubi in the interior, but the Catholic Claretian missionaries then set up a kind of mission theocracy to protect their wards from the planters. Bubi lands were thus saved from further encroachments, and the Bubi took to growing some cocoa to meet their needs for cash. An attempt in 1907 to apply the 1904 forced labor code in modified form to those Bubi not cultivating more than a hectare of land had disastrous consequences, for they rose in revolt three years later (Liniger-Goumaz 1979:85–87). The 1913 labor code then expressly excluded the Bubi from forced labor (United Kingdom 1919:32–33).

In the Kamerun Berg area, neither the coastal Creoles, often immigrants from Fernando Po, nor the local African population would perform regular plantation labor. Local Africans were not numerous and were able to retain sufficient land to prevent their proletarianization. After the first great wave of land alienation, Berlin intervened in 1902, largely under missionary pressure. Not only did the German government prevent further loss of land by the local inhabitants, but it even forced the plantation companies to give back some of the wide swaths of land they had seized or bought in unscrupulous ways. The little reservations, islands in the sea of plantation land, produced some cocoa and provided the planters with casual labor (Michel 1969:193–97; Rüger 1960:182–92).

The traditional answer to the shortage of local labor was to employ slaves, as the Portuguese had done in São Tomé and Príncipe for centuries, but the slave system entered into a period of crisis from the middle of the century, as Lisbon struggled to meet insistent British demands for the abolition of slavery. The slaves became frustrated as one form of procrastination followed another, and rebellions broke out. When Lisbon finally took the plunge in 1875 and decreed the abolition of slavery throughout the empire, the existing slave population was entirely freed. The planters agreed to immediate liberation, instead of waiting for the expiry of the three-year period of grace, and some even waived the obligation of former slaves to serve a two-year apprenticeship with their former masters. In return, the government promised to protect the lives and property of the planters and to help them obtain an alternative source of free labor. The apparent magnanimity of the planters mainly resulted from the turmoil and violence surrounding the issuing of the new legislation, although some entrepreneurs seem to have been genuinely convinced that free labor might prove more efficient than unfree labor (Sá da Bandeira 1873:96; Seixas 1865:13; Banco Nacional Ultramarino 1890:346, 437–38).

The attempt to replace slavery with free immigration was short-lived, and the planters rapidly fell back on renewed importations of slaves. The Portuguese government agreed unofficially to allow slavery to be reestablished for the new arrivals, while in public it stuck to its story that this was contract labor. This was partly because the Portuguese treasury was bankrupt and thus could not envisage paying the compensation it owed to owners of slaves freed in 1875 and partly because it was thought that the plantation economy would otherwise collapse. Isolated government employees attempted to enforce the law against slavery, but until the republican revolution of 1910, the planters always had enough clout in Lisbon to have these troublesome individuals transferred to other posts.

The process of disguising slavery as contract labor had three key elements. The purchase of slaves from African dealers, who operated outside Portuguese authority, was termed the price of redeeming slaves from servitude. The theoretically freed slaves were then obliged to sign five-year contracts, binding them to their "redeemer." So far, the process was against the spirit but not the letter of the law. The real illegality, which for a time the Portuguese authorities hesitated to condone, came at the end of the five-year contract, when the laborers were "automatically recontracted." To maintain a functioning market in slaves, the authorities allowed money to change hands for the transferring of a contract from one master to another, or for the subcontracting of a laborer by one master to another. British abolitionists quickly grasped the fact that the key way to penetrate this web of deceit was to see whether the laborers were ever repatriated (Duffy 1967; Clarence-Smith 1976: 214–23).

A new generation of slaves was thus transplanted to São Tomé to replace those freed in 1875. As the slave trade still raged unchecked in the interior of Africa, slaves were both plentiful and cheap, especially in Angola. Benguela and Novo Redondo were the great slave marts where the agents of São Tomé planters bought their laborers (Duffy 1967:98). The coastal plantations of Angola also relied on slaves from the interior, but market forces ensured that the bulk and the best of the slaves were reserved for São Tomé. In the 1890s it was said that the Angolan planters had to content themselves with children, as adult slaves all went to the São Tomé cocoa planters, who were able to pay higher prices (Contreiras 1894:90 n. 2).

Slaves were also obtained from Dahomey and Gabon. In 1884–85 the Portuguese attempted to expand out from their little fort in Whydah by declaring a protectorate over the whole Dahomey coast. One of the central reasons for this expansion was to obtain slaves for São Tomé. A clause in the treaty establishing the protectorate stipulated that two hundred captives a year would be provided for the Portuguese islands, with no guarantee of repatriation. The Portuguese explained to the indignant British that the slaves would otherwise be immolated in Dahomey's infamous human sacrifices (Esparteiro 1962:12–13; Almeida 1978–79, 2:239–40). Although Portugal was forced to withdraw the protectorate in 1887, Dahomey continued to export slaves to the Portuguese islands until the French conquered the kingdom in 1892. Thus, a batch of two hundred slaves left for São Tomé in November 1890 (Newbury 1961:130 n. 4). On some plantations, a high proportion of slaves originated from Dahomey in the 1890s, and Dahomeyans were often employed as foremen or drivers (Möller 1974:7; Chevalier 1907:54). The other traditional current of slaves from the nearby Gabon coast had been repressed by the French from the mid-1870s, but it was so easy to slip over to the Portuguese islands in small boats that this trade lingered on until at least 1900 (Patterson 1975:134–35, 141).

The laborers in this "modern slavery" enjoyed two advantages over an older generation of slaves. First, in order to keep the British antislavery lobby at bay, the Portuguese authorities insisted on the payment of a wage. The 1880 regulations set out that during the first two years of a contract, men were to receive 700 reis a month and women 500, sums which after two years were to rise to 1,400 and 1,000 reis respectively (Banco Nacional Ultramarino 1890:709). At this time, 4,500 reis equaled one pound sterling, so the sums were small. Moreover, masters sometimes got around the regulations by paying in kind or in bonds redeemable only at the plantation store or by creating a kind of perpetual debt. All food, clothing, shelter, medical attention, and other needs were provided by the planters in addition to the meager wages, and even the most vociferous British opponents of the system generally conceded that from this point of view the laborers were not too badly off (Cadbury Papers 4/20, W. Cadbury, March 17, 1903, and A. Ceffala, April 20, 1904; Almeida 1978–79, 2:306–7). Second, the planters no longer had any more than minor disciplinary rights over their laborers, who had to be turned over to the authorities for any major alleged offenses. Thus, the more barbaric aspects of masters' social power over their slaves were curtailed. Plantation life still entailed rigorous control over aspects of the slave's life, however, such as the ability to leave the plantation and the right to marry. Twelve hours of grinding labor were extorted from the laborers, six days a week, in a trying tropical climate (Muralha n.d.:24–26, 32, 36–37; Almeida 1978–79, 3:24).

The greatest problem for the slaves was the appallingly high death rate, which the statistics graphically illustrate. Some 120,000 workers were imported between 1876 and 1914, of whom about 20,000 were repatriated (Roçadas 1914: 18, 33; Almeida 1978–79, 3:11, 113; Duffy 1967:181 n. 24, 209–11). As the overwhelming majority were adolescents and young adults, the natural death rate should have been small. Moreover, as sex ratios were not too uneven, one would have expected a new generation of laborers to have been born on the islands. Yet the figures for 1914 indicate that fewer than 40,000 laborers lived on São Tomé and Príncipe (United Kingdom 1920b:4). In 1882 the Banco Nacional Ultramarino reported that 19 percent of the recently imported male slaves and 28 percent of the female slaves had perished (1890:669). In 1897 the British consul estimated that about a fifth of all Angolan slaves died in their first year and a half, during the period of their initial five-year "contract" (Almeida 1978–79, 2:306–7). Very high infant mortality rates also frustrated the planters' desire to make themselves independent of the trade through natural reproduction (Almeida 1978–79, 3:24; United Kingdom 1920b:23).

The high mortality rate does not seem to have resulted from the conditions of sea transport or ill treatment on the plantations. Although conditions on board the Portuguese steamers from Angola were far from ideal, the distance by sea was short, and the ships were closely watched by the British. On the plantations, the employers did their best to keep their scarce and threatened labor supply alive and healthy, as well as to promote breeding. They were in no position to work their slaves to death and replace them with new imports, for no one knew when the British would finally blow the whistle on this "modern slavery" (Duffy 1967: chap. 7). The terrible death rates resulted rather from two interrelated factors, the conditions of enslavement and the diseases of the Gulf of Guinea. Slaves came increasingly from deep in the interior of Central Africa, including areas nominally in the Congo Free State or British Central Africa. After brutal capture, the captives were marched to the Angolan coast by African dealers through the dreaded Hungry Country, a barren region of Kalahari sands, in conditions so revolting that they provoked the most powerful denunciations in the writings of abolitionists (Nevinson 1968). Enfeebled and traumatized by this experience, the slaves were in no shape to face their next ordeal, exposure to the microbes of the Gulf.

The immigrants themselves involuntarily made the situation worse by importing new diseases. Sleeping sickness broke out in Príncipe in the 1890s, causing extremely high death rates. The Portuguese countered by treating the victims with new arsenic-based drugs and by conducting a vigorous campaign to eradicate the tsetse fly. By 1914 Príncipe was free of sleeping sickness, one of the first victories against the dreaded scourge in Africa. But this was not before thousands of unfortunate workers had paid with their lives (*Antologia* 1946:283–96). Similarly, the Mozambicans, who began to come to the cocoa plantations in the 1900s, brought with them tuberculosis, which had itself been spread in southern Mozambique by migrant laborers returning from the South African gold mines (Muralha n.d.:96–97).

As the flow of labor to the cocoa plantations grew in volume, the whole system came under strain. One problem was that prices for slaves were rising fast, partly because of growing demand but partly also because European officials in the heart of Africa were curbing slave raiding. In the mid-1860s a good adult slave cost about twelve pounds sterling on the islands, a figure which had risen to twenty-five pounds by 1899 and thirty-five pounds by 1907 (Sá da Bandeira 1873:30; Hammond 1966:319; Duffy 1967:196). There seems little doubt that the attraction of slavery was diminishing in the planters' eyes, as the cost of purchase began to outweigh the cost of repatriation.

At the same time, the agitation of the British antislavery movement began to mesh with the colonial ambitions of Germany. After the 1898 agreement for a partition of Portugal's empire between Britain and Germany, Lisbon became much more sensitive to accusations of practices which might make Portugal appear to be "unfit to colonize." In 1902 matters came to a head when part of the Ovimbundu peoples of central Angola rose against the Portuguese. This rebellion was wrongly but effectively characterized by the Protestant missionaries as a rising against the slave trade. Portugal was obliged to promise reforms, which were decreed in 1903. About 40 percent of laborers' salaries was to be paid into a fund, which would finance the workers' repatriation at the end of their contracts. The fact that contracts could still be renewed after five years was a weakness, however, and nothing changed in the old system. It was yet another decree "for the Englishman to see." After a slight pause, the slave trade to São Tomé resumed and reached new heights.

The cynicism of this maneuver aroused the British abolitionists to fever pitch, and international sanctions proved their effectiveness for the first time in Africa. In 1909 the British and German chocolate manufacturers (though not the American ones), agreed to impose a boycott on cocoa from São Tomé and Príncipe. This jolted the Portuguese into action. All exports of labor from Angola were halted, and a few slaves at last began to be freed and repatriated.

The process of reform was accelerated by the new republican authorities in Lisbon, who swept to power in 1910. Desperately needing international recognition, they stood for a program of modernization and rationalism. The slave trade from Angola to São Tomé was thus intolerable. Africans in the interior of Angola were progressively conquered and stopped from slave raiding and trading, thus destroying one of the pillars of the system. Automatic recontracting of laborers was banned, and the ban was enforced. The right to repatriation from São Tomé was also decreed (Duffy 1967: chaps. 7 and 8). Recruiting in Angola, however, was allowed to begin again in 1913, and contracts still lasted five years. Repatriation was not automatic but depended on a laborer's declaring the desire to return. Abuses quickly followed, with planters expelling their old and sick laborers and pressuring their healthy workers to remain. It was not until 1921 that compulsory repatriation was introduced, after worrying reports that only about half of the laborers imported into São Tomé between 1910 and 1917 had returned home (Almeida 1978–79, 3:83–84, 90; Newitt 1981:208).

Spain was little involved in slave labor on Fernando Po. Although slavery continued in Cuba up to 1886, the Spaniards abolished the institution in Fernando Po in 1859. Paradoxically, this move was in part aimed at attracting labor, by encouraging slaves to escape from neighboring Príncipe. It was also a gesture to placate the British, who were attempting to put an end to Spanish slave exports to Cuba (Sundiata 1977:90–94). The lack of substantial continental possessions made it difficult for Spain to emulate the Portuguese in disguising the slave trade as the cocoa boom gathered way.

The importation of contract labor from Liberia, however, at times took on strong overtones of a slave trade. There are clear indications that the gangs of laborers rounded up by chiefs in up-country areas were in fact bought and sold as slaves, and there were persistent accusations of nonrepatriation of laborers from Fernando Po (Sundiata 1974:103–5). Even more akin to a slave trade was the clandestine importation of labor from southeastern Nigeria from about 1900, organized by African canoe owners who had for centuries been deeply involved in the slave trade of the "Oil Rivers" (Osuntokun 1978:27). Nor was slavery entirely absent from the Kamerun plantations. In 1899 the commander of the German armed forces was told not to free slaves when he conquered an African kingdom but to send them down to form villages of laborers in the plantation zone. Whether this ever was done is not clear, but it is certain that many of the workers known as volunteers were actually slaves subcontracted by the Bali and other chiefs to the planters. The slaves were sent back at the end of their contracts, and their masters confiscated their meager salaries. It is possible that survivors were returned for further contracts in the plantations. The result was intensified slave raiding, especially at the expense of the dense populations of the "Grassfields." The Bali and others thus strongly opposed the slow progression of German colonial pacification and its corollary, the ending of slave raiding (Rüger 1960:196; Michel 1969:199).

The costs, legal uncertainties, and moral opprobrium attaching to the slave trade led to a constant experimentation with new forms of labor. At the beginning of the period there was widespread optimism that free contract labor could be substituted for slave labor, and the first choice fell on the people known as Krumen or Kru. These coastal peoples from the area from Sierra Leone to the Ivory Coast specialized in maritime and dock work in western Africa. During the nineteenth century they traveled as voluntary wage laborers on long contracts as far away as Walvis Bay and the Guianas. They were famed for their physique and aptitude for hard labor in tropical climates (Brooks 1972; Schuler 1986:155–201). The term Kru then came to be applied even more widely, sometimes to any coastal West Africans engaging voluntarily in contract labor. Although the distinction became increasingly blurred with the expansion of colonial rule, this kind of labor is treated here as a separate category from short-term, tax-induced migratory labor, which remained within one colonial empire and functioned under close administrative supervision.

It was in São Tomé and Príncipe that the first recourse to free contract labor occurred. In 1875 the planters made a concerted effort to break with the slave-based past, partly because of the violent slave uprisings of this period and partly because of a belief that free labor might be more efficient (Banco Nacional Ultramarino 1890:346). Some São Tomé planters had already experimented with Kru labor in the 1860s, sensing the winds of change blowing through the continent. Brought in for two- or three-year contracts, the Kru had proved more productive than slaves, but also more expensive to recruit and pay (Sá da Bandeira 1873:90; Rebello da Silva 1969:154). The experiment with Kru labor from 1875 was not a success. Communications with Liberia and British possessions were precarious, and at least half the 1876 coffee crop was lost because the three thousand or so workers arrived too late. There were complaints about the poor quality of the labor, contrasting with the myth of the strong and productive Kru. The planters disliked paying salaries and complained of high overhead costs, especially the cost of repatriation after a contract period as short as eighteen months. The financially hard-pressed Portuguese authorities made things worse in 1877 by insisting on a one-pound passport fee for all returning Kru. Because of this, the planters kept their laborers on after the end of their contracts. This immediately triggered a hostile reaction in Britain, where the Portuguese were suspected of being incapable of running a free labor system, and the British authorities began to hamper recruitment. It also created a very bad impression in the homelands of the laborers, who had long been wary of enslavement. By 1878 most of the Kru had been repatriated, and very few new recruits were forthcoming (Banco Nacional Ultramarino 1890:368–69, 386, 409–10, 437–43, 463, 486–87, 712). It is hard to say whether the system might have worked better if the British had been less suspicious and if the planters had not felt that they could fall back on slaves from Angola and elsewhere.

The Germans in Kamerun also experimented with free contract labor. In the earliest days it was the obvious source of workers, and one German commentator in 1876 declared that no other Africans should be considered as laborers. From about the mid-1890s, when cocoa cultivation began to take off in the Kamerun Berg area, the Germans became alarmed at the labor shortage and made a considerable effort to step up the recruitment of "foreign Africans." By a mixture of force and bribery, they managed to obtain a labor-recruiting monopoly in independent Liberia in 1897. Further supplies were obtained from German Togoland, southern Nigeria, and the French Congo. But the French cut off the supply of laborers, alleging that death rates were too high, and in 1900 the British did the same in Nigeria. Even Togoland prohibited labor exports to its sister colony, presumably because the labor was needed locally. In Liberia, the British pulled out every stop to put an end to the German labor monopoly and to have more restrictive regulations imposed. Both goals were achieved by 1904. The Germans became disillusioned with the precariousness and escalating cost of this imported labor and decided to rely as far as possible on labor from within Kamerun (Rüger 1960:193–94, 197, 208–11).

The Spaniards relied the most on Kru labor. Imports were facilitated by the fact that many of the Fernandinos were of Sierra Leonean origins, having come to the island early in the century, when the British had leased it as an anti-slave trade base. These men made frequent trips to their home area and organized the flow of labor to Fernando Po. The British monitored the flow of labor very carefully. Wives and families were not allowed to come to Fernando Po, and repatriation at the end of contracts was scrutinized with care (Sundiata 1974:102–3). At the very end of the century, laborers from southwestern Nigeria were also recruited (Osuntokun 1978:25). But relations with the British deteriorated sharply in 1900. Years of allegations of bad treatment culminated in a strike in 1900 by some of the Nigerian and Liberian workers. The Spanish authorities repatriated 450 Nigerian laborers at their own expense, but London imposed a ban on all recruiting in British possessions (Liniger-Goumaz 1979:458–59; Sundiata 1974:103).

Liberia thus became the chief source of labor for Fernando Po. The "Kru proper" generally refused to come to the Spanish island, for they wanted to be paid in British money, so Africans from inland began to make up the bulk of the recruits. Initially the Spanish and Fernandino planters were obliged to work through the German monopoly. Later Liberians were appointed recruiters, and they obtained a handsome bonus for each laborer. In theory, the Liberian government demanded bonds for return passages and insisted that contracts were to be made in front of the authorities and were to be for no longer than two years. But the corrupt Liberian administration was enticed into waiving these requirements. In 1905 the Spaniards ceased to give three-month advances to laborers and instead began to pay a fixed sum per laborer to a Liberian treasury hovering on the edge of bankruptcy. As labor from Sierra Leone began to be drawn over the border into Liberia for this trade, British accusations of a new slave trade became louder (Sundiata 1974:103–5).

Under British pressure, the Liberians made a new agreement with Spain in 1914. Contracts were to be for a maximum of two years and a minimum of one; recruiters were to be licensed by both countries; there was to be no recruiting for individual planters, but the laborers were instead to be consigned to the Liberian consul in Fernando Po; the Liberian consul and the Spanish labor inspector were to assign the laborers to planters who were suitable and solvent; there were detailed regulations for treatment and repatriation; and wages were to be paid in British coin, half on the island and half as deferred pay. Although Liberia continued to be a major source of labor for over a decade, the planters found this new system expensive and began to cast about for alternatives (Sundiata 1974:105–7; United Kingdom 1919:29–33).

Schemes to import European indentured labor proved even more disappointing. Both the Spaniards and the Portuguese noted that some of their poor peasants were emigrating to foreign parts to engage in plantation labor in tropical or subtropical climes and thought it would be more profitable to the mother country if these men could be directed to the cocoa plantations of the Gulf of Guinea. In 1881 the Portuguese persuaded twenty-seven emigrants intending to go and work in the Hawaiian sugar plantations to go to São Tomé instead, tempting them with the offer of state lands at the end of their contracts. But the diseases of the Gulf of Guinea took their usual terrible toll, and white labor was declared unsuitable (Banco Nacional Ultramarino 1890:670–71). The Spaniards encountered the same problem when they tried to divert emigrants bound for Algeria to Fernando Po in the 1890s. Nor did the Spanish utilization of Fernando Po as a penal colony help the labor problem, as transportation to the Gulf of Guinea was the equivalent of a sentence to death by disease (Moreno Moreno 1952:51–53, 64–65, 101).

Asian laborers were seen as another possibility. The Spaniards thought of importing Chinese and Filipinos, but apart from a few Filipino convicts, no importations of Asian labor are recorded (Nosti 1948:36; Liniger-Goumaz 1979:458; Moreno Moreno 1952:101). Similarly, German plans to bring Indians and Chinese never left the drawing board, because Berlin feared that high mortality would lead to adverse world reactions (Ruger 1960:211). The Portuguese were the only ones to take the plunge. In 1895 some three hundred Chinese "coolies" were brought from the Portuguese colony of Macao to São Tomé on an experimental basis with official help. But they were no more resistant to the virulent African diseases than the Europeans were, and the experiment does not appear to have been followed up, although 1903 regulations made provision for labor from Macao. Those who survived were employed for light work until the ends of their contracts and then became market gardeners (*Portugal em Africa* 3 (1896):35–36, 5 (1898):346; Möller 1974:7; United Kingdom 1920b:29).

The only partial success with free contract labor came in the 1900s, with the importation of Cape Verdeans, mainly to the island of Príncipe. The Cape Verdeans were in an ambiguous position in the Portuguese imperial system. Their archipelago was legally a colony, but the population was of mixed race, spoke a Creole form of Portuguese, was entirely Catholic, and possessed Portuguese citizenship. Cape Verdeans were thus in a better position to defend their rights than most of the inhabitants of the Portuguese empire and could not be reduced to de facto slavery.

The Cape Verdeans were pushed out of their homes by a series of terrible droughts and famines, which repeatedly swept through the archipelago. The droughts of 1850–66 had already resulted in a first wave of emigration to São Tomé, and renewed famine led to another wave from 1902. Those who could, however, went to the United States, Brazil, or other places which already had established communities of Cape Verdeans. It was the poorest, the least educated, and often the most physically African in appearance who accepted the insistent suggestions of the administration that they should offer their services to the planters of São Tomé and Príncipe. The poorest could not pay their passages to other destinations but were offered free transport to São Tomé. Moreover, many countries would not admit them, on grounds of illiteracy or color. For a time, the Portuguese authorities deliberately increased the pressure by refusing to issue passports for emigration to Dakar, a center for poor Cape Verdean laborers at this time. In 1909, when the labor crisis in São Tomé and Príncipe became acute because of the suspension of labor recruitment in Angola, the government in Cape Verde temporarily banned all emigration to foreign countries.

The Cape Verdeans were more successful than other indentured laborers because they were more desperate and because they proved to be fairly resistant to the diseases of the Gulf of Guinea, especially to the sleeping sickness which was decimating the population of Príncipe at this time. This said, the mortality rates of Cape Verdeans were high, and only the famine at home and the difficulties of emigrating elsewhere brought these men and their families to São Tomé and Príncipe. They went out on one- to three-year contracts, and some of them recontracted themselves there or came back for a second contract after returning home. The numbers of Cape Verdeans emigrating to São Tomé and Príncipe, however, remained insufficient to meet the planters' needs. Some 13,000 passages were recorded between 1902 and 1914, including about 150 children and an unknown number of men on second or third contracts (Carreira 1982: chap. 4; United Kingdom 1920a:19–20).

As the slave trade slowly ground to a halt and free contract labor failed to fill the gap, the planters turned to the administration to provide them with forced labor. The Germans were the first to move in this direction, using their superior financial and military resources to conquer the interior of Kamerun. During the 1890s these campaigns took on the aspect of massive forced labor recruitment. Prisoners of war were packed off to the coastal plantations, public works, or porterage duty, and "rebellious" peoples had a tribute in labor imposed upon them. The conditions of this punitive labor varied, but in many cases the laborers were not even paid the minimum wage of five marks a month (Rüger 1960:195–96). Thus, in 1899–1901 the savage repression of the Bulu revolt in south central Kamerun was followed by the imposition of six-year periods of compulsory and unpaid forced labor on the Bulu, thousands of whom were sent to work on the plantations of Kamerun Berg (Michel 1969:199–200). This kind of massive forced labor ended with the reforms of 1902, but administratively coerced laborers, especially tax defaulters, continued to be provided to the planters until the end of the German period (Rüger 1960:203–6).

The Spaniards moved toward forced labor later and much less effectively. The legislative turning point was the decree of 1904 whereby all Africans had to do two years' labor on the plantations in lieu of military service. Planters were obliged to look after the laborers but were not expected to pay them

(Ndongo Bidyogo 1977:67–68). The main result of these measures was a major Bubi revolt. The 1913 labor code thus proceeded somewhat differently. All vagrant and unemployed Africans, except the Bubi, were to labor for wages, and this could be either for the state or for private employers. Contracts were between one and two years in duration. The employer paid for repatriation, and laborers could choose a concession of two hectares of land in lieu of returning home (United Kingdom 1919:29, 32–33). There is little indication that the coercive aspects of this legislation had much impact, given the Spaniards' lack of control over Río Muni. In reality, the growing numbers of "Bata Boys" in Fernando Po would not work without a sufficient wage (Sundiata 1974:107–9).

The Portuguese were stirred to consider forced labor by the Ovimbundu rebellion of 1902, though they turned to other colonies rather than disturbing the established slave trade of Angola. In 1903 contracts for São Tomé were authorized for between one and two years. Although the legislation did not specify the use of force in recruitment, it is clear that the laborers were not volunteers (Duffy 1967:176–77). Only a handful of laborers came from Portuguese Guinea, where the local administration protested strongly and on the whole successfully against the idea of sending forced labor to São Tomé. Those who did come were prisoners of war and other "troublemakers" (Almeida 1978–79, 3:24, 43; Chevalier 1907:3–4).

Mozambique came to supply a modest flow of forced labor. The "prazo" legislation of central Mozambique forced peasants to pay part of their annual rent to estate holders in the form of labor services. How this was to be reconciled with yearlong contracts in São Tomé is unclear, but one of the greatest planters of São Tomé, Francisco Mantero, subleased a prazo in central Mozambique in 1906, and by 1909, 900 of the 1,200 laborers sent from Mozambique were consigned to Mantero. It is likely that the ancient and only recently suppressed slave trade of the Zambezi Valley was reactivated for this purpose, and it is not clear whether the Mozambicans were repatriated (Vail and White 1980:166). When the Anglo-German cocoa boycott was imposed in 1909 and imports of labor from Angola were banned, contracts for São Tomé were suddenly extended to three years, and the authorities made a major effort at coercive recruitment, resulting in outbreaks of violence in Mozambique (Duffy 1967:207).

The republicans after 1910 swept away slavery and replaced it with a system of forced labor. The interior of the mainland colonies was conquered, and the population was made to pay tax and to perform obligatory labor duties (Clarence-Smith 1985: chap. 5). The usual contract period was fixed at six months, but the authorities rapidly made exceptions to this, with contracts of up to five years authorized for São Tomé. In effect, being sent to São Tomé became a special form of punishment. The threat of a long contract in the "islands of death" was a convenient way to discipline the labor force and the population at large (Penvenne 1982).

The greater autonomy granted to the colonies by the republic, however, created problems for the São Tomé planters. Over time, both Mozambique and Angola shortened the contracts, insisted on repatriation, and limited the numbers of laborers they allowed to go to the islands. At times they even cut off the flow of labor altogether, on the grounds that it was needed at home (Vail and White 1980:184–85, 215, 236; Morna 1944:228, 240–41). Forced labor was thus never as effective for the São Tomé planters as the old free market in slaves.

Finally, we must consider tax-induced migratory labor, which was becoming the norm in parts of Africa but which played almost no role in the cocoa plantations. One need look no further than the terrible death rates prevalent on all the plantations to understand why laborers would avoid the cocoa plantations if they possibly could. Only the Germans made any kind of effort to induce labor migration. Owing to the repeated protests of missionaries, traders, and concession companies worried at the decimation of their clients and porters, the Germans promulgated labor reforms in 1902 and slowly and cautiously imposed taxation from 1903. This stimulated both production of cash crops and wage labor, but there is little indication that the cocoa plantations ever received more than a trickle of laborers who truly made the free choice to come there to meet their tax obligations (Rüger 1960:203–7).

The fact that laborers in the cocoa plantations were mainly coerced might give the impression that this was "cheap labor." It is certain that wages were minuscule or nonexistent and that the standard of living of the workers was low. The real cost of labor to the employers, however, was determined as much by recruitment costs and productivity as by the level of wages in cash or in kind. In fact, it seems clear that the chief weakness of the plantations was high real labor costs and that this was the fundamental reason why peasant production overtook plantation production after the First World War.

Recruitment costs were affected partly by the steeply rising price of slaves and the distances over which coerced labor of every kind had to be transported, but they were affected even more fundamentally by excessive mortality. Not only was the total number of deaths high, but death also tended to occur right at the beginning of a worker's service, when the laborer had hardly begun to be productive (Banco Nacional Ultramarino 1890:667–69). High mortality was not confined to the Portuguese islands, and it was made worse by persistently high rates of serious illness. The French authorities calculated that death rates among laborers from south central Kamerun sent to the cocoa plantations in the German period averaged at around 10 percent a year, while the number of workers off sick at any given time often stood as high as

30 percent. Even the Victoria Pflanzung, often cited as a model for health care, suffered a death rate of 10.24 percent among its workers in 1912. Malaria was one of the worse problems, as workers from the highlands had little or no resistance to the disease (Michel 1969:200–203).

When the high recruitment costs and the mortality figures were considered in calculations of labor costs, the coerced labor of the Gulf of Guinea no longer appeared cheap. Chevalier estimated that the total real cost of a laborer in São Tomé in the 1900s, including recruitment costs and losses due to mortality, came to around 32 shillings a month. This compared with an average of 26.5 shillings in Surinam at the same time (Van Hall 1932:317; see also Faro 1908:163). It also stands to reason that the labor costs of African peasants, with greater resistance to disease and lower or nonexistent recruitment expenses, must have been much lower.

Moreover, productivity was not considered in these calculations. Not only did the high incidence of illness lower the productivity of labor considerably, but employers were also faced with the sullen resistance of a deeply alienated body of workers. Although few overt acts of open rebellion occurred after the São Tomé troubles of 1875–76, the more desperate laborers committed suicide and went on collective hunger strikes (see Cadbury Papers 4/21). An even more generalized passive resistance by workers seems to have accounted for the high supervisory costs that employers were obliged to bear, especially through hiring European staff (Faro 1908:163). While it is not even possible to estimate the losses caused by shirking, deliberate damage to cocoa trees, illegal sales of part of the cocoa crop, and other forms of resistance, a strong contrast existed between African peasant families eager to increase household incomes and forced laborers.

It is true that other factors contributed to the stagnation of the cocoa plantations after the First World War, in contrast with the spectacular rise of peasant output in West Africa. Sun-drying of cocoa was possible in the Gold Coast and Nigeria, whereas most of the Gulf of Guinea plantations required expensive drying machinery and sheds (Van Hall 1932). The São Tomé plantations were devastated by an insect plague from 1918, whereas on the mainland a parasite checked the spread of the insect. Soil exhaustion was becoming a problem on lands where planters had naively believed in the inexhaustible fertility of volcanic soils and had not used fertilizers (Dias 1961:26–27; United Kingdom 1920b: 27; Urquhart 1956:126–27). Moreover, it was not just the cost of labor which affected the planters but also a new uncertainty about supplies of labor, resulting from the almost simultaneous abolition of the Angolan slave trade to São Tomé, the reform of Liberian labor exports to Fernando Po, and the reforms in Kamerun after the expulsion of the Germans.

It is also true that tariff factors affected the evolution of cocoa planting. The Portuguese islands clung to cocoa, but the protected metropolitan market in Portugal was small and saturated, so that exports stagnated and then fell. The planters thus turned to oil palms and other substitute crops (Portugal 1936:126). In contrast, the Spanish planters had a large, protected home market, which was not satiated with colonial cocoa until the economic crisis of the 1930s. Fernando Po thus rapidly outstripped São Tomé and Príncipe as a producer of plantation cocoa. The Spanish planters, however, were unable to compete on the world market (Nosti 1948:43-44; Liniger-Goumaz 1979:93).

In Kamerun, plantation cocoa did maintain itself to some extent, in spite of the absence of a protected market, which suggests that the plantations had one comparative advantage in their competition with peasants, namely quality (see Epale 1985: chaps. 3 and 4). Better drying and fermenting of the cocoa beans was especially important in this respect, although this was offset by the failure of all attempts to acclimatize the fine cocoa trees of Venezuela or Ecuador in the Gulf of Guinea (Van Hall 1932:314, 325, 394-95). This said, the German planters who repurchased their lands in the British Cameroons placed much less emphasis on cocoa than they had previously. This one partial exception cannot detract from the extraordinary victory of peasants over planters on a vastly expanded world market in the interwar years.

Thus, the chief advantage of coerced labor was not that it was cheap, but rather that it was available. When prices were high on the world market and producers had difficulties in keeping up with booming demand, planters who could acquire labor were at an advantage. In contrast, when prices stabilized at a lower level and reducing costs became the chief imperative, the advantage passed to peasants, who disposed of truly cheap labor.

References

Almeida, Pedro Ramos de. 1978-79. *História do colonialismo Português em Africa.* 3 vols. Lisbon: Editorial Estampa.

Antologia colonial Portuguesa. 1946. Vol. 1. Lisbon: Ministério das Colonias.

Austen, Ralph, and Rita Headrick. 1983. Equatorial Africa under colonial rule. In *History of Central Africa*, ed. David Birmingham and Phyllis Martin. London: Longmans.

Banco Nacional Ultramarino. 1890. *Relatórios do Banco Nacional Ultramarino desde o anno de 1865 a 1889.* Lisbon: Banco Nacional Ultramarino.

Brooks, George. 1972. *The Kru mariner in the 19th century.* Newark, N.J.: Liberian Studies Association.

Cadbury, Papers. Birmingham University Library. Birmingham, England.

Carreira, António. 1982. *The people of the Cape Verde Islands: Exploitation and emigration.* London: C. Hurst.

Chevalier, A. 1907. *A ilha de São Tomé*. Lisbon: Revista Portugueza Colonial e Marítima.

Clarence-Smith, William Gervase. 1976. Slavery in coastal southern Angola, 1875–1913. *Journal of Southern African Studies* 2, no. 2:214–23.

Clarence-Smith, William Gervase. 1985. *The third Portuguese empire, 1825–1975*. Manchester: Manchester University Press.

Contreiras, M. 1894. *A província de Angola*. Lisbon: Livraria Ferreira.

Cooper, Frederick. 1977. *Plantation slavery on the east coast of Africa*. New Haven: Yale University Press.

Dias, M. Nunes. 1961. O cacau luso-brasileiro na economia mundial: Subsídios para a sua história. *Studia* 8:7–93.

Duffy, James. 1967. *A question of slavery: Labour policies in Portuguese Africa and British protest, 1850–1920*. Cambridge: Harvard University Press.

Epale, S. 1985. *Plantations and development in western Cameroon, 1885–1975*. New York: Vantage Press.

Esparteiro, A. Marques. 1962. *Portugal no Daomé, 1471–1961*. Lisbon: Agência Geral do Ultramar.

Faro, Conde de Sousa e. 1908. *A ilha de S. Thomé e a roça Agua-Izé*. Lisbon: Typ. do Annuario Commercial.

Fincke, Heinrich. 1936. *Handbuch der Kakaoerzeugnisse*. Berlin: Julius Springer.

Galvão, Henrique, and Carlos Selvagem. 1951. *Império Ultramarino Português*. Vol. 2. Lisbon: Empresa Nacional de Publicidade.

Hammond, Richard. 1966. *Portugal and Africa, 1815–1910*. Stanford, Calif.: Stanford University Press.

Liniger-Goumaz, Max. 1979. *La Guinée Equatoriale, un pays méconnu*. Paris: Harmattan.

Mantero, Francisco. 1910. *A mão d'obra em S. Thomé e Príncipe*. Lisbon: Privately printed.

Michel, Marc. 1969. Les plantations allemandes du Mont Cameroun, 1885–1914. *Revue Française d'Histoire d'Outre-Mer* 57, no. 2:183–213.

Möller, P. A. 1974. *Journey in Africa, 1895–1896*. Cape Town: C. Struik.

Moreno Moreno, J. A. 1952. *Reseña histórica de la presencia de España en el Golfo de Guinea*. Madrid: Instituto de Estudios Africanos.

Morna, Alvaro de Freitas. 1944. *Angola, um ano no governo geral, 1942–1943*. Lisbon: Livraria Popular.

Muralha, Pedro. N.d. *Terras de Africa: S. Tomé e Angola*. Lisbon: Publicitas.

Ndongo Bidyogo, Donato. 1977. *Historia y tragedia de Guinea Ecuatorial*. Madrid: Editorial Cambio.

Nevinson, Henry. 1968. *A modern slavery*. New York: Schocken Books.

Newbury, Colin. 1961. *The western slave coast and its rulers*. Oxford: Clarendon Press.

Newitt, Malyn. 1981. *Portugal in Africa: The last hundred years*. London: C. Hurst.

Nogueira, A. F. 1893. *A ilha de São Thomé*. 2d ed. Lisbon: Jornal As Colonias Portuguezas.

Norero, Agustin. 1910. *El cacao y su cultivo*. Madrid: Librería General de Victoriano Suárez.

Nosti, Jaime. 1948. *Agricultura de Guinea, promesa para España*. Madrid: Instituto de Estudios Africanos.

Osuntokun, A. 1978. *Equatorial Guinea-Nigeria relations: The diplomacy of labour*. Ibadan: Oxford University Press.

Othick, J. 1976. The cocoa and chocolate industry in the nineteenth century. In *The making of the modern diet*, ed. D. Oddy and D. Miller. London: Croom Helm.

Patterson, K. D. 1975. *The northern Gabon coast to 1875*. Oxford: Clarendon Press.

Penvenne, Jeanne. 1982. A history of African labor in Lourenço Marques, Mozambique, 1877 to 1950. Ph.D. diss., Boston University.

Portugal. Ministério das Colonias. 1936. *Primeira conferência económica do império colonial português: Pareceres, projectos de decreto e votos*. Vol. 1. Lisbon: Ministério das Colónias.

Portugal em Africa. 1896, 1898. (Periodical published in Lisbon.)

Rebello da Silva, Luis. 1969. *Relatórios do ministro e secretário de estado dos negócios da marinha e do ultramar*. Lisbon: Ministério do Ultramar.

Roçadas, J. Alves. 1914. *La main d'oeuvre indigène à Angola*. Lisbon: Imprensa Nacional.

Rudin, Harry. 1938. *Germans in the Cameroons, 1884-1914*. New Haven: Yale University Press.

Rüger, Adolf. 1960. Die Entstehung und Lage der Arbeiterklasse unter dem deutschen Kolonialregime in Kamerun (1895-1905). In *Kamerun unter deutscher Kolonialherrschaft*, vol. 1, ed. Helmuth Stoecker. Berlin: Rütten und Loenig.

Sá da Bandeira, Marquês de. 1873. *O trabalho rural Africano e a administração colonial*. Lisbon: Imprensa Nacional.

Schuler, Monica. 1986. Kru emigration to British and French Guiana, 1841-1857. In *Africans in bondage*, ed. Paul Lovejoy. Madison: University of Wisconsin Press.

Seixas, António de. 1865. *As colónias Portuguesas*. Lisbon: Typ. Universal.

Stollwerck, Walter. 1907. *Der Kakao und die Schokoladenindustrie*. Jena: Fischer.

Sundiata, Ibrahim. 1974. Prelude to scandal: Liberia and Fernando Po, 1880-1930. *Journal of African History* 15, no. 1:97-112.

Sundiata, Ibrahim. 1977. "Cuba Africana": Cuba and Spain in the Bight of Biafra, 1839-1869. *The Americas* 34, no. 1:90-101.

Tenreiro, Francisco. 1961. *A ilha de São Tomé, estudo geográfico*. Lisbon: Junta de Investigações do Ultramar.

United Kingdom. Foreign Office, Historical Section. 1919. *Spanish Guinea*. London.

United Kingdom. Foreign Office, Historical Section. 1920a. *Cape Verde Islands*. London.

United Kingdom. Foreign Office, Historical Section. 1920b. *San Thomé and Principe*. London.

Urquhart, Duncan. 1956. *Cocoa*. 3d ed. London: Longmans, Green.

Vail, Leroy, and Landeg White. 1980. *Capitalism and colonialism in Mozambique*. London: Heinemann.

Van Hall, C. J. J. 1932. *Cocoa*. 2d ed. London: Macmillan.

7 *Martin A. Klein*

Slavery and Emancipation in French West Africa

Slavery was abolished in the French colonial empire in 1848. At the time, the major concern of French abolitionists was the Caribbean. France's domain in Africa consisted of two small islands—St. Louis in the mouth of the Senegal River, Gorée in what is now Dakar Harbor—and a series of posts strung out along the Senegal River. Emancipation caused few difficulties in these areas (Gueye 1966; Pasquier 1967). The major problem faced by the colonial state and by commercial interests based on the coast of Senegal was not their own slaves, but those of their neighbors. For the next fifty-seven years, the colonial administration did its best to limit the impact of French abolition on its African neighbors and subjects and to prevent their slaves from fleeing to French territories (Renault 1972).

The Nature of Sudanese Slavery

The area that today makes up Senegal, Mali, and Guinea was a major slave-using area. Slaves constituted a majority of the population near commercial towns, each of which was surrounded by a belt of slave-worked farms (Bernus 1960:239–324; Peroz 1889:353; Baillaud 1902:294). Powerful states like Segou, the Futa Jallon, and Sikasso depended on slave labor both to produce food and to staff the machinery of the state. In desert-side areas, where slaves produced grain and textiles for exchange with Saharan nomads, the population

171

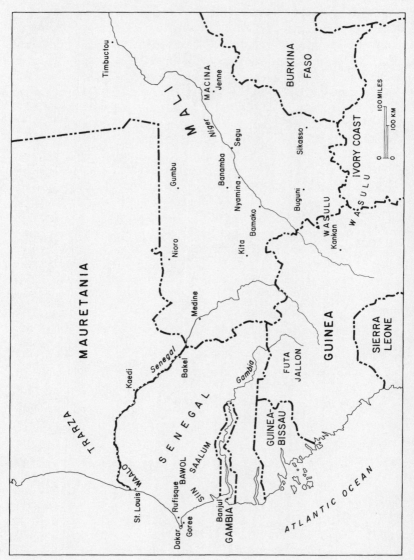

7.1 Senegal, Guinea, and Mali

172

ran about 50 percent slave. Only in the southern part of what is now Mali and in a part of eastern Senegal were slave concentrations small, and these areas largely offered sources of slaves for more centralized societies further north. The colony of Haut Sénégal-Niger (now Mali and Burkina Faso) was between a quarter and third servile.[1] Though not as great as slave percentages in the West Indies, the percentage of the population in slavery was greater than that of most known slave societies.[2]

Two different kinds of slavery predominated. In those societies with large slave concentrations, slaves tended to live in separate settlements and worked in a very systematic way under the direction of others. Manumission was rare, and slavery was hereditary. These tended to be Muslim societies, not because of a predisposition of Islam to slavery, but rather because these were societies open to the market, where slaves were used to produce commodities. Slaves tended to work five days a week from sunrise to early afternoon prayer (about 2:00 P.M.). If these hours were not as long as the "sunrise to sunset" schedule of American slaves, it was partly because the productivity of West African hoe agriculture was low and slaves had to work their own plots in order to feed themselves (Klein and Lovejoy 1979; Klein 1977, 1983a; Lovejoy 1983; Meillassoux 1975b, 1986; Roberts 1987: 112–28). The second kind of slavery is the more benign kind often described as lineage slavery. It existed where the slave concentrations were low, usually less than 10 to 15 percent, and where slaves worked alongside the master and his kin. Within these societies, the offspring of slaves tended to be absorbed into the free population within a generation or two, often creating junior branches of the master's lineage. While the second form has attracted considerable scholarly attention, the first involved much larger numbers of people (Miers and Kopytoff 1977: introduction; Lovejoy 1983:12–15; Miller 1981).

Senegal and Its Neighbors

All states on the Senegalese mainland had long raided for slaves, traded slaves, and exploited slave labor. Slaves manned the caravans that brought trade goods into St. Louis. Slaves of Mauritanian nomads produced the gum which was St. Louis' major export (Webb 1985). In 1848 slave labor was already producing the peanuts that would become the economic base of the colony. African leaders responded quickly. The emirate of Trarza suspended the gum trade. The kingdom of Waalo seized a herd of cattle destined for St. Louis. The chiefs of Cape Verde villages refused to sell fish to Gorée (ANSOM 1849a).

French authorities in Paris refused to suspend the law, but governors were reminded of their police powers (ANSOM 1848). By 1857 Governor Louis Faidherbe had worked out a way of dealing with slave flight from friendly states (Renault 1972). First, the prohibition against owning slaves applied only to French citizens and to areas under French sovereignty in 1848. Residents of areas conquered later were to be considered subjects and thus immune from the provisions of the 1848 act. Second, the principle that French soil freed was to apply only to slaves fleeing enemies. Other runaways were to be expelled as "vagabonds dangerous for order and public peace" on the complaint of their masters. Slaves accompanying chiefs visiting St. Louis or Gorée were also to be expelled if they sought their freedom (ANS 1855, 1857a, b). A system of wardship was set up that authorized the purchase of children on the condition that they be freed and registered within twenty-four hours after reaching St. Louis. Until 1904 there was a regular trade in children from upper river posts to St. Louis. Finally, Faidherbe set up rules for distributing booty: one-third went to the state, and two-thirds to the soldiers, but soldiers and allies "were allowed to take and keep captives from their enemies" (Barrows 1974, 1978). Ironically, Faidherbe successfully projected the image of himself as an abolitionist.

Abolition and Expansion

This system could work only if Senegal could be insulated from French public opinion. This was not always possible. The economy was growing rapidly. The prohibition of slavery was belatedly extended to the new port of Dakar in 1877 and to nearby Rufisque in 1879. The structure of the colonial state also caused problems. During the 1870s the communes of coastal Senegal were recognized as French municipalities, and their residents were given the right to elect a deputy, a general council, and municipal councils (Idowu 1968). This made Senegal a more open society than most other colonies. Within the communes, the judicial authorities depended not on the governor but on the Ministry of Justice. In the 1870s a prosecuting attorney with a reverence for the law that the military authorities did not share brought a series of prosecutions on slave-related charges (Renault 1972; ANSOM, Senegal 15 and 17; ANS, K 11). Finally, the presence of missionaries created difficulties. Protestant missionaries were running a sanctuary in St. Louis where they tried to hide runaways during the three-month waiting period. They also fed information to allies in Paris. In 1880 Victor Schoelcher, the aging dean of French abolitionists, gave a speech in the French Senate, using information provided by missionaries to document the toleration of slavery in Senegal. He talked of the slave trade at French posts, described the expulsion of runaways from St. Louis, and even showed a copy of the form printed for the expulsion of runaways (*JORF* 1880; Schoelcher 1880).

The minister of colonies first denied the charges, but 1880 was also the year that the conquest of the Sudan began. Many strong supporters of imperial expansion were sometime supporters of abolition. In 1881, for example, Léon Gambetta, Jules Simon, and Admiral Cloué, the minister of the navy and colonies, attended an abolitionist banquet (Schoelcher 1882:270; *MS*, Feb. 7, 1881; ANS, K 12). An expansionist colonial administration depended on appropriations coaxed with difficulty from a stingy Parliament. By 1883 the law in Senegal decreed that all runaways coming into areas of direct administration were to be immediately freed. The number of slaves freed increased. Between 1875 and 1881 from 350 to 674 a year were freed. Between 1881 and 1889 it oscillated between 1,058 and 2,198 (Renault 1972:37).

These numbers would have been much higher had the administration not once again limited the application of its laws. Between 1881 and 1885 a railroad was completed across the lands of Kajoor, connecting St. Louis and Dakar and opening up prime peanut lands, where slave labor was being imported to expand production (Diouf 1990; N'Diaye 1968). In the Senegal River area, the new laws also posed a threat. Between 1881 and 1889 the number of Fulbe in the cercle of St. Louis dropped from about fifty thousand to fewer than ten thousand as Fulbe migrated east to the lands of Ahmadu of Segu, then France's major opponent in the Sudan (Renault 1972:38–43; ANS 1889a, b, Cons. Gen. 1892; Hansen 1989; Robinson 1985). The French response was to disannex large areas and place them under a protectorate, in the process insulating them from French law.

Thus, once again the law seemed to say much more than it actually said. A slave could flee to St. Louis or Gorée and claim freedom. Elsewhere flight was not encouraged. In many areas, runaways were freed only if they showed signs of mistreatment, such as severe beatings or underfeeding. Ironically, French reluctance to free slaves meant that Italian labor had to be used to build the Dakar-St. Louis railroad. The growing investment of capital in Senegal increased the demand for slaves. It had been important in Waalo after the French conquest in 1855 (Barry 1972), it was particularly intense along the rail line (Moitt 1983, 1989), and it was important in the middle Senegal River area, where slave labor produced millet to feed St. Louis and the Mauritanian nomads (Delaunay 1984).

Persistence of the Slave Trade

Slave ownership was not actively discouraged. Employees of the colonial state could own slaves as long as they did not trade them or bring them into areas of direct administration. They could even do those things if the slaves did not complain. Europeans were not supposed to own slaves, but many seem to have done so. In the Senegal River area and on the upper

Guinea coast, the owner of record was usually the European's wife or a concubine, often herself a slave (Renault 1972:18–20). Army officers in the Sudan recruited servants and concubines from their human booty.

The army was also recruited largely from slaves. In 1866, when recruitment was slow, Governor Pinet-Laprade raised the enlistment bonus from fifty to two hundred francs, the price demanded for most able-bodied male slaves. Payments were often made directly to masters, and this was acknowledged in account books and journals at river posts: "An enlistment bonus of 300 francs was paid to masters of 40 slaves as price of their redemption" (ANS 1885a). Dependence on slaves disturbed some military commanders. In 1880 Governor Canard tried to reform the system in order to attract free men. To do so, he raised the bonus: 300 francs for six years, 120 for four, 60 for two. The volunteers still remained largely slaves (Renault 1972:21–23; Echenberg 1986, 1991). Payment to the master was probably desirable because the river's shallowness gave masters the capacity to block the movement downriver of boats carrying freed slaves (ANS 1885b).

Both enslavement and slave raiding increased dramatically in the Sudan during the 1880s. The most important slave market was Banamba, north of Bamako, where Samory and his rival, Tiéba of Sikasso, exchanged slaves for horses. The slaves were then traded either into desert-side towns like Goumbou (Meillassoux 1971, 1975), into the desert, into Senegal. For a period between December 1888 and November 1889, nine commercial reports are available for Médine. They indicate the importation of 10,130 slaves and the exportation of 3,924 (ANM 1889). This would suggest that more than twelve thousand a year moved through, four or five times the number at the peak of the Atlantic trade.

The existing literature on Senegalese history says little about a massive flow of slaves into lower Senegal, but there are enough archival references to suggest that it was important. Most of the slave dealers in the upper Senegal River area and some further east were from lower Senegal (ANS 1898). In the last years of the trade, the administrator at Dagana wrote that "the river crossed, the wretched having been sold, are immediately taken into the interior by the juula, who will sell them principally in Kajoor, Bawol and the outskirts of St. Louis" (ANS 1904a). Most were probably moved either by boat or overland down to Dagana and then overland into the "peanut basin." Toward the turn of the century, Kaedi, on the north bank of the river, became the major market for this trade: "Moors coming from the desert sell large numbers of slaves to juula coming from all parts of the colony, particularly from Cayor. Some of them buy such large numbers that they can only be trading" (ANS 1899b; Moitt 1983, 1989).

Some of these slaves were undoubtedly absorbed in the river states, which in 1904 had the highest slave percentages reported for Senegal (Delaunay

1984: chaps. 1 and 2).[3] Some were absorbed into the urban or southern desert economies. None of these, however, had the capacity to absorb large numbers. The most significant economic growth in Senegal during this period was along the rail line, which had a strong demand for labor (Moitt 1983, 1989). Today this is the most densely populated part of Senegal. Into the area came both slave caravans and new forms of labor migration, but even the new migrants were probably largely servile. Most early migrants were probably slaves moved in large groups down to Senegal and the Gambia by slave-owning entrepreneurs, early labor contractors, as it were (David 1980; Curtin 1975).

The Dilemma of the Colonial Regimes

The late 1880s saw the establishment of French sovereignty in most of what is now Senegal. This meant an end to slave raiding, though some kidnapping continued, particularly in the Senegal River area, and slavery continued in peripheral areas until the beginning of the twentieth century. In the wake of the Brussels convention of 1890 (Miers 1975), an agreement was signed with the chiefs of the cercle of St. Louis in which the chiefs promised that slaves would no longer be traded, that all existing slaves would be considered domestic slaves and be protected by safeguards in the Koran, and that slaves would have the right to buy their freedom for five hundred francs each. This sum was more than twice the price of the most valuable slaves. The chiefs also kept the right to purchase slaves in areas not under French authority (ANSOM 1895c; Renault 1972:44).

In the following years, most other chiefs in Senegal were induced to sign this agreement. The agreement seems to have had an unintended consequence. It gave chiefs an interest in stopping caravans, because the chief who did so was usually entrusted with the freed slaves, who became his dependents (Klein 1968:168–69; ANS 1893b, 1894a, 1895). One chief even complained to an administrator that no important slave routes crossed his territory (ANS 1893b). Slaves did run to the Gambia and, from about 1893, were being freed there. Likewise, slaves fleeing the Gambia were likely to be freed in Senegal.

Thus, in Senegal slavery was being undermined, but very slowly. Slaves could and did flee, and it was not always easy to replace them. The slave trade did, however, continue into the first years of the twentieth century (Delaunay 1984:43; ANS 1904a, b), and slavery itself was still thriving in 1904 (ANS 1904a).

The Conquest of the Sudan

The vulnerability of Senegal to pressures from France lay in its openness and the existence of groups with political rights. The military men who conquered the Sudan were careful from the first to insulate their efforts from French public opinion. They had neither a political nor a business community rooted in the metropole, and they chose their missionaries carefully. They also controlled the information that St. Louis and Paris received about their efforts (Kanya-Forstner 1969).

The French approach to slavery and the slave trade was shaped by limitations of military force and geography. The first military campaigns in the Sudan involved between two hundred and five hundred soldiers, mostly Africans under the command of French officers. Goals were at first quite limited. Borgnis-Desbordes was operating during the first years among people interested in independence from Segu. His troops were thus often welcome. The French army operated only during the dry season, the campaign beginning in December or January and ending before the rains, when the bulk of the army would return to Senegal, leaving garrisons behind in various forts. They thus depended heavily on their alliances. This made slavery an important question. Both allies and enemies of the French were involved in the slave trade and in the exploitation of slave labor, and this shaped the way the French fought. After a victory, auxiliaries were free to take as many prisoners as they could. Some prisoners taken by the army itself were given to local elders (ANM 1887), but most were divided among the officers, their soldiers, and their allies. The French were particularly helpful to those called agents, who worked as spies, sources of information, and representatives. Many slaves were sold, sometimes right on the field of battle, but others were incorporated into soldiers' households. Like the slave warriors of African armies, French *tirailleurs* lived largely off the labor of female slaves. French officers also enjoyed the services of slave servants. The letters of the White Fathers, for example, frequently refer to the accumulation of women by French soldiers.

Another problem presented itself early. The heart of the new colony was what Denise Bouche has called the "dorsal spine of the French Soudan," the supply line that ran from Kayes through Bafoulabé and Kita to Bamako. Through this underpopulated area the French army every year had to move enough supplies for its military campaigns. In 1887 Gallieni ordered *villages de liberté* set up near most French posts (Bouche 1968). Archinard soon afterward spelled out how these were to be used. The villages were to receive slaves fleeing France's enemies. Others could also be received, but they were to be returned to their owners if claimed within three months, one month for those willing to enlist in the French army (ANS, 15 G 154–56, 1 D 102). Of course, the runaways developed their own tactics. One commandant complained that two-thirds of the runaways did not know their names, their parents' names, or their places of birth. When the master came to claim the runaway, he rarely knew the name the slave had given (ANM 1894b).

These villages might have repopulated an area that had suffered from a generation of warfare if the demand for labor, especially for porters, had not been so heavy. Residents could be pulled from their fields even while planting or harvesting. Army commanders constantly tried to limit the demands made on the villages but could often not control local officers. The attitude of the administration is best demonstrated by the fact that refugees from the villages were called runaways. Many left as soon as they could get away, and the population of many *villages de liberté* remained low (Roberts 1988).

Thus, while the military commanders of the Sudan used the ideology of antislavery to justify the conquest, they argued that it was necessary to tolerate not only slavery but also the slave trade. Caravans of slaves moved through the colony with passes from the French administration. The few surviving tax records indicate that slaves were by far the most important item being traded (see table 7.1). Taxes were collected in kind, which meant that the administration held and distributed large numbers of slaves (ANM 1894a, b).

In 1893 a civilian governor, Albert Grodet, was appointed in a reaction against the refusal of Archinard to accept instructions from Paris (Ghomsi 1968; Kanya-Forstner 1969: chap. 8). Grodet's response to the continued slave trade was strong: "I cannot admit that on the territory of the Republic, in the headquarters of a cercle, representatives of the human species are among the articles bought and sold" (ANS, 1894c). The result was a series of orders banning the slave trade, prohibiting the use of children as porters, and trying to regulate caravan organization in order to prevent porters' being sold (ANM 1895a). Paul Marty charged years later that these orders were "faite pour la galerie," but a number of caravans seem to have been stopped and several thousand slaves freed (Marty 1920, 4:170). In 1893 only 641 slaves were freed; in 1894 it was 1,258 (ANSOM 1894a, 1895b). Grodet also confiscated 140 slaves owned by Commandant Quiquandon (ANSOM 1895a) and ordered thirty days of confinement for Lieutenant Mangin, who had distributed 16 slaves, mostly to his servants (ANS 1894b).

The military detested Grodet and tried to ignore him. The campaign of 1894 was begun early so the troops could get into the field before he arrived. Colonel Trentinian, who replaced Grodet in 1895, could not repeal Grodet's orders without risking censure from Paris, but he sent out several carefully coded circulars which made it clear that it would be indiscreet to do anything about the trade. He gave instructions that slaves were to be freed only when there was evidence of mistreatment, but he told the White Fathers that change would come: "As for the question of slaves, it is with reluctance that he spoke. He assured us that resale is forbidden, he confessed to us that there are written orders, there are verbal orders, which are less severe and less strict. It is necessary, it would seem, to be careful with the masters, the Muslims. But in a little time, the commandant assured us, we will see our

Table 7.1. Slaves as a percentage of total trade

Post	Period	Number of slaves	Value of slaves (francs)	Total trade value (francs)	Percentage of slave value
Kountou	June–Oct. 1885	749	187,250	257,173	73
Bakel	Jan.–Mar. 1885	465	105,000	137,698	76
Médine	Feb. 1885	2,048	409,600	676,000	61
Bafoulabé	June–Sept. 1885	386	77,200	101,582	76
Bamako	Mar. 1887	703	140,600	379,490	37
	July 1887	323	64,600	104,200	62
Nioro	Feb. 1892	106	18,550	128,752	14
	Apr. 1892	100	15,000	40,715	37

Sources: ANM, 1 E 60; 1 Q 4, 44, 70, 74.

wishes fulfilled. It will be enough to seize Kenedougou [Sikasso], from which most of the slaves come" (AWF, *Diaires*, Segou, Mar. 12, 1897; ANM 1897).

Within a year, both Samory and Ba Bemba had fallen. The seizure of Ba Bemba's powerful fortress at Sikasso wrote a brutal finis to an age of horror: "A large caravan of slaves from Sikasso is passing between our house and that of the nuns. For some time they have been coming through every day. It is said that the lieutenant governor has taken three thousand slaves and has had them distributed to his soldiers" (AWF, *Diaires*, Segou, May 31, 1898). Trentinian was still reluctant to put teeth into his pious denunciations of slavery. The time, he wrote, was still not ripe. There were many slaves on the market, but it was a temporary phenomenon, the results of the victories of 1898 (ANS 1899a).

Abolition

In December 1899 another civilian, William Merlaud-Ponty, was appointed to command the Sudan. Ponty was very different from Grodet. A former secretary to Archinard, he knew the Sudan, understood the soldiers, and had good political sense. For most of his term, he served under Ernest Roume, whom he succeeded as governor-general in 1908. During the Ponty-Roume years, senior and junior administration differed sharply on the slavery question. Local administrators tended to believe more in the property rights of masters than in the human rights of slaves. They opposed any policy that would undermine their African intermediaries, and they seem to have genuinely believed that neither slaves nor masters would work if slavery ended. They were often reluctant to act and frequently had to be badgered by their superiors to carry out policy. At the same time, they constantly complained about the time spent on the claims of relatives, on slave flights, and on the claims of masters.

Once again, French politics pushed the administration to act. In December 1899 Abbé Lemire, a Catholic deputy, gave a speech denouncing the continued slave trade in the Sudan (*JORF*, Dec. 11, 1899).[4] Within weeks, Decrais, the minister of colonies, wrote all governors:

My attention has recently been called by a member of Parliament to the persistence of slaving practices, which the administration seems impotent to suppress in certain of our colonies. . . . It is important to the progress of civilization and to the honor of our country that within all countries where our dominion is established the natives should be led to completely renounce the practice of slavery. It is especially necessary that the trade in slaves and their export from one country to the next confronts a surveillance and a repression so severe that it disappears quickly in areas where it still exists. (ANSOM 1900)

Ponty distributed the letter to all administrators with instructions that they were to be guided by its principles. Specifically, he insisted that caravans taking slaves out of the colony be stopped. He followed the letter a year later with a circular, which remarked that many tax rolls enumerated the slave and the free separately and suggested that this seemed to give slavery official recognition. Administrators were no longer to receive claims in slave questions and were henceforth to treat slaves the same as other persons (ANM 1901). This circular became the basis of Ponty's policy on slavery. To the degree that it was enforced, it undercut slavery by withdrawing the support of the courts.

In 1903 another circular imposed penalties for slave trading. Caravans were to be stopped, and slaves placed in *villages de liberté*. Slave traders were to be jailed for fifteen days and fined one hundred francs for each slave being traded (ANS 1903a). In some areas, caravans were already being stopped. Large-scale raiding and trading had ended. Kidnapping and slave raiding continued, however, on the desert's edge and in the Mossi-Gurunsi area, and slaves, usually children, were traded secretly.

During the same period, the adoption system was being ended in Senegal (Moitt n.d.), and a new law code was enacted. Martial Merlin, the secretary-general of the federal government, used the occasion to assert some of the same principles Ponty was using in the Sudan: "Do not hesitate to reject any claim by a supposed master under the title of slavery over the person of other natives, whomever they are. You will warn them that any effort to seize those they say to be their slaves, any act of force against such persons, will expose them to prosecution. To those who come to complain of their masters, or simply to claim their liberty, you will explain that they are adults . . . that they are free under the law, and that the French authority will have their liberty respected" (ARNS 1903b, 1904c). A month later Merlin sent out a questionnaire requesting information about slavery and the opinion of administrators on how to deal with it. In the interim, he asked administrators to avoid "a propaganda which might provoke among natives still living in captivity a movement of a collective character." They were also no longer to issue certificates of liberty. All were free, but they were not to be told so. If not for the slaves, it might have been the quietest emancipation in history (ANSOM 1903).

On paper, Merlin's instructions of 1903 seem decisive, much like the law of 1848. There is no evidence, however, that they changed the procedures used in the cercles. The questionnaire was distributed with the idea of drawing up a comprehensive law on slavery. In the interim, slave trading was prosecuted under an 1831 law that had been written with the maritime trade in mind. The 1948 law was of limited use because the only sanction involved was the loss of French citizenship (ANS 1903b). In 1904 a French appeals court threw out a conviction under the 1831 law. The administration suddenly found itself without the legal tools it needed. As a result, a new, comprehensive law was speedily written and proclaimed on December 12, 1905. It made illegal both the alienation of any other person's liberty and any transaction in persons. It did not expressly prohibit slavery, though it is often interpreted as having done so (Renault 1972). Roume claimed that "there is no longer an institution of captivity in any form whatsoever in our colonies of West Africa" (*BCAF*, Jan. 1906, p. 15).

The Exodus

The colonial administration wanted to distance itself from slavery without disrupting social structures. It did not consider the slaves themselves, but should have done so. Slave flight had always been the most significant form of resistance to slavery. The response of slaves to the disruptions of conquest was to take advantage of the opportunity by fleeing even more than before. They fled to *villages de liberté*. They fled from *villages de liberté*. They fled to earlier homes. They fled to other masters and rival political leaders (Roberts 1988). Railroads were being built in both the Sudan and Guinea by forced labor. The laborers were mostly slaves, and no matter what was done to prevent flight, most simply disappeared (ANM, 1 E 16 and 47). There were slave revolts in some areas, most notably near Bakel in 1896 (ANS, 13 G 197 and 199) and Nyamina in 1901. With the defeat of Samory and Ba Bemba in 1898, most of the Sudan was peaceful. Refugees and slaves from Wasulu, probably the most ravaged area in the Sudan, sought to go home from the moment of French victory.

The most vulnerable of the slave-owning societies were the Soninke and Maraka towns of the desert-side region. Here a harsh form of slavery had developed, marked by a low rate of manumission, high labor obligations, and frequent underfeeding (Meillassoux 1975a; Pollet and Winter 1971). Nowhere was this slave mode of production more marked than around the market town of Banamba. Founded in the mid-nineteenth century, Banamba profited from the destruction of other market centers and from the patronage of major slavers (Roberts 1988; Roberts and Klein 1980; McDougall 1988). It was a horse-exporting region and was ideally suited for the distribution of slaves into desert-side towns and into Senegal. Much of the profit was redirected into a prosperous slave-worked agricultural economy. As a result of its rapid growth, Banamba had a homogeneous slave population: many of them came from Wasulu, were recently enslaved, and spoke a common language. Thus, conditions were ideal for resistance. In most slave communities, ethnic diversity, the lack of kinship ties, and divisions between old and new slaves combined to make effective coordination difficult.

In the spring of 1905, when a group of slaves were prevented by force from leaving Banamba, a detachment of soldiers was sent in under an administrator who had orders to mediate the differences and dissuade slaves from leaving. He was successful, but the following year the slaves were ready to go again. This time Ponty said to let them go as long as they had paid their taxes and had passes (Roberts and Klein 1980). Slaves were most likely to leave their masters in the spring, when granaries were low and planting would soon commence. That same spring, slaves began to leave other places. In 1907 there were massive departures from Segou and elsewhere in western Mali. The movement then moved further east and south into Guinea and the Ivory Coast. In 1911 in Kankan, about 1,800 slaves showed up at the commandant's office to request passes in a single day (ANS, K 28). Before the movement slowed in 1912 and 1913, it touched most of the western savanna, Bella and Harratin in desert-side areas, and the Guinea coast (ANS, ser. 2 G; see also Roberts 1988; Klein 1988).

There is no clear evidence that Ponty fully understood what the effect of his actions would be. He simply realized that he could not stop the movement and that it would be politically disastrous to try to do so. Within a year of the Banamba exodus, he realized that the departures were not hurting productivity but were probably increasing it. Most important, they were creating a reservoir of laborers, who were moving into towns, working as porters in rubber-growing areas of Guinea, and cultivating peanuts in Senegal. As governor, and after 1908 as governor-general, Ponty constantly pressed on subordinates the idea that emancipation was contributing and could contribute to economic growth. For example, in opening the Conseil Général in 1908, he said that "the exodus of former slaves toward their native land has taken place with calm and without the slightest incident. The principle of individual liberty having been put above discussion, the former masters were at first disconcerted, but have accepted the new state of things. Thus a new class of free and salaried workers has been created" (*JOAOF*, Dec. 14, 1908).

Most colonial administrators did not come to social revolution comfortably. The French were only willing to go so far. There was to be no emancipation in the desert. Slavery persisted in the Sahara with the open cooperation of the colonial administration until the end of colonial rule (McDougall 1988; Derrick 1975: chap. 2; Maugham 1961). Equally important, local administrators were frequently disturbed to see much of their labor supply going elsewhere. The careers of administrators depended on the well-being and economic growth of their commands, measured mostly in tax receipts. Thus, there were constant efforts to tie freedmen down and to keep them from leaving. The frequency and the vigor with which Ponty belabored the issue was probably more a result of the immobility of local administration than of abolitionist fervor. The area that most concerned the administration was Masina, the inner delta of the Niger (Johnson 1976). A large flood plain, it was controlled by Fulbe pastoralists, whose slaves produced large surpluses of rice. Rice and cattle from Masina were important in feeding Bamako and various garrison towns. Many feared that slaves would flee and that the pastoralists would ignore agriculture, leaving Bamako hungry (Roberts 1980).

The result was an effort from 1908, approved by Ponty, to impose sharecropping contracts (Klein 1983b), which attempted to shift from control over persons to control over land and, at the same time, to reduce the obligations of slaves. In Masina, sharecropping contracts were reluctantly accepted, but almost from the first, both slaves and masters began undercutting them. The masters often tried to collect both traditional dues and the new rents. The slaves could see no reason to pay anything. They were, however, not interested in leaving a fertile area. After a period of bitter controversy, the subject disappeared from the archives, but control over land gave the Fulbe masters control over the former slaves, which has remained effective in the modern period (Cissé 1978; Gallais 1967, 1:160–61). In other areas, however, efforts to impose sharecropping were less successful. In Fulbe areas north of the delta, population densities were low, and land had little value. Masters could not prevent their former slaves from simply moving out. Only in the densely populated Futa Toro and Futa Jallon did local elites make a similar shift.

How They Did It

This leaves us with a number of key questions. The first is how they did it. No one was helping them. They lived and worked in a relatively unproductive economy that made it difficult for them to save. They often had to walk long distances to get home: from Banamba to Bougouni, the center of Wasulu, for example, was about 230 kilometers; from Nioro, it was over 400. When they got there, often in tatters, they found uncertain conditions. Land had returned to bush. They had no seed and no tools. They had no savings and no possessions to pawn.

The missions might have helped. In earlier years, they had often provided refuge for runaways and for slave children freed in military or police operations (Bouche 1968: pt. 2), but the separation of church and state led to a period of open warfare between the two hitherto allied institutions from 1904 to 1906 (Benoist, 1987: chaps. 3 and 4). Missions trying to help slaves were often harassed. They were also deprived of subsidies, which meant that they lacked resources. It is then all the more surprising that there are no references to massive starvation among freedmen, though undoubtedly periods of low nutrition made them susceptible to disease.

For Senegal, the question is not difficult. Numerous slaves were found and redeemed by kin. People often found relatives long distances away, and sometimes they used the colonial administration to make contact. This was a period of rapid economic growth. Peace and order made possible the extension of trade and production. From 1908 the railroad inched east from Thiès, every year opening new areas to peanut production, which rose in the well-watered cercle of Sine-Saloum from eight thousand metric tons in 1895 to one hundred thousand in 1914 (Klein 1968: chap. 9). Work was available in the peanut fields, on the railroad, in the cities, and in the station towns.

It is probable, however, that the most significant variable was the Mourides. A religious order formed in the 1880s by Amadou Bamba, the Mourides early developed an emphasis on submission and on work as a substitute for other religious obligations (Cruise O'Brien 1971; Copans 1980). From the first, the Mourides rallied those most dislocated by colonization: the aristocracy, the slave warriors, and the agricultural slaves. It is probable that most early converts were slaves. The key institution for them was the *dahra*, a colony of young male disciples. Young men would submit to a Mouride shaikh and go with him to a frontier settlement. As the rail line moved east, Mouride colonies sprang up around the stations, often arriving before the stations opened and seizing the most valuable land (Klein 1968:223–29). The disciples worked for the shaikhs for about eight years and then were given land and freed to marry. Joining the Mourides was the most effective way for a freedman to get access to land. Not surprisingly, early recruitment was heaviest in areas of high population density.

For the Sudan, the question of how the slaves did it is more difficult. The role of the missions was a limited one, oriented to kin, spouses, and would-be spouses of converts. Certain mechanisms were clearly important. The first was the use of the *villages de liberté*. The data on admissions and departures suggest that in some areas, the villages were used not for resettlement purposes but to hold women and children until the men could establish themselves elsewhere. In the villages, the French provided work, land, and seed, often assigning newcomers to established families. Only a minority of the returning slaves, however, used the villages, and only in a few areas.

Second, Senegal provided an outlet. The development of migrant labor in Senegal and the Gambia dates to the 1840s and probably involved slave traders becoming labor contractors. By the 1880s migrant labor had assumed forms it would maintain until independence. Migrants came in from outside the peanut basin and were given plots of land, seed, lodging, and food. They would pay for all this by working five mornings a week on the lands of the head of the family. The migrant from the Sudan needed only to get to Senegal to be assured food and work. He could then use the money to get established back home or, later, to pay taxes. The number of migrants in the Gambia increased from 4,657 in 1904 to 21,979 in 1914 (David 1980:33–34, 467). There is no similar early data for Senegal, but the number was clearly increasing dramatically (David 1980:114). By 1902 there were also harvest migrants called *firdous*, most of whom came from the area of that name on the upper Gambia.

Third, significant growth in economic activity was occurring within the Sudan. Perhaps most interesting, Richard Roberts' research (1984) shows an increase in weaving even though importations of textiles from Europe were also increasing. Weaving was traditionally slave work in those Sudanese societies marked by the importance of slave-based production. In most areas, it remained slave work until the drought years of the 1970s began to break down such barriers. Weaving is also an activity for which credit was probably available. Finally, it uses more female labor than male. Women spun, and men wove. It took about eight hours of spinning to produce enough thread for one hour of weaving. It is probable that many slaves survived by spinning and weaving, especially during the difficult years. More people left the desertside cercles than actually settled in the areas from which slaves had been taken. Interviews suggest that many settled in the towns instead of going home. The increase in textile production followed the expansion of the grain market and the general stimulus provided by the completion of the railroad in 1904.

The rubber boom in Guinea also provided a demand for laborers, particularly for porters. Lacking an all-water route to the sea, Guinea depended heavily on porters, of which there were never enough. The railroad's moving into the interior did not diminish the importance of porterage but rather shifted the focus of trade routes. By 1909 over 1,800 metric tons of rubber a year were being exported from Guinea (Suret-Canale 1971:43–45). Similarly, in the Sudan, when the rubber boom hit Bougouni about 1903, there was not enough labor to carry rubber to the railhead (ANM 1903). By 1908 this problem was solving itself. Archival sources describe "these Bambaras who come every year from Bamako and even further to work as porters between the last harvest and the beginning of the sowing" (ANG 1910). Further, "Although it used to be difficult to find porters and laborers, they now present themselves, and when they do not find work, they go elsewhere to look for it, sometimes very far" (ANG 1914).

People interviewed in Wasulu stressed none of these mechanisms, or rather stressed all of them but insisted that they were important not to get reestablished but to pay taxes. Oral accounts stress a period of difficulty in which returnees lived by gathering and perhaps hunting small animals. Hunting and gathering remained important in the area because the continuing flow of returnees heavily burdened the area's limited reserves of seed. People remember the period as one of hunger, in which wild animals were as much a threat as a source of nourishment. Though colonial administrators knew how poor the returnees were, an effort was made to collect a head tax from 1895, the year after a post was created at Bougouni.[5]

How Many Went?

A precise estimate of the size of the slave exodus is difficult. For Senegal it is impossible. There was no single, massive departure. Slaves drifted off or moved in small groups. Those who left are not remembered. Those who descended from slaves prefer not to talk about it. No good social surveys exist that would facilitate an estimate. Even administrative correspondence offers little help. For the Sudan an estimate is difficult, but possible (Roberts 1988). In 1911 Ponty estimated the departures at half a million in a letter to the British consul (ANS 1911). This is our best working estimate.

We can approach the question by looking at two sets of statistics. First, we can examine changes in census reports. The problem here is that French counting methods were becoming more rigorous. The era of eyeballing was over. An increase in population often meant simply that counting was more efficient. This was particularly true of those cercles in the southern Sudan to which slaves were returning. We have to search, therefore, for declines or dramatic increases (table 7.2). The declines in Kita and Bafoulabé are striking, because both were railroad stations and old cercles, well organized before the exodus. It is not surprising that the cercle of Bougouni shows the most dramatic increases (table 7.3). Over 40 percent of those leaving many desert-side cercles gave Bougouni as their destination. They did not all end up there, but many did. When the cercle was first created, only four villages existed, and most of the population clustered around the post. Between 1894 and 1898 the cercle was much reduced in size, while the return of refugees and runaway slaves began to repopulate villages.

Table 7.2. Population of selected cercles

Cercle	1905	1906	1913	1914
Northern				
Bafoulabé	65,273	71,230	60,811	–
Kita	56,624	–	46,633	–
Gao	46,011	–	34,703	–
Goumbou	66,947	–	63,117	–
Southern				
Sikasso	164,410	–	223,719	–
Koury	224,266	–	322,719	–
Koutiala	134,264	–	–	221,277

Sources: ANM, 1 E 17, 38, 43, 48, 73; 5 D 51.

A second source of data is the reported requests for passes. The problems here are that many left without seeking passes, data are available for only a few cercles and data are only available for limited periods. In evaluating these figures, we have to assume that others left without asking for passes. We can also assume that in most areas the estimated slave population was lower than the actual slave populations. Modern social surveys suggest that the 1904 figures underestimated slave population. For example, Djenné reported a population that was 23-percent servile. Surveys taken in the 1950s and 1960s suggest that Macina, most of which was within the cercle, was at least half servile (Klein 1987; Gallais 1967). In those cercles of which an estimate is possible, somewhere between 20 and 40 percent of the slave population left. If we try to project that over the Sudan as a whole, an area with a slave population somewhere between 1 and 1.3 million, we end up with about three hundred thousand to five hundred thousand leaving. In other words, Ponty's estimate was probably close to the truth.

Who Left and Who Stayed?

This was a massive population movement, but on second glance, it is clear that most slaves stayed in place. Who left? Departures were most numerous

Table 7.3. Population growth, cercle of Bougouni

Year	Population
1894	6,709
1896	8,977
1898	14,425
1899	68,830
1905	95,592
1913	162,343

Source: ANM, 1 E 27.

Table 7.4. Slave departures, selected cercles

Cercle	1907	1908	1909	1910	1911
Bamako	2,146	608	39	–	–
Goumbou	–	2,956	2,598	652	240
Kayes	–	397	30	262	–
Kita	78	849	1,438	over 500	–
Segou	2,609	–	–	–	–

Sources: Bamako, ANM, 1 E 19. The data for 1907 includes ten months, for 1908, six months, for 1909, one month.

Goumbou, ANM, 1 E 38. This is the only cercle for which data are just about complete, at least during the major period of the exodus. There is no estimate of clandestine departures.

Kayes, ANM, 1 E 44. The data for 1909 include only two months, for 1910, only three months.

Kita, ANM, 1 E 48. Data are complete only for 1909. The figure for 1907 refers only to February. The annual report for 1909 estimates that there were about 4,000 clandestine departures.

Segou, ANM, 1 E 72. The 1907 data are for the first six months. Over 10,000 departures are estimated to have occurred by April 1908. After that, no statistics are available.

from those societies that were harshest in their exploitation of slave labor (see table 7.4). "That which is emptying Muslim centers like Segou," a missionary wrote, "has caused no difficulty in our Bambara villages in the bush" (AWF, *Chroniques*, Banankorou, Nov. 1907). Migration was also greatest among those who remembered an earlier home. From the first, a significant group had no desire to leave the regions where they had long lived but wanted to farm for themselves. Thus in Nioro, as early as 1910, freedmen were setting up separate villages in new locations (ANSOM 1910). We can also assume that the young, the strong, and the most daring were most likely to leave. Those afraid of uncertainty found it safer to remain. Yet some people tracked down missing relatives, found them, and brought them home.

Those who remained faced a complex process of negotiating new social relationships. With the end of slaving and slave trading, masters could no longer replace slave losses. Furthermore, increasing demands on the slaves could only force them out. Thus, there seems to have been a tendency for freedmen to establish control over both their productive activity and their offspring. In this, the experience in the Sudan resembled that of the Americas (Foner 1983). The question of control over children was the most frequent source of conflict in the emancipation process. Masters sometimes tried to seize the children of fleeing parents, but the administration generally came down on the side of the parents.

The masters won other battles. A Soninke informant told Pollet and Winter: "Today, among the Soninke, the slaves can do anything but forget that they are slaves" (Pollet and Winter 1971:259) Oliver de Sardan (1984:201) makes a similar assertion. Deprived of the support of the state, masters struggled to maintain social and economic hegemony. They were most successful where they could establish control over scarce land (Cissé 1978). They were also successful in the desert and desert-fringe areas, where slavery-based social relations were shattered only with the drought years of the 1970s and 1980s. In other areas, they used control over Islam to maintain social ascendancy. In many places, no person of slave descent can become an imam, and the descendant of a slave is expected to "buy" freedom before making the pilgrimage to Mecca. In some areas, class struggle involved such symbolic acts as the obligation of former slaves to engage in licentious dances, to cook at weddings and funerals, and to run errands. Michael Samuel describes a revolt of Soninke "slaves" who refused to do all of the cooking in a migrant hostel in Paris (Samuel 1976:101–19). In economic terms, the obligations of the former slaves were often reduced to token gifts, such as several bunches of millet (Olivier de Sardan 1984).

Conclusion

In 1915 two peasants showed up at the office of the administrator of Matam in Senegal dragging a third peasant, who was tied up. They had been asked to provide a recruit for the French army. None of their sons wanted to go, so they went out and bought a slave (ANS 1915). The fact that they could easily do so suggests that change was not as profound as Ponty liked to claim in his letters to his superiors. In some areas, slaves could be bought up to the end of the colonial period (Maugham 1961). Ponty had not tried to abolish slavery. He had merely tried to distance the state from it. He also wanted to reduce the power of the large slave owners and to create a reservoir of labor. It is a measure of Ponty's success that scholars find it difficult to do research on slavery during the interwar years. As far as the colonial state was concerned, slavery was finished and consequently was rarely mentioned in any official correspondence. Only after World War II did a more open and progressive group of administrators discover that they still had a problem.

After the dust had settled, something less than a free labor market existed. To the degree that slaves were emancipated, it was because they saw the possibility and grabbed it. In doing so, they destroyed slavery as a system of economic exploitation. In the process, some did reasonably well economically. Those who left were free and were often more open to opportunity than their one-time masters. Those who stayed often found themselves caught up in a dependent relationship. For them, emancipation involved a struggle that often lasted generations. Outside of the desert, most rapidly gained control of their reproductive lives, but they remained economically and socially dependent. Not surprisingly, while individual noble families were destroyed by the loss of their human capital, many of the masters did well. This is particularly true of Muslim commercial elites like the Banamba Maraka, who used Islam to maintain their ideological hegemony and used commerce to create new wealth. It is also true of elites like the Masina Fulbe, who were able to make the transition from control over persons to control over land.

Notes

1. The source of these figures is the study of slavery done by the French colonial administration in early 1904. The figures have been checked against later census data and surveys by French social scientists. See Klein 1987.

2. The term *slave society* is Moses Finley's (1968). I prefer to speak of slave modes of production, because such accumulations resulted from slave labor's becoming the basis of the system of production. In societies with large concentrations of slaves, slave labor produced the surplus on which the privileges of the elite and the functioning of the state depended.

3. David Robinson believes that the high concentration of slaves in the Futa Toro is explained not by the river trade but by the return of slave-owning Futanke, who served the Umarian states and were expelled by the French after the conquest of Kaarta and Segou in 1890 and 1891.

4. From the moment of the creation of a Catholic antislavery movement in 1888, the Church and its representatives became prime movers in slavery questions. There is almost no literature available on the post-1848 antislavery movement in France or on the clerical-anticlerical division within it. On the founder, however, see Renault 1971.

5. This paragraph is based on interviews conducted by the author in 1989. The tapes have been deposited at the Institut des Sciences Humaines in Bamako.

References

Periodicals

BCAF   Bulletin du Comité de l'Afrique Française
JOAOF   Journal Officiel de l'Afrique Occidentale Française
JORF   Journal Officiel de la République Française
MS   Moniteur du Sénégal

Archival Sources

ANG: Archives Nationales de la Guinée, Conakry.
  1910: Political Report, Mamou, April 1910. 7 G 63.
  1914: Administrator Dinguiraye to Lieutenant Governor, April 26, 1914. 2 D 75.
ANM: Archives Nationales du Mali, Bamako.
  1887: Commandant Bafoulabé to Commandant Kayes, August 2, 1887. 1 E 168.
  1889: Commercial reports. 1 Q 70.
  1894a: Commandant Northeast to Governor Sudan, April 25, 1894. 1 E 177.

1894b: Commandant Nioro to Commandant Supérieur, July 2, 1894. 1 E 164.
1894c: Commandant Supérieur to Governor Sudan, January 23, 1894. 1 E 191.
1894d: Commandant Northeast to Governor Sudan, August 4, 1894. 1 E 177.
1895a: General Order 301, June 29, 1895. 1 E 183.
1895b: Minister to Governor General, December 5, 1895. 1 E 232.
1897: Circular 92, March 17, 1897. 1 E 183.
1898: Political Report, Bafoulabé, December 1898. 1 E 16.
1899a: Political Report, Kayes, March 2, 1899. 1 E 44.
1899b: Political Report, Kita, March 1899. 1 E 47.
1899c: Annual Report, Bamako. 1 E 19.
1901: Circular, February 1, 1901. A 20.
1903: Annual Report, Bougouni, 1903. 1 E 27.
1906: Circular, June 25, 1906. 1 E 182.
ANS: Archives Nationales du Sénégal, Dakar.
1855: Decree of October 18, 1855. K 11.
1857a: Confidential Circular of November 14, 1857. K 11.
1857b: Decree of December 5, 1857. K 11.
1885a: Journal, Bakel, 1885–86. 13 G 185.
1885b: Dr. Collomb to Commandant des Cercles, March 4, 1885. 13 G 185.
1888: Order 185, December 18, 1888. 15 G 154.
1889a: Governor to Minister, February 5, 1889. K 12.
1889b: Governor to Minister, December 18, 1889. K 12.
1893a: Order 120, May 3, 1893. 15 G 155.
1893b: Administrator Sine-Saloum to Governor Senegal, September 27, 1893. K 13.
1894a: Administrator Dakar-Thiès to Director of Political Affairs, April 21, 1894.
        K 13.
1894b: Governor to Diverse Administrators, September 11, 1894. 15 G 142.
1894c: Governor Sudan to Commandant East, September 24, 1894. 15 G 168.
1895: Administrator Sine-Saloum to Governor General, October 1895. 13 G 325.
1898: Commandant Médine to Commandant Kayes, August 24, 1898. 15 G 116.
1899a: Circular 87, January 27, 1899. 15 G 162.
1899b: Commandant Kaedi to Director of Native Affairs, December 30, 1899. Fonds
        Sénégal, 2 D 136.
1902: Monthly Political Report, Segou, April 1902. 2 G 2/6.
1903a: Circular to all administrators, October 11, 1903. K 15.
1903b: Merlin letter with new law code. November 1903. K 16.
1904a: Reports on Slavery. K 18.
1904b: Commandant Niani-Ouli to Secretary General, June 24, 1904. 2 D 136.
1904c: Secretary General Merlin to Lieutenant Governors, no. 72, August 1904.
        M 72.
1911: Governor General to British Consul, February 22, 1911. K 26.
1915: Administrator Matam to Lieutenant Governor, Senegal. 13 G.
Conseil Général, Débats
ANSOM: Archives Nationales, France, Section Outre Mer, Aix en Provence.
1848: Minister to Governor, October 26, 1848. Sénégal XIV 15a.

1849a: Governor to Minister, February 3, 1849. Sénégal XIV 15a.
1849b: Report of April 18, 1849. Sénégal XIV 15 a.
1894: Governor to Minister, July 18, 1894. Soudan XIV 1.
1895a: Governor to Minister, January 10, 1895. Soudan I 7.
1895b: Governor to Minister, July 8, 1895. Soudan XIV 1.
1895c: Governor General to Minister, December 5, 1895. AOF XIV 1.
1900: Minister to all governors, January 6, 1900. Sénégal XIV 28.
1903: Circular, December 10, 1903. Sénégal XIV 28.
1910: Governor General to Minister, no. 2734, September 28, 1910.
AWF: Archives of the White Fathers, Rome.
    Diaires, Segou, March 12, 1897; May 31, 1898
    Chroniques, Banankorou, November 1907
PRO: Public Record Office, Banjul

Other Sources

Baillaud, Emile. 1902. *Sur les routes du Soudan*. Toulouse: Privat.

Barrows, Leland. 1974. General Faidherbe, the Maurel and Prom Company, and French Expansion in Senegal. Ph.D. diss., UCLA.

Barrows, Leland. 1978. Louis Léon Cesar Faidherbe (1818–1889). In *African proconsuls*, ed. Lewis Gann and Peter Duignan. New York: Free Press.

Barry, Boubacar. 1972. *Le royaume de Waalo*. Paris: Maspero.

Barry, Boubacar. 1988. *La Sénéqambie du XVe au XIX siècle*. Paris: Harmattan.

Barry, Ismail. 1971. Contribution a l'étude de l'histoire de la Guinée: Le Hubbu du Fitaba et les almami du Futa. Memoire de maitrise, Institut Polytechnique Julius Nyerere, Kankan.

Benoist, Joseph-Roger de. 1987. *Eglise et pouvoir colonial au Soudan Français*. Paris: Karthala.

Bernus, E. 1960. Kong et sa region. *Etudes Eburnéennes* 8:239–324.

Bouche, Denise. 1968. *Les villages de liberté en Afrique Noire Française, 1887–1910*. Paris: Mouton.

Cissé, Salmana. 1978. L'esclavage "domestique" dans la partie Gourma du Moyen Niger (Mali): Structure Sociale et comportement de classe. Thèse du 3e cycle. Université de Paris-VII.

Copans, Jean. 1980. *Les marabouts de l'arachide, la confrérie mouride et les paysans du Senegal*. Paris: Sycamore.

Coulon, Christian. 1981. *Le marabout et le prince*. Paris: Pedone.

Cruise O'Brien, Donal. 1971. *The Mourides of Senegal*. Oxford: Oxford University Press.

Curtin, Philip. 1975. *Economic change in precolonial Africa: Senegambia in the era of the slave trade*. Madison: University of Wisconsin Press.

David, Philippe. 1980. *Les Navetanes: Histoire de migrants saisoniers de l'arachide en Sénégambie des origines à nos jours*. Dakar: Nouvelles Editions Africaines.

Delaunay, Daniel. 1984. *De la captivité à l'exil: Histoire et démographie de migrations paysannes dans la Moyenne Vallée du fleuve Sénégal*. Paris: ORSTOM.

Derrick, Jonathan. 1975. *African slaves today*. London: George Allen and Unwin.

Diouf, Mamadou. 1990. Le Kajoor au XIXe siècle. Paris: Karthala.

Echenberg, Myron. 1986. Slaves into soldiers: Social origins of the Tirailleurs Senegalais. In *Africans in bondage*, ed. Paul Lovejoy. Madison, Wis.: African Studies Program.

Echenberg, Myron. 1991. *Soldiers of empire: France and the African tirailleur army, 1857–1960*. London: Heinemann.

Finley, Moses. 1968. Slavery. In *International encyclopedia of the social sciences* 14:307–13. New York: Macmillan.

Foner, Eric. 1983. *Nothing but freedom: Emancipation and its legacy*. Baton Rouge: Louisiana State University Press.

Gallais, Jean. 1967. *Le delta intérieur du Niger*, 2 vols. Dakar: IFAN.

Ghomsi, Emmanuel. 1968. Le gouverneur Albert Grodet au Soudan Français (Novembre 1893 à Juin 1895). Memoire de maitrise, Université de Dakar.

Gueye, Mbaye. 1966. "La fin de l'esclavage à St. Louis et à Gorée en 1848." *Bulletin de l'IFAN* 28:637–56.

Hansen, John. 1989. Umarian Karta (Mali, West Africa) during the late nineteenth century: Dissent and revolt among the Futanke after Umar Tal's holy war. Ph.D. diss., Michigan State University.

Idowu, H. O. 1968. The establishment of elective institutions in Senegal, 1869–1920. *Journal of African History* 9:261ff.

Johnson, G. Wesley. 1978. William Ponty and republican paternalism in French West Africa (1866–1915). In *African proconsuls*, ed. Lewis Gann and Peter Duignan. New York: Free Press.

Johnson, Marion. 1976. Economic foundations of an Islamic theocracy: The case of Macina. *Journal of African History* 17:481–95.

Kanya-Forstner, A. S. 1969. *The conquest of the western Soudan: A study of French military imperialism*. Cambridge: Cambridge University Press.

Klein, Martin A. 1968. *Islam and imperialism in Senegal: Sine-Saloum, 1847–1914*. Stanford, Calif.: Stanford University Press.

Klein, Martin A. 1977. Servitude among the Wolof and Sereer of Senegambia. In *Slavery in Africa*, ed. Suzanne Miers and Igor Kopytoff. Madison: University of Wisconsin Press.

Klein, Martin A. 1983a. Women in slavery in the western Sudan. In *Women and slavery in Africa*, ed. Claire C. Robertson and Martin A. Klein. Madison: University of Wisconsin Press.

Klein, Martin A. 1983b. From slave to share-cropper: An effort at controlled social change in the French Soudan. *Itinerario* 8:102–15.

Klein, Martin A. 1987. The demography of slavery in the western Soudan during the late 19th century. In *African population and capitalism: Historical perspectives*, ed. Dennis Cordell and Joel Gregory. Boulder: Westview.

Klein, Martin A. 1988. Slave resistance and slave emancipation in coastal Guinea. In *The end of slavery in Africa*, ed. Richard Roberts and Suzanne Miers. Madison: University of Wisconsin Press.

Klein, Martin A., and Paul Lovejoy. 1979. Slavery in West Africa. In *The uncommon* market: *Essays in the economic history of the Atlantic slave trade*, ed. H. A. Gemery and Jan Hogendorn. New York: Academic Press.

Lovejoy, Paul. 1983. *Transformations in slavery: A history of slavery in Africa*. Cambridge: Cambridge University Press.

McDougall, Ann. 1988. A topsy-turvy world: Slaves and freed slaves in the Mauritanian Adrar, 1910–1950. In *The end of slavery in Africa*, ed. Suzanne Miers and Richard S. Roberts. Madison: University of Wisconsin Press.

McDougall, Ann. 1990. Banamba and the salt trade of the western Sudan. In *West African economic and social history: studies in memory of Marion Johnson*, ed. David Henige and T. C. McCaskie. Madison, Wis.: African Studies Program.

Marty, Paul. 1920. *Etudes sur l'Islam et les Tribus du Soudan*. 4 vols. Paris: Leroux.

Meillassoux, Claude. 1971. Commerce précoloniale. In *The development of indigenous trade and markets in West Africa*, ed. Claude Meillassoux. London: Oxford University Press.

Meillassoux, Claude. 1975a. Esclavage à Goumbou. In *L'esclavage en Afrique precoloniale*. *See* Meillassoux 1975b.

Meillassoux, Claude, ed. 1975b. *L'esclavage en Afrique precoloniale*. Paris: Maspero.

Meillassoux, Claude. 1986. *Anthropologie de l'esclavage: Le ventre de fer et d'argent*. Paris: PUF.

Miers, Suzanne. 1975. *Britain and the ending of the slave trade*. New York: Africana.

Miers, Suzanne, and Igor Kopytoff, eds. 1977. *Slavery in Africa*. Madison: University of Wisconsin Press.

Miller, Joseph. 1981. Lineages, ideology and the history of slavery in western central Africa. In *The ideology of slavery in Africa*, ed. Paul Lovejoy. Beverly Hills: Sage.

Moitt, Bernard. 1983. Peanut production and social change in the Dakar hinterland: Kajoor and Bawol, 1840–1940. Ph.D. diss., University of Toronto.

Moitt, Bernard. 1989. Slavery and emancipation in Senegal's peanut basin: The nineteenth and twentieth centuries. *International Journal of African Historical Studies* 22:27–50.

Moitt, Bernard. N.d. From slavery to guardianship in Senegal: Minors in *tutelle*, 1848–1905. Unpublished manuscript.

N'Diaye, Francine. 1968. La colonie du Sénégal au temps de Brière de l'Isle (1876–1881). *Bulletin de l'Institut Français d'Afrique Noire* 30:463–512.

Olivier de Sardan, Jean-Pierre. 1975. Captifs ruraux et esclaves imperiaux du Songhay. In *L'esclavage en Afrique précoloniale*. *See* Meillassoux 1975b.

Olivier de Sardan, Jean-Pierre. 1984. *Les sociétés Songhay-Zarma (Niger-Mali)*. Paris: Karthala.

Pasquier, Roger. 1967. A propos de l'emancipation des esclaves au Sénégal en 1848. *Revue Française d'Histoire d'Outre-Mer* 54:188–208.

Pelissier, Paul. 1966. *Les paysans du Sénégal*. St. Yreix: Fabrègue.

Peroz, Etienne. 1889. *Au Soudan Français*. Paris.

Pollet, Eric, and Grace Winter. 1971. *La société Soninke*. Brussels: Editions de l'Institut de Sociologie, Université Libre de Bruxelles.

Renault, François. 1971. *Lavigerie, l'esclavage africain et l'Europe, 1868–1892.* 2 vols. Paris: Boccard.

Renault, François. 1972. *L'abolition de l'esclavage au Sénégal: L'attitude de l'administration française, 1848–1905.* Paris: Société Française de l'Histoire d'Outre-Mer.

Roberts, Richard. 1980. The emergence of a grain market in Bamako, 1883–1908. *Canadian Journal of African Studies* 14:37–54.

Roberts, Richard. 1984. Women's work and women's property: Household social relations in the Maraka textile industry in the nineteenth century. *Comparative Studies in Society and History* 26:229–50.

Roberts, Richard. 1987. *Warriors, merchants, and slaves: The state and the economy in the Middle Niger Valley, 1700–1914.* Stanford, Calif.: Stanford University Press.

Roberts, Richard. 1988. The end of slavery in the French Soudan, 1905–1914. In *The end of slavery in Africa*, ed. Suzanne Miers and Richard Roberts. Madison: University of Wisconsin Press.

Roberts, Richard, and Martin A. Klein. 1980. The Banamba slave exodus of 1905 and the decline of slavery in the western Sudan. *Journal of African History* 21:375–94.

Robinson, David. 1985. *The holy war of Umar Tal: The western Sudan in the mid-nineteenth century.* Oxford: Oxford University Press.

Samuel, Michel. 1976. Les contradictions internes à la paysannerie continuent à agir au sein de la migration en France. In *Capitalisme Négrier: La marche des Paysans vers le Prolétariat*, ed. Pierre-Philippe Rey. Paris: Maspero.

Schoelcher, Victor. 1880. *L'esclavage au Sénégal en 1880.* Paris: H. E. Martin.

Schoelcher, Victor. 1882. *Polemiques coloniales.* Paris: Dentu.

Suret-Canale, Jean. 1971. *French colonialism in tropical Africa.* New York: Pica.

Webb, James. 1985. The trade in gum arabic: Prelude to French conquest in Senegal. *Journal of African History* 26:149–68.

Webb, James L. 1986. Shifting sands: An economic history of the Mauritanian Sahara, 1500–1850. Ph.D. diss. Johns Hopkins University.

8 *Mohamed Mbodj*

The Abolition of Slavery in Senegal, 1820–1890: Crisis or the Rise of a New Entrepreneurial Class?

Studies of the abolition of the slave trade and of slavery in Africa often focus on the political consequences of abolition. When they deal with the social and economic questions, they rarely take a long view. Many nineteenth-century authors writing on Senegal, for example, limited themselves to a broad general view of economic problems and failed to analyze the data in detail. They also tended to see only the immediate aftermath of emancipation and thus failed to examine the larger patterns of change (Bouet-Willaumez 1848, 1852; Carrère and Holle 1855; Raffenel 1856; Faidherbe 1889). A later group of authors during the 1960s and 1970s provided more detail in their explanation of the mechanisms at work during emancipation and their consequences for the second half of the nineteenth century (Gueye 1966; Pasquier 1967), as well as for the development of the colonial economic system (Amin 1969). This literature argues that a profound economic crisis occurred from 1817, which ended with the displacement of local merchants by metropolitan entrepreneurs. Abolition is thus seen as part of a crisis which created many of the characteristics of the twentieth-century colonial economy, and local slave owners are viewed as prisoners of the local economic situation who submitted passively to colonial policy. Thus, the conjunction of political and economic realities is seen as having been unfavorable to them from 1817 to 1890, if not throughout the nineteenth and twentieth centuries.

I would like to call into question a good part of this vision or, at a minimum, to introduce some very strong qualifications. I believe that the crisis was less profound and that the former slave owners still possessed a great deal of initiative at the end of the nineteenth century. The fluctuations of colonial policy, the penetration by the French of the markets of the Senegambian interior, and the development of the peanut trade rendered the postemancipation crisis less dramatic and provided improved opportunities for Senegalese traders. Many local entrepreneurs made the transition from slave trade to commodity trade with ease, and some even increased their fortunes, especially in transport. In most cases, local entrepreneurs preserved an intermediary role essential to metropolitan capital. Most important, the former slave owners maintained control of the labor of their former slaves through the control of wage employment. Of course they had problems, caused, for example, by the bitter competition among local businessmen, their inability to control commodity prices, which were set in Europe, the lack of specie, the increasing importance of European industrial products, and the persistence of the system which gave French nationals a monopoly in commerce. In the economic crisis, local entrepreneurs, especially the former slave owners of St. Louis and Gorée, were not eliminated. On the contrary, they increased their power because they continued to control the supply of labor.[1]

At the beginning of the nineteenth century the French colonial empire in Africa consisted essentially of St. Louis, Gorée, and several posts like Bakel on the upper Senegal River and Albreda at the mouth of the Gambia. By 1890 French control had been established over most of what is now Senegal. I will limit myself to those territories under French authority when slavery was abolished in 1848, because this was a homogeneous area for which excellent documentation exists. This area was almost identical to that which the French controlled at the beginning of the nineteenth century.

In looking at St. Louis and Gorée, we must distinguish between domestic slavery and trade slavery. The trade slave was purchased to be sold, while the domestic slave was not for sale. Many of the trade slaves brought into the colony, however, were not sold and were absorbed among the domestic slaves. In my usage, domestic slaves are those, either born or introduced into St. Louis and Gorée, who remained in the service of their masters either within or outside the towns. This slave population was completely black. It was mostly Muslim in St. Louis and Christian in Gorée, since the slaves in each case adopted the religion of their masters. In town, most of the slaves worked as artisans, as domestic servants, or as crew members on the boats that went upriver or along the coast. In the interior, they were agricultural laborers and provided the bulk of the army and administration of the various states, especially the Wolof.

Slaves were owned by free persons at all social levels. There were three important groups of slave owners: Senegalese male traders, a group of female entrepreneurs known as *signares*, and the *pileuses*, who prepared food. The traders were Senegalese, sometimes of servile origin, who were able to stake out a middle position for themselves during the period of the slave trade. They were mostly Muslim along the Senegal River and Catholic along the coast. They traded from their boats, which gave them a flexibility the female traders lacked. The signares gained their power when French officials and Senegalese women formed temporary liaisons called *mariages à la mode du pays*. During the period of the slave-trading monopoly companies, these officials were not allowed to trade for themselves, but they circumvented this prohibition through their Senegalese "wives." Many of the Frenchmen died of various tropical maladies, leaving the signares with boats, trade goods, and urban property, which many managed shrewdly. The male offspring of these marriages either went into trade or worked for the colonial administration. Finally, the pileuses, or "pounders," prepared millet for workers in town or on board boats. Originally servile, they often became petty entrepreneurs and frequently owned slaves.

Abolition of the Slave Trade

The slave-trading and slave-using societies of the interior found it difficult to understand the abolition first of the trade in 1817 and then of slavery itself in 1848. Their former European trading partners had taken these actions for philanthropic and economic reasons that Africans could not accept (Coupland 1933; Martin 1948; Williams 1944). Africans felt that the rules of their traditional life had been called into question by initiatives which destabilized the bases of their society. Each of these acts, the prohibition of the trade from 1817 and the abolition of slavery in 1848, produced a crisis.

When France regained its Senegambian trading stations in 1817 after the Napoleonic wars, it had two obligations concerning the slave trade. First, England had insisted on prohibition of the trade in the Treaty of Paris of 1815. In fact, the trade was already abolished at these posts. England had occupied Gorée from 1800 and St. Louis from 1809 and had banned the trade in those locations in 1808. It was thus difficult for France to regress, especially since the three French trading posts in the region, St. Louis, Gorée, and Albreda, were all prosperous. Free trade, the extension of commercial transactions in the interior, and the development of a commerce in new products such as gum arabic inspired this prosperity (Barry 1972; Pasquier 1983; Webb 1985). An illegal Atlantic slave trade, however, persisted in Senegambia and did not end definitively until 1831 (Daget 1986).

The arsenal of laws used to suppress the trade was extensive: four acts between 1817 and 1831. The last two acts were the most important. An 1823 decree made it illegal to bring captives to St. Louis and Gorée unless they came in as indentured laborers, that is to say, as freed persons. This decree permitted French citizens to bring slaves they had purchased to St. Louis and Gorée. Slaves were then freed on the condition that they accepted fourteen-year contracts. During this period they worked for their new masters (*BAS* 1831). An 1831 law made it illegal to either introduce slaves into the colony or to ship them out (*BAS* 1831). These measures were not immediately effective because officials often demonstrated ill will in applying them (Kane 1984).

France and England ended the Atlantic trade, but the trade within Senegambia remained active until the end of the nineteenth century. A major factor was the continued existence of slavery at French posts. This made possible the maintenance and renewal of large stocks of slaves in the interior and in areas near French possessions, often with the cooperation of local rulers. Those slaves who remained within the trading stations were used in diverse crafts and in trade. As traders, they played a major role in the expansion of commercial relations between French possessions and the rest of the region. The artisans in the towns, the sailors and soldiers, and even many of the traders were slaves. Thus, Gorée in 1825 had 237 slave owners and free traders, but 235 slaves were also licensed to trade. The slaves without a doubt constituted a majority of the traders, because the free slave owners were certainly not all traders (ANS, 22 G 4, 1825). Those slaves who commanded boats or were entrusted with responsibility for trading stations were a relatively privileged group, capable of accumulating wealth and living in comfort. Unfortunately, archival sources only provide information about the social origins of Gorean merchants for 1825. The system of indentured labor also perpetuated the institution, because the indentured laborers were indistinguishable from slaves (Zuccarelli 1962). The end of the slave trade increased the servile presence in the colony. Thus, in Gorée in 1767 slaves constituted 69 percent of the population, but that increased to 81 percent in 1823 and 83 percent in 1832 (Sané 1978). The abolition of slavery in 1848 had much greater consequences because it destroyed the institution itself (Gueye 1966).

Abolition and Local Entrepreneurs

On April 27, 1848, a decree of the French National Assembly abolished slavery in all French possessions. By this time French dominion had been established at a series of posts along the various rivers of the region: Merinaghène on Lake Guiers; Dagana, Bakel, and Sénoudébou on the Senegal; Albreda on the Gambia; and Sédhiou on the Casamance. The decree did not affect slavery in neighboring territories, either independent or under French protection. Slave owners exploited this fact, though they could no longer benefit from the labor of slaves within Gorée or St. Louis. Masters used a series of solutions suggested by an administration anxious not to disturb the regional economic system (Renault 1972). These mostly involved the use of servile labor and its renewal. Some slaves were sold or moved to villages outside French territory, where they could be exploited as farm laborers. Just outside the towns, especially near St. Louis, slaves could be used to grow food crops for the growing urban market. They could also be trained as apprentices or could engage in artisanal activities, particularly in cloth production. In addition, a system was developed whereby children could be purchased in the interior, "freed," and then adopted.

The slave owners also received what many of them considered a very low indemnity: 330.15 francs for each slave freed. Between 1830 and 1841 the price of a slave averaged 744 francs (ANS, 2 B 31, 1852; Sané 1978). Instead of accepting the promised indemnity, many slave owners settled their slaves on the mainland either as cultivators or traders. Those who did so lost two of their best sources of revenue: skilled labor in town and service on the river fleet. The situation was made more difficult because those redeemed and freed had a tendency to remain where they were and to continue their traditional activities for their own profit. The crisis was particularly difficult between 1848 and 1852. Many slave owners responded to the low indemnity by selling their rights at a loss rather than waiting out the formalities necessary to convert their property into bonds from the Bank of Senegal. Others gave these rights to their creditors or mortgaged them (Pasquier 1983:157). These transactions took place over a short period of time and in an atmosphere reminiscent of a fire sale from December 1849 to December 1851 for St. Louis and from February 1851 to December 1852 for Gorée (Pasquier 1967:201). The atmosphere was determined by the economic conjuncture, but also by the massive flight of slaves (426 in 1848 alone), by the departure of slave owners to the mainland with their slaves, and by the arrogance of the recently freed (Gueye 1966:641–45; Ka 1981:51). These sales proved especially beneficial to the European commercial houses, the major purchasers, who profited from the transactions to establish their control over the Bank of Senegal. Many authors see this as the moment when metropolitan domination was established over the Senegalese economy and the power of the African bourgeoisie was destroyed (Amin 1969; Pasquier 1967). They forget that such transactions only involved 1,575 slaves out of 10,075 (15.6 percent) and that the indemnification involved only 6,703 slaves (66.5%) (ANS, 2 B 31, 1852). These transactions thus constituted only one important aspect of economic evolution from 1848 to 1855, but not a decisive one.

Redemption by the slaves themselves or settlement on the mainland was more important. Self-redemption meant that the slaves were freed not only in the eyes of French law but also within their own society, and thus they could move more freely. Settlement on the mainland involved two very different kinds of slaves, farm laborers and commercial agents who were the trusted representatives of St. Louis and Gorée traders. Thus Bouet-Willaumez reported that from Gorée to the Gambia "on almost every point . . . there were black traders from Gorée established in native villages without any protection other than their French nationality" (1848:61) The tendency to settle on the mainland thus seems to have been significant, though we have no statistics on the actual number. We can get some idea by examining the number of inhabitants in St. Louis. Archival sources mention a definite increase in population, although available data indicate a rather slow rate of growth (table 8.1). The most important data are thus not quantitative. We must make a qualitative analysis based on the new relations of production of the former slaves and the commercial networks linked to those new relationships. The movement of slaves out of St. Louis and the growth of slave-based production in areas near the town probably meant that population growth was greater there than within St. Louis.

The masters developed another strategy based on the indenture system. They purchased young children in the interior, freed them, and accepted responsibility for raising them before a guardianship council in St. Louis. Under law, these children were wards and not slaves, but they met the demand for domestic servants and apprentices. Once grown up, they could be either sold in the interior or kept in St. Louis, since the guardianship council set up in 1849 exercised no actual supervision.

Within the administration, periods of abolitionist fervor occurred, but without significant results. There was a particular acceleration when emancipation was decreed in Dakar in 1877 and in Rufisque in 1879 (ANS, K 12). A press campaign and a major speech by abolitionist senator Victor Schoelcher (Schoelcher 1880:56–59) also pushed the administration to make some changes. From 1875 to 1881 between 350 and 674 slaves were freed each year. From 1881 to 1889 the number fluctuated between 1,058 and 2,198 per year (Renault 1972:37). In 1890, the administration decided to move against the trade by signing conventions with protectorate chiefs forbidding the resale of slaves, who thus all became domestic slaves (ANS, K 12).

Abuses continued even after 1890. Finally, in 1903 the French administration decided that all individuals were free by right (Renault 1972:56–59). This left to slaves the decision to remain, to leave, or to reorganize their relations with their masters. Slavery no longer had a juridical base, and time was expected to widen the breach in the system. At the same time, the adoption of minors was suppressed, and the administration took charge of the children. France was able at this time to fight more vigorously against the trade because of the control it had established over its colonial domain (Gueye 1966). Thus, between 1890 and 1905 the slave system essentially withered away.

Table 8.1. Population of St. Louis, 1817–1900

Year	Population	Slaves and former slaves	Percentage
1817	9,000	–	–
1837	12,137	6,061	49.9
	17,641	10,096	57.2
1850	12,336	6,651	53.9
1869	15,480	–	–
1894	19,160	–	–
1900	20,173	–	–

Sources: Zuccarelli 1962:437–48; Mbaye 1974:92; Boilat 1853:207; Camara 1968:64–65; Courtet 1903:141. The first set of numbers for 1837 are from Zuccarelli; the second, from Mbaye.

Slave Labor and Wage Labor

The length of the abolition process suggests either that the former masters had little power or that the former slaves were weak, and perhaps both at the same time. Relations of servitude at the beginning of the century were transformed into patron-client relations toward the end. A community once founded on the authority of the master evolved into one based on access to training, housing, and wage employment. In analyzing this evolution, we see how the former slave owners were able to control salaried labor in Gorée and St. Louis up to the end of the nineteenth century, successfully transforming themselves into intermediaries necessary to both employers and employees. In 1894, when the governor of Guiana requested four thousand laborers from Senegal, he asked explicitly that former slave owners and not the administration take charge of recruitment (ANS, K 30).

Control of Apprenticeship

If we examine the deployment of labor, we see that slaves monopolized certain activities from 1820 to 1830 (table 8.2). For example, at Gorée in 1825 they constituted 89.1 percent of all workers counted. More precisely, slaves were 50 percent of all those who engaged in commerce; 75 percent of the blacksmiths; 86 percent of the cooks; between 90 and 96 percent of the masons, sailors, carpenters, and cabinet-makers; and virtually all of the coopers, leather workers, bakers, weavers, tailors, dressmakers, and domestic servants (ANS, 22 G 4, 1825). These data can only be compared with those of Courtet (1903:1) on St. Louis in 1900. Courtet, however, does not give data on origins.[2] A comparison of the 1825 and 1900 data shows that with a population

Table 8.2. Craft skills of workers at Gorée and St. Louis, 1825–1900

| Occupation | Gorée (1825) | | | St. Louis | |
	Free	Slave	Total	Totals, 1837	Totals, 1900
Landlords and merchants	237	–	237	–	–
Trader	–	235	235	–	–
Carpenter	10	198	208	115	227
Cabinetmaker	3	79	82	33	–
Mason	12	112	124	–	195
Sailor	30	508	538	–	–
Caulker	–	–	–	60	83
Blacksmith	16	47	63	15	95
Jeweler	–	–	–	–	42
Cooper	–	23	23	–	–
Harnessmaker, saddler	–	–	–	–	6
Leather worker	–	7	7	–	6
Baker	–	11	11	–	–
Cook	5	32	37	–	–
Weaver	–	229	229	320	42
Tailor	–	27	27	–	–
Dressmaker	–	2	2	–	–
Unskilled laborer	83	–	83	–	–
Laptot	–	–	–	–	–
Marabout	7	7	14	–	–
Servant	–	2,211	2,211	–	–
Indentured worker	17	–	17	–	–
Painter	–	–	–	–	14
Mechanic	–	–	–	–	36
Driver	–	–	–	–	110
Unclassified	73	300	373		
Total for 1825	493	4,028	4,521		

Sources: ARS, 22 G 4; Courtet 1903:141.

a fourth that of St. Louis in 1900, Gorée had more artisans in 1825. Gorée's number of artisans in 1825 also exceeded that of St. Louis in 1900. Slavery was clearly favorable to the development of a class of artisans, a class that dwindled as soon as it was no longer supported by the slave system. The masters organized enterprises that provided services (masonry or cabinetmaking controlled by men) or produced goods for the local market (weaving and smithing controlled by the signares).

This phenomenon is largely explained by the way artisans were integrated into the labor force. With the abolition of the slave trade and then of slavery itself, former masters used their control over access to artisanal skills to restrict apprenticeship to the children they had adopted. By placing these minors in apprenticeship in their workshops and enterprises, they guaranteed themselves a free supply of labor and at the same time controlled the market for future workers. They were able to do this largely because of the permissiveness of the colonial administration, which did not seek to protect apprentices from exploitation. This quasi monopoly over the training of craftworkers ended only toward the end of the century, when the development of peanut-trading networks increasingly transferred workers from one area to another. Then in 1903 the Ecole Professionnelle Pinet-Laprade was founded on Gorée to provide training in various crafts.

Control of Urban Housing

Control over the labor force was maintained through control over the laborers themselves. Given that space was not free in the colony, that lots for construction were rare, and that the investment demanded was large, former slave owners only needed to control housing in order to channel social mobility and migratory movement and, thus, the stock of workers, former slaves or newcomers, in the urban labor market. This control was exercised through the management of urban property and the monopoly of construction enterprises. Urban property on Gorée and St. Louis had been developed from the seventeenth century. By the middle of the nineteenth century these two small islands were completely covered with buildings. Urbanization began to extend onto the mainland with the filling-in of marshes to the north of St. Louis. Buildings were owned by traders or by signares, and even the administration was forced to pay rent for buildings housing public services. According to Raffenel, St. Louis landowners were pocketing a million francs a year in rents by 1850 (1856:181). Although a lively market in urban property existed, transactions took place largely among the same group of people. Only toward the end of the century did the administration and metropolitan interests open a breach in local control of urban property. This patrimony was maintained and extended thanks to construction enterprises, which were staffed largely by workers of servile origin. Slave labor clearly played a major part in the construction of the port and city of Dakar, and the French authorities were aware of it (Gov. Sen. to Com. Gorée, Feb. 22, 1865, ANS, K 11). Also important was St. Louis, which doubled its population during the nineteenth century.

In 1825 the population of St. Louis was lodged in about 880 brick buildings and more than 2,000 straw huts (ANS, 22 G 4, 1825). In 1871 the only difference was that most of the buildings were of brick (Dupère 1871:55). The same was true in 1882. A housing crisis was evident in 1882, when the governor wrote that "in St. Louis, most houses are refuges which shelter an unbelievable number of individuals: courtyards, ground-floor flats, even the space beneath staircases are inhabited, each room housing as many as twenty individuals" (ANS, 2 B 74, 1882:131). Construction enterprises concentrated on transforming huts into brick buildings. Freed slaves who founded families tended to move to Ndar Toute, a new quarter north of St. Louis, or to Sor on the mainland. The improvement of the infrastructure made these movements possible: in particular, the northern part of the island, where Ndar Toute was built, was drained, and a bridge to the mainland was built. Former slave owners, however, gained control of many of the new properties. Only toward the very end of the century did the changes in the infrastructure lower rents by 40 percent (Pasquier 1960:421). Up to that time, control of housing contributed to control of the labor market by the former slave owners.

Transport

If control of housing was a major asset for the St. Louis bourgeoisie, transport and the peanut-marketing network were important in both Gorée and St. Louis. Local traders helped develop peanut production, first in the Gambia, then in the Casamance and on the Petite Côte (ANS, 13 G 315, 13 G 375). Goreans were the most active (Boilat 1853; United Kingdom 1827, 1842), but St. Louisians developed areas further north from about 1860. Both archival and oral sources designate the traders as the major actors up to 1880 and then, with the penetration of European firms, as the major intermediaries. Thus, their monopoly lasted until about 1890.

During the colonial period they were not able to maintain their position. Their domination between 1820 and 1890 rested on three pillars. First, they had participated in trade along the coast at least as far back as the seventeenth century. They knew the regions where navigation was difficult, and they knew the peoples and their varied political systems. Thus, they maintained dependable patron-client ties, forged by trade and reinforced by slave commercial representatives kept in place even after the abolition of the trade. They controlled both the river and the coastal trade. Gorée alone had 538 sailors in 1825, 508 slaves and 30 free blacks (ANS, 22 G 4, 1825). Both St. Louis and Gorée were home to a large fleet of small, locally owned commercial craft. Cutters from Gorée worked the coastal trade almost as far south as Sierra Leone. From St. Louis a fleet of small boats traveled up the Senegal River to Bakel every year. In addition, numerous people used dugouts and other smaller boats to fish and to work the local trade. Both islands had boatyards that used mostly local materials, local woods for the ribbing and planking, and rope made from baobab bark for cord and nets. Sails, masts, hardware, brass instruments, pitch, and tar were imported from France. At Gorée, American fir was imported for the planking of the larger boats. These boats were of such good quality that the administration was not reluctant to arm them and integrate them into the fleet (ANS, MF8: 590). Shipbuilders remained active to the end of the 1870s, resisting for a while the introduction of steel hulls and steamboats (Ka 1981:96). The railroad and the truck only began to replace water transport after 1910 (Mbodj 1978). In the meantime, Senegalese traders gradually became transporters of commodities for other parties. The nature of shipping remained the same, and former slaves remained employed by their former owners. The low cost of shipbuilding and the absence of energy costs made local shipping very competitive throughout the nineteenth century. In 1818 a small steamboat cost 125,000 francs and consumed 26,000 francs per year in coal (ANS, MF8: 2). The largest schooners cost only 10,000 francs, and a cutter could be found for as little as 600 francs, with about the same size crew as a steamboat would require (Sané 1978). Thus, up to 1910 local entrepreneurs kept control of regional transport. This in turn proved decisive in the diffusion of the peanut, which meant that former slaves and their offspring found it advantageous to remain clients of their one-time masters.

Slave Salaries and Modern Salaries

One of the principal uses of slave labor at Gorée and St. Louis was as wage labor. In effect, slave owners rented out the services of their slaves. They kept a part of the slave's salary based on the cost of maintenance, the slave's wage level, and the slave's status, that is, whether the slave was fully enslaved, in the process of being freed, or already freed. Well after 1848 former slave owners, particularly the signares, continued to operate as placement agents. They were especially important in providing domestic servants and sailors for shipping on the river and along the coast. The major employer was the colony. In the eighteenth century it had been the Company of Senegal.

In 1820 a sailor employed by the government was paid 240 francs per year plus rations (ANS, MF8:470). His master kept half of his salary and provided lodging. Nothing seems to have changed, because sixty-two years later a sailor received a salary of 20 francs a month, of which his master kept half (ANS, 2 B 74, 1882: fol. 131). An indentured laborer hired by the government received only 5 francs a month plus rations. Thus, the indentured laborer found himself in conditions much more precarious than did the slave. An 1882 source indicates that the free laborer earned 1 to 1.5 francs per day, that is, 25 to 37.5 francs per month, with 15 francs going to the "signare" for food and lodging (ANS, 2 B 74, 1882: fol. 131). In 1903 wages still remained at 1 to 1.5 francs per day for the unskilled or semiskilled laborer (Courtet 1903:141). Thus, we see a strong similarity between the wages paid to slaves and those paid to free laborers during the second half of the nineteenth century.

In the first half of the nineteenth century the slave kept for himself 10 francs per month above and beyond the cost of food and lodging. The free worker of 1903 received 0.45 francs per day with rations or 1 to 1.5 francs per day without rations, thus 11.25 francs a month above and beyond the cost of food. Though we must be cautious about these figures, the slave owners seem to have been more successful in negotiating for their slaves than the free workers of a triumphant capitalism were in negotiating for themselves. In addition, the latter were not always sure of working, and thus of eating, unlike the slaves.

The liberation of the slaves therefore did not lead to the emergence of a free labor market based on wage labor. On the contrary, there was a tendency to retreat from this possibility because of the capacity of the former slave owners to adapt to the changed economic situation. Some visitors to Senegambia in the early twentieth century even spoke of the "reticence" to wage labor (ANS, K 32).

Conclusion

Slave owners evidently were able to change enough during the crisis of 1840 to 1860 that they remained prosperous through the 1890s. They did not disappear, but successfully kept their positions. The number of brick houses and boats they owned increased. The situation of entrepreneurs whose slaves specialized in the construction of housing and boats remained attractive. These entrepreneurs continued to control the urban labor market. They took the initiative in creating new posts along the southern coast. If the household of the average slave owner contained about thirty to forty slaves at the beginning of the nineteenth century, it rarely held more than twenty after 1850. This did not represent an impoverishment, but a redeployment, which enabled former slave owners to maintain their control over the labor market and the trade on the mainland. This successful reconversion is demonstrated by the strength of ties with former slaves. Thus, the bourgeoisie of St. Louis and Gorée successfully exploited the various abolitions.

Some jolts undermined and eventually destroyed the structure, however. From the time of Faidherbe, for example, the government began to build the buildings it needed and to develop urban sites. This reduced the value of the urban landholdings of former slave owners. The government also threatened their control of transport by creating a modern transport system and modern commerce by introducing industrial products which competed with the production of local artisans. This began in the 1860s, but the former slave owners only began to lose their ascendancy in the 1890s.

Notes

1. This study uses archival sources exceptional in Africa to supplement the existing literature. I have consulted the notarial archives of St. Louis and Gorée, series Z of the Archives Nationales du Sénégal (ANS). I have also consulted subseries 2 B (correspondence of the governor of Senegal), 3 G (Municipal Institutions), 13 G (Political Affairs), 22 G (Statistics and Census Data), and K (Slavery and Labor), as well as printed sources dealing with economic and social life, such as the *Bulletin Administratif du Sénégal* (1819–1908), the *Moniteur du Sénégal et Dépendances* (1856–87), and the *Journal Officiel du Sénégal* (from 1888). This written documentation has yet to be explored in depth. My effort here is only a first attempt. I have tried to supplement it with oral inquiries, particularly in coastal areas between Joal and Banjul.

2. Courtet also gives a somewhat different list of craft skills. He lists more, twenty-two instead of eighteen, and does not mention, probably because of the method of inquiry, traders, bakers, cooks, tailors, dressmakers, unskilled laborers, marabouts, and domestic servants. He adds, as a result of technical change, painters, mechanics, and drivers.

References

Archival Sources

ANS. Archives Nationales du Sénégal
  2 B: Correspondence of the Governor of Senegal
      2 B 31. Governor Protet to Navy Minister, 287 of June 8, 1852.
      2 B 74. Governor to Navy Minister, fol. 131.
  13 G: Political Affairs
      13 G 315. Correspondance Albreda, 1822–24.
      13 G 375. Correspondance Sédhiou, 1837–38.
  22 G: Statistics and Census Data
      22 G 4. Population of Gorée in 1825.
  K: Slavery and Labor
      K 11. Esclavage et Captivité, 1854–80.
      K 12. Esclavage et Captivité, 1881–92.
      K 13. Captivité au Sénégal, 1893–94.
      K 30. Captivité au Sénégal, 1878–94.
      K 32. Esclavage et Main-d'Oeuvre, 1906–14.
  MF: Microfilms
      MF8. Annales inédites de la flotille du Fleuve Sénégal de 1819 à 1854 par Delattre s.d.

Official Publications

Bulletin Administratif du Sénégal (*BAS*), 1819–1908
Moniteur du Sénégal et Dépendances (*MOS*), 1856–87
Journal Officiel du Sénégal (*JOS*), from 1888

Other Sources

Amin, Samir. 1969. *Le monde des affaires sénégalais*. Paris: Editions de Minuit.

Barry, Boubacar. 1972. *Le royaume du Waalo*. Paris: Maspero.

Boilat, P. D. 1853. *Esquisses Sénégalaises*. Paris: P. Bertrand.

Bouet-Willaumez, Louis-Edward. 1848. *Commerce et traite des Noirs aux cotes occidentales d'Afrique*. Paris.

Bouet-Willaumez, Louis-Edward. 1852. Les colonies françaises en 1852. *Revue des Deux Mondes* 14 (June): 930–51.

Bour, Charles. 1885. *Les dépendances du Sénégal*. Paris: L. Baudoin et Cie.

Camara, C. 1968. *Saint Louis-du-Sénégal: Evolution du úne ville en milieu africain*. Dakar: Institut Fondamentale d'Afrique Noire.

Carrére, F. and P. Holle. 1855. *De la Sénégambie française*. Paris: Firmin Didot Frères.

Coupland, Reginald. 1933. *The British anti-slavery movement*. London: Oxford University Press.

Courtet, M. 1903. *Etude sur le Sénégal*. Paris: A. Challamel.

Daget, Serge. 1986. Les Aléas de l'abolition de la traite au Sénégal (1817–1831). Paper presented to the Colloque international pour le tricentenaire du Code Noir. July. Dakar.

Dupère, N. D. 1871. "La Sénégambie française." *Bulletin de la Société de Géographie* (July).

Faidherbe, Louis. 1889. *Le Sénégal: La France dans l'Afrique Occidentale*. Paris: Hachette.

Gueye, Mbaye. 1966. L'affaire Chautemps (Avril 1904) et la suppression de l'esclavage de case au Sénégal. *Bulletin de l'IFAN* 27:543–59.

Ka, I. 1981. L'évolution sociale à Saint-Louis du Sénégal, du XIXe siècle au début du XXe siècle. Mémoire de maîtrise, Université de Dakar.

Kane, M. 1984. L'esclavage à Saint Louis et à Gorée à travers les archives notariées: 1817–1848. Mémoire de maîtrise, Université de Dakar.

Martin, Gaston. 1948. *Histoire de l'esclavage dans les colonies françaises*. Paris: PUF.

Mbaye, Saliou. 1974. Le Conseil Privé du Sénégal de 1819 à 1854. Thèse, Ecole des Chartes.

Mbodj, Mohamed. 1978. Un exemple d'economie coloniale, le Sine-Saloum (Sénégal), de 1887 à 1940: Culture arachidière et mutations sociales. Thèse de 3e cycle, Université de Paris-VII.

Pasquier, Roger. 1960. Villes du Sénégal au XIXe siècle. *Revue Française d'Histoire d'Outre-Mer* 47:387–426.

Pasquier, Roger. 1967. A propos de l'émancipation des esclaves au Sénégal en 1848. *Revue Française d'Histoire d'Outre-Mer* 54:188–208.

Pasquier, Roger. 1983. Les traitants des comptoirs du Sénégal au milieu du XIXe siècle. In *Entreprises et entrepreneurs en Afrique, XIXe et XXe siècles*, ed. Catherine Coquery-Vidrovitch. Paris: Harmattan.

Raffenel, A. 1856. *Nouveaux voyages dans les pays des Nègres*. Paris: Chaix.

Renault, François. 1972. *L'abolition de l'esclavage au Sénégal: L'attitude de l'administration française, 1848–1905*. Paris: Société Française de l'Histoire d'Outre Mer.

Sané, O. 1978. La Vie économique et sociale des Goréens entre 1817 et 1848. Thèse de 3e cycle, Université de Dakar.

Schoelcher, Victor. 1880. *L'esclavage au Sénégal en 1880*. Paris: H. E. Martin.

United Kingdom. Parliament. 1827. *Report on the Gambia by Major Rowan*. Parliamentary Papers No. 52, pp. 211–25.

United Kingdom. Parliament. 1842. *Minutes on evidence before the Select Committee on West Coast of Africa*. Parliamentary Papers No. 2.

Webb, James. 1985. The trade in gum arabic: Prelude to French conquest in Senegal. *Journal of African History* 26:149–68.

Williams, Eric. 1944. *Capitalism and Slavery*. Chapel Hill: University of North Carolina Press.

Zuccarelli, François. 1962. Le régime des engagés à temps au Sénégal, 1817–1848. *Cahiers d'Etudes Africaines* 2:420–61.

Index

Index

215